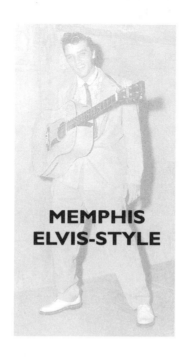

MEMPHIS ELVIS-STYLE

Jan

welcome to Memphis!

Mike Freeman

Cris Hey

MEMPHIS ELVIS-STYLE

Cindy Hazen
and
Mike Freeman

JOHN F. BLAIR, PUBLISHER

WINSTON-SALEM, NORTH CAROLINA

Maps provided by the Memphis Convention and Visitors Bureau

Cover Photographs

Union Avenue, Courtesy of the Memphis and Shelby County Room,
Memphis/Shelby County Public Library

Elvis by Opal Walker

Library of Congress Cataloging-in-Publication Data

Hazen, Cindy.
    Memphis Elvis-style / Cindy Hazen and Mike Freeman.
        p.   cm.
    Includes bibliographical references (p.   ) and index.
    ISBN 0-89587-173-4 (alk. paper)
        1. Presley, Elvis, 1935–1977—Homes and haunts—Tennessee—Memphis—
Guidebooks.   2. Memphis (Tenn.)—Guidebooks.   I. Freeman, Mike, 1956–
II. Title.
ML420.P96H53   1997
782.42166'092—dc21
[B]   97–2715

*"Someone asked me this morning
what I'd missed about Memphis.
I said everything."*

Elvis upon his return
from Germany
March 8, 1960

**Dedicated to all
who search for the
spirit of Elvis in Memphis.**

Elvis on South Main Street
Courtesy of Linda Everett

CONTENTS

Acknowledgments   xi
Preface   xiii

Part I
Teenage Dreams (1948–1954)

Homes   1
  572 Poplar Avenue
  185 Winchester Avenue
  698 Saffarans Avenue
  462 Alabama Avenue

Parent's Employment   9
  United Paint Company
  St. Joseph's Hospital

School   12
  L.C. Humes High School

High School Prom   17
  The Peabody Hotel

Hangouts   19
  Market Mall
  The Triangle
  The Recreation Hall
  Odd Fellows Hall
  Water Works
  Hall's Grocery

Elvis's Employment   27
  Loew's State Theater
  MARL Metal Manufacturing Company
  Tennessee Employment Security Office
  M.B. Parker Company
  Precision Tool Company, Inc.
  Crown Electric Company

Career Influences   36
  Suzore #2 Theater

The Green Owl
Beale Street
Palace Theater
Home of the Blues Record Shop
The Blues Shop
Pop (Poplar) Tunes

Gospel and Religious Influences   46
  Blackwood Brothers' Record Shop and
    Offices
  First Assembly of God Church
  Centenary A.M.E. Church
  East Trigg Baptist Church

Restaurants   54
  Culpepper's Chicken Shack
  K's Drive-In
  Earl's Hot Biscuits
  The Peanut Shop
  Taylor's Cafe

Part II
A Young Rock-and-Roller
(1954–1958)

Recording Studio   60
  Memphis Recording Service/Sun
    Records

Radio Stations   64
  WHBQ Radio
  WDIA Radio
  WMPS Radio

Local Performances   71
  The Bon-Air Night Club
  The Bel-Air Night Club
  The Eagle's Nest
  Lamar-Airways Shopping Center
  Overton Park Shell

Ellis Auditorium
Russwood Park

Homes   85
2414 Lamar Avenue
1414 Getwell Road
1034 Audubon Drive
Graceland

Musicians and Friends   94
Scotty Moore's Homes
Bill Black's Homes
Sam Phillips's Home
Ace Appliance Company
University Park Cleaners
Anita Wood's Home

Publicity and Promotion   102
Bob Neal's Office
Blue Light Studio
Speer Photography

Train Stops and Stations   107
White Station Train Stop

Stores   109
Harry Levitch Jewelers
Lansky Brothers' Men's Store
O.K. Houck & Company

Restaurants   113
Krystal
State Café

Court Appearance   116
Shelby County Courthouse

Movie Theaters   119
Plaza Cinema
Strand Theater

Motorcycles   122
Tommy Taylor's Memphis Harley-Davidson

Football   124
Crump Stadium

Playgrounds   126
Mid-South Fairgrounds and Libertyland
Rainbow Roller Skating Rink

Hair Cuts   131
Jim's Barber Shop

Departure for the Army   133
Local Draft Board 86
Kennedy Veterans Hospital

Elvis's Mother's Death   136
Methodist Hospital
Forest Hill Cemetery
Burke's Florist

A Grand Welcome   139
Union Station

Part III
The City That Never Sleeps
(1961–1977)

Recording Studios   142
American Sound Studio
Stax Records
Hi Records/Royal Sound Studio

Performances   148
Mid-South Coliseum

Awards   151
Claridge Hotel
Holiday Inn-Rivermont

Restaurants   156
Four Flames Restaurant
Chenault's Restaurant
Leonard's Barbeque

Colletta's Italian Restaurant
Western Steakhouse and Lounge
Gridiron Restaurant
Hickory Log Restaurant and Beef and
Liberty Restaurant
McDonald's

Parties   166
Manhattan Club
Thunderbird Lounge
T.J.'s Lounge

Movie Theaters   170
Memphian Theater
Crosstown Theater

Priscilla's School   173
Immaculate Conception High School

Ranching   175
Circle G Ranch

Football   178
Graceland School
Whitehaven High School

Boating   180
McKellar Lake

Automobiles   182
Hull-Dobbs Ford
Southern Motors/Madison Cadillac
Schilling Lincoln-Mercury
Robertson Motors
Sid Carroll Pontiac

Motorcycles   191
Super Cycle

Airplanes   193
Memphis Aero

Stores   195
Goldsmith's Department Store
Lowell Hays Jewelers
Sears Roebuck and Company

Police Department   199
Memphis Police Station

Karate   201
Kang Rhee Institute for Self-Defense
Tennessee Karate Institute

Racquetball   205
Presley Center Courts

Hideaway   207
Howard Johnson's Motor Lodge

Family and Friends   209
Vernon Presley's Homes
Linda Thompson's Home
Sam Thompson's Home
Elvis's Other Properties

Banking   214
National Bank of Commerce

The Loss of a Legend   216
Baptist Memorial Hospital
Memphis Funeral Home

The Legacy Continues   221
Elvis Presley Trauma Center
Le Bonheur Children's Hospital
St. Jude Children's Research Hospital

Appendix   224
Bibliography   234
Index   236

Elvis driving on South Main Street
Courtesy of Linda Everett

ACKNOWLEDGMENTS

Writing a book is, for the most part, a solitary endeavor, but a project like this cannot be realized without the help of a great many people. In particular, we would like to thank the following people: Stephen Shutts, Robert Dye, Jr., Doris Pieraccini, Carolyn Scarberry, Linda Everett, Sam Thompson, Henrik Knudsen, Ernie Barrasso, James Blackwood, Lil Thompson, Ron Elliot, Mark Bell, Ron Burgess, Will McDaniel, Anna Hamilton, William and Vancil Speer, Charles Bramlett, Mrs. J.C. Bramlett, Joyce Bradley Bramlett, Pam and James Godsey, Anna May Bradley, Skip and Jean Wallin, Opal Walker, Joel Hurley, Jean Lazenby Foster, Fred Woloshin, Charles Russell, Mary Greer, Dr. Jim Johnson and the staff of the Memphis/Shelby County Public Library, and Ed Franks and the staff at the Mississippi Valley Collections of the Ned McWherter University of Memphis Library. Special thanks to our editor, Andrew Waters, and the good folks at John F. Blair, Publisher.

Elvis backstage at the Orpheum
Courtesy of Stephen Shutts

PREFACE

If there is a single name synonymous with Memphis, Tennessee, it is Elvis Presley. As the premier superstar of this century, he could have lived anywhere in the world. And having risen up from the Lauderdale Courts housing project in Memphis, he would have been justified in doing so. Instead, he chose Graceland, the mansion in his hometown where he lived from 1957 until his death in 1977.

That he chose to remove himself from the glamour of Hollywood says a lot about him. His tastes remained very simple, if not almost childlike. He preferred many of the same foods, pastimes, and friends as he did in his youth. He longed for the familiar, as if trying to hold anchor while the perils of fame rushed to sweep him away.

He felt comfortable in Memphis where people tended to give him a little more privacy. There were certainly ardent fans watching out for his every move, but by and large, Memphians were accustomed to his presence. Seeing him on the street was not an everyday occurrence, nor was it a traffic-stopping event. If anything, a lot of the locals wanted their town to be known for something *besides* Elvis.

The part of Memphis most people automatically associate with Elvis is Graceland. With seven hundred thousand visitors each year, Graceland is second only to the White House in the number of tourists who pass through its doors. By seeing how Elvis lived and viewing the things that he valued and kept close to him, a tour of Graceland provides an intimate perspective of his life. At the same time, a visit through Graceland's trophy room offers a glimmer of his extraordinary accomplishments: his three Grammy awards, 113 gold and platinum records, and countless other awards.

Yet for all that Graceland can possibly say about Elvis, it can never be the last word. To fully appreciate Graceland, you have to see where he came from. Elvis knew this. Throughout his life, he would drive his friends to old neighborhoods and haunts. After all, if he had been born to any different circumstances, could he have still been Elvis? It was precisely the sum of his youthful experience that burst forth as rock-and-roll.

In his youth, Elvis was exposed to two different cultures, that of the working-class whites and the segregated blacks. He was raised in a world where politeness still mattered and where no one was too busy or too poor to help someone in need. He was deeply influenced by the fire-and-brimstone services of his Assembly of God church, and he was so profoundly moved by their sacred music that he considered devoting his life to making his own joyful version of it.

It's little wonder that the young Elvis turned to music. This environment practically demanded creativity, so great was the conglomeration of music and opportunity. Before the days of canned top forty, radio shows played a wide variety of music. Independent record stores were spread all over downtown Memphis, each carrying their own particular forte. Why, one could even walk into a recording studio and buy a short recording session, then walk into a radio station and ask for the demo to be played over the airwaves.

However, this opportunity did not necessarily mean an instant path to glory. Elvis's career was launched with extraordinary speed; less than four years after his high school graduation, his appearance on the *Ed Sullivan Show* set records for television ratings. Yet to look at his career as it unfolded, progress must have seemed agonizingly slow. Could Elvis have imagined where he would be in two years while standing on the stage of the Bon-Air Club or the Eagle's Nest in front of less-than-enthusiastic crowds? We're fairly certain not, no more than he could imagine himself twenty years later.

The one constant during his twenty-three-year career was his affection for his hometown. And it is through this context that we will let Elvis's story unfold. While guiding you through more than a hundred sites important in Elvis's life and career, we hope to present more than a travelogue. We hope, instead, to offer some insights into his relationship with the city, both in the ways that Memphis influenced him and the ways that he related to the city. We hope that his personality will emerge, and that occasionally his sense of humor will come through.

As Memphians, we will attempt to show you Elvis's Memphis, while pointing out how it differs today. You will find many of the places we discuss are no longer in existence. Owners of businesses have retired and passed on. Moreover, all of the social issues that have changed America in the last forty years have also changed Memphis. Urban renewal projects have forever altered the landscape of Elvis's downtown neighborhoods.

But for all of the places that are no longer in existence, there are many that still are. You can still eat at some of the same restaurants Elvis frequented and see sites like his high school, his various homes, and the stages where he performed. We hope you enjoy these sites, but our larger goal is to paint a historical picture of Memphis so that you can better understand the city Elvis knew.

LEGEND FOR MAPS

1   572 Poplar Avenue
2   185 Winchester Street
3   698 Saffarans Avenue
4   462 Alabama Street
5   United Paint   446 Concord Avenue (North Parkway)
6   Saint Joseph's Hospital   264 Jackson Avenue
7   L. C. Humes High School   659 Manassas Street
8   Peabody Hotel   149 Union Avenue
9   Market Mall   Lauderdale Courts
10 Triangle   Lauderdale Courts
11 Recreation Hall   Winchester Avenue and Lauderdale Street
12 Odd Fellows Club   Main Street at Court Avenue
13 Water Works   North Parkway and Dunlap Street
14 Hall's Grocery   1588 Mississippi Boulevard
15 Loew's State Theater   152 South Main Street
16 MARL Metal Mfg. Co.   208 West Georgia Avenue
17 Tennessee Department of Employment Security
        122 Union Avenue
18 M.B. Parker Company   1449 Thomas Street
19 Precision Tool Co. Inc.   1132 Kansas Street
20 Crown Electric   353 Poplar Avenue
21 Suzore #2 Theater   279 North Main Street
22 The Green Owl Nightclub   260 North Main Street
23 Palace Theater   324 Beale Street
24 Beale Street
25 Home of the Blues Record Shop   107 Beale Street
26 The Blues Shop   286 North Main Street
27 Pop Tunes Record Shop   306 Poplar Avenue
28 Blackwood Brothers' Record Shop & Offices
        186 Jefferson Avenue
29 First Assembly of God   1084 East McLemore Avenue
30 Centenary A.M.E. Church   878 Mississippi Boulevard
31 East Trigg Baptist Church   1189 East Trigg Avenue
32 Culpepper's Chicken Shack   204 Hernando Street
33 K's Drive-In   166 Crump Boulevard
34 Earl's Hot Biscuits   179 Crump Boulevard
35 The Peanut Shop   134 South Main Street and 24 South
        Main Street

36   Taylor's Restaurant   *710 Union Avenue*

37   Sun Studio   *706 Union Avenue*

38   WHBQ/Hotel Chisca   *272 South Main Street*

39   WDIA Radio   *2074 Union Avenue*

40   WMPS   *112 Union Avenue*

41   Bon-Air Night Club   *4862 Summer Avenue*

42   Bel-Air Night Club   *1850 South Bellevue Boulevard*

43   Eagle's Nest   *Lamar Avenue at Winchester Road*

44   Lamar-Airways Shopping Center   *Lamar Avenue*

45   Overton Park Shell   *1928 Poplar Avenue in Overton Park*

46   Ellis Auditorium, Cook Convention Center
        225 North Main Street

47   Russwood Park   *914 Madison Avenue*

48   2414 Lamar Avenue

49   1414 Getwell Road

50   1034 Audubon Drive

51   Graceland   *3764 Elvis Presley Boulevard*

52   Scotty Moore's Homes   *983 Belz Avenue, 1248 Meda Street*

53   Bill Black's Homes   *971 Belz Avenue, 4188 Pike's Peak Avenue,*
        3890 North Watkins Street.

54   Sam Phillips's Homes   *1028 McEvers Road, 79 South*
        Mendenhall Road

55   Ace Appliance   *3431 Summer Avenue*

56   University Park Cleaners   *613 North McLean Boulevard*

57   Anita Wood's House   *2186 Monroe Avenue*

58   Bob Neal's Office   *160 Union Avenue*

59   Blue Light Studio   *130 Beale Street, 115 Union Avenue*

60   Speer Photography   *1330 Linden Avenue*

61   White Station   *Poplar Avenue*

62   Harry Levitch Jewelers   *176 South Main Street,*
        5100 Poplar Avenue

63   Lansky Brothers' Men's Store   *126 Beale Street*

64   O.K. Houck & Co. Music Shop   *121 Union Avenue*

65   Krystal   *135 Union Avenue*

66   State Café   *84 Beale Street*

67   Shelby County Courthouse   *Adams Avenue*

68   Plaza Cinema   *3402 Poplar Avenue*

69   Strand Theater   *138 South Main Street*

70   Tommy Taylor's Memphis Harley-Davidson
        235 Poplar Avenue

71   Crump Stadium   *Cleveland Street at Linden Avenue*

72 Libertyland, Mid-South Fairgrounds   *940 Early Maxwell Boulevard*

73 Rainbow Roller Skating Rink   *2881 Lamar Avenue*

74 Jim's Barber Shop   *201 South Main Street, 7 North Third Street*

75 Local Draft Board 86   *198 Beale Street*

76 Kennedy Veterans Hospital   *Getwell Road and Park Avenue*

77 Methodist Hospital Central   *1265 Union Avenue*

78 Forest Hill Cemetery   *1661 Elvis Presley Boulevard*

79 Burke's Florist   *1609 Elvis Presley Boulevard*

80 Union Station   *199 East Calhoun Avenue*

81 American Sound Studio   *829 Thomas Street*

82 Stax Records   *928 East McLemore Avenue*

83 Hi Records/ Royal Sound Studio   *1329 South Lauderdale Street*

84 Mid-South Coliseum   *Early Maxwell Boulevard*

85 Claridge Hotel   *109 North Main Street*

86 Holiday-Inn Rivermont   *200 West Georgia Avenue*

87 Four Flames Restaurant   *1085 Poplar Avenue*

88 Chenault's Restaurant   *1404 Elvis Presley Boulevard*

89 Leonard's Barbeque   *1140 South Bellevue Boulevard*

90 Colletta's Italian Restaurant   *1063 South Parkway*

91 Western Steakhouse and Lounge   *1298 Madison Avenue*

92 Gridiron Restaurant   *4101 Elvis Presley Boulevard*

93 Hickory Log Restaurant   *3795 Elvis Presley Boulevard*
Beef and Liberty Restaurant   *3765 Elvis Presley Boulevard*

94 McDonald's   *4237 Elvis Presley Boulevard*

95 Manhattan Club   *1459 Elvis Presley Boulevard*

96 Thunderbird Lounge   *750 Adams Avenue*

97 T.J.'s Lounge   *94 North Avalon Street*

98 Memphian Theater   *51 South Cooper Street*

99 Crosstown Theater   *400 North Cleveland Street*

100 Immaculate Conception High School   *1725 Central Avenue*

101 Circle G Ranch   *Highway 301 and Goodman Road*

102 Graceland School   *3866 Pattie Ann Drive*

103 Whitehaven High School   *4851 Elvis Presley Boulevard*

104 McKeller Lake

105 Hull-Dobbs Ford   *115 South Third Street*

106 Southern Motors/ Madison Cadillac   *341 Union Avenue*

107 Schilling Lincoln-Mercury   *987 Union Avenue*

108 Robertson Motors   *2950 Airways Boulevard*

109 Sid Carroll Pontiac   *1011 Union Avenue*

110   Super Cycle   *624 South Bellevue Boulevard*
111   Memphis Aero   *Memphis International Airport*
112   Goldsmith's Department Store   *123 South Main Street*
113   Lowell Hays Jewelers   *4872 Poplar Avenue*
114   Sears Roebuck and Company   *495 North Watkins,*
         Southland Mall
115   Memphis Police Station   *128 Adams Avenue*
116   Kang Rhee Institute for Self-Defense   *1911 Poplar Avenue,*
         706 Germantown Parkway
117   Tennessee Karate Institute   *1372 Overton Park Avenue*
118   Presley Center Courts   *Mendenhall Road at Mt. Moriah Road*
119   Howard Johnson's Motor Lodge   *3280 Elvis Presley Boulevard*
120   Vernon Presley's Homes   *3650 Hermitage Road,*
         1266 Dolan Drive
121   Linda Thompson's House   *1254 Old Hickory Road*
122   Sam Thompson's House   *1317 Farell Road*
123   Elvis's Other Properties   *1576 Lehr Street, 4152 Royalcrest*
         Place
124   National Bank of Commerce   *45 South Second Street*
125   Baptist Memorial Hospital   *899 Union Avenue*
126   Memphis Funeral Home   *1177 Union Avenue*
127   Elvis Presley Trauma Center   *877 Jefferson Avenue*
128   Le Bonheur Children's Hospital   *50 North Dunlap Street*
129   St. Jude Children's Research Hospital   *332 North Lauderdale*
         Street

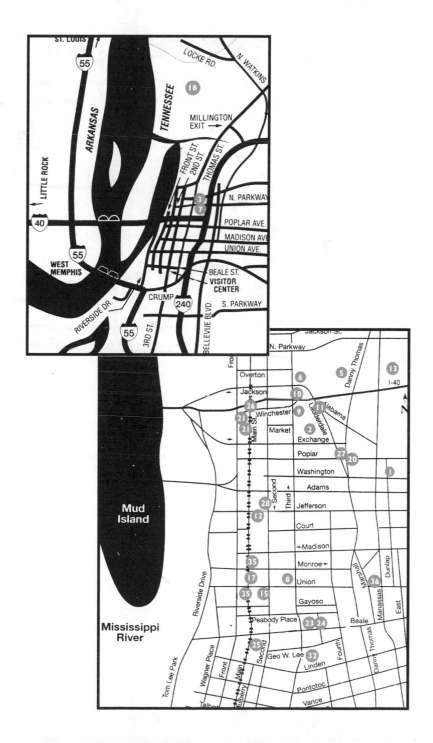

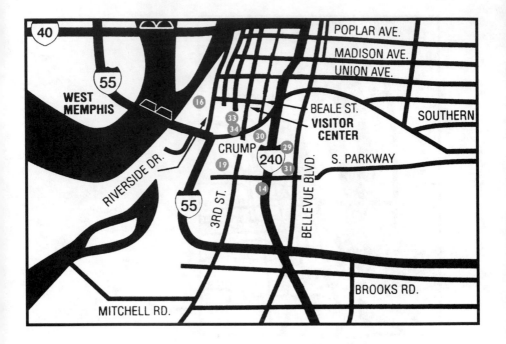

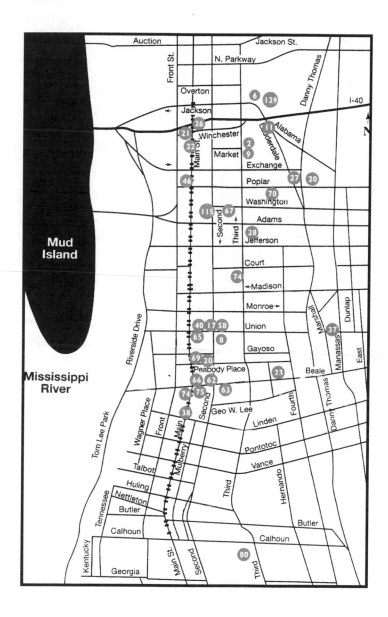

PART TWO — CENTRAL MEMPHIS

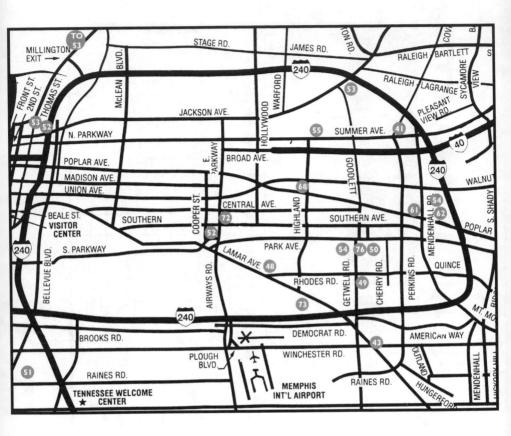

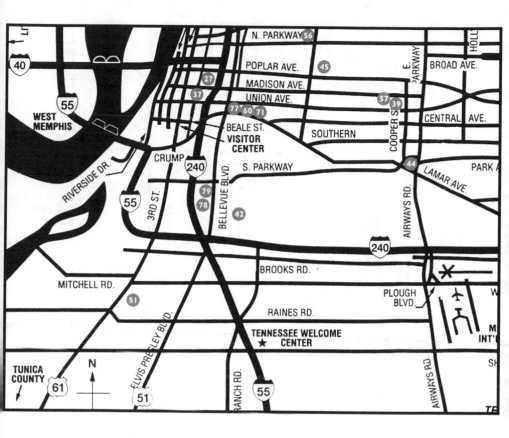

PART THREE — CENTRAL MEMPHIS

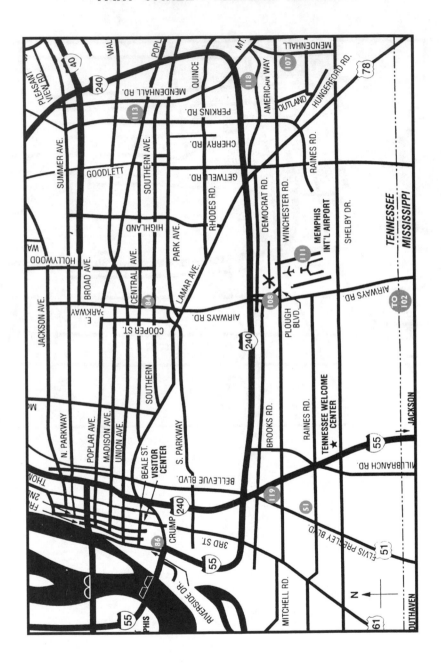

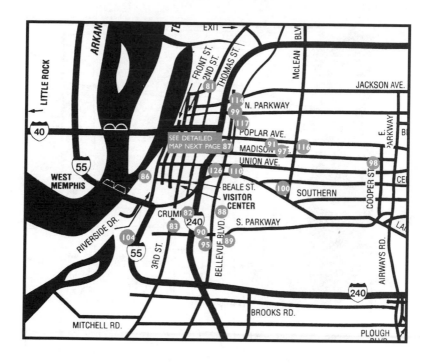

PART THREE — WHITEHAVEN

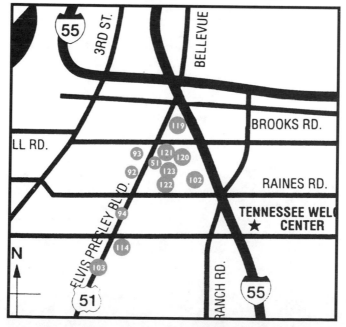

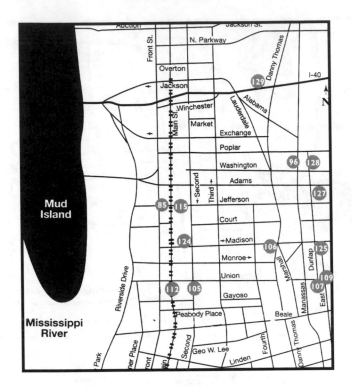

PART I
TEENAGE DREAMS
(1948–1954)

HOMES

572 Poplar Avenue

It's been said that to understand a man you should look at his childhood. This is certainly true of Elvis because at the very heart of his appeal is his rise from the depths of poverty he knew as a child to phenomenal success. His birth in a two-room sharecropper's house in Tupelo, Mississippi, lies in sharp contrast to his death at his Graceland mansion. His family's apartment at the Lauderdale Courts housing project in Memphis, where Elvis spent his high school years, reminds us of how quickly and drastically his life changed during his rise to stardom. Yet for all of the difficulties and disadvantages met by the Presley family in Elvis's youth, none seem more horrific than their tenure at 572 Poplar Avenue.

The year was 1948. Elvis was thirteen and just starting a new school year when his father, Vernon, was fired from his job in Tupelo. In postwar America the northern industries were booming, but jobs were scarce in the rural South. Vernon, following Gladys's two brothers who had found work here, moved the family to Memphis.

Even with relatives living in Memphis, the transition to urban life was not easy. The Presleys, nearly destitute when they arrived, settled into a boarding house at 572 Poplar Avenue. The neighborhood was full of hard-luck tales. Just a few blocks down the road, the Union Mission fed and preached to the homeless. Housing projects were around the corner. Though the Presleys' boarding house was set some distance from the road, it was far from protected from street noise. Even then, Poplar Avenue was a busy thoroughfare leading to downtown Memphis. Ambulances wailed as they drove down the street toward the downtown hospitals, and police sirens could be heard screaming as the patrol cars left the station or the nearby jail.

Even worse was the racket within the house. Sixteen families rented rooms, and in all more than sixty people resided in the house. Elvis's family of four (which included his grandmother, Minnie Mae Presley) lived in one ground-floor room. They shared the bathroom down the hall with three other families. The lack of privacy was bad enough, but it was the filth that was most unbearable. Cockroaches were so plentiful they boldly climbed the walls, even in daylight. Plaster was knocked loose in places, exposing gaping holes and ancient lathe work, and aside from the ornate but neglected woodwork, little remained of the once fine house.

Given the condition of the house when the Presleys lived there, it is not surprising that the property was eventually razed. The site is now a vacant lot. A neighboring house that survived until the early '90s has been mistakenly identified as the house where the Presleys lived; however, the city directories last list the 572 Poplar Avenue address in 1970. While this vacant lot, nestled among pawn shops and tenements, is all that remains of Elvis's first year in Memphis, the site still speaks loudly of the trials of his childhood and the wonder of his rise to stardom.

DOWNTOWN. THE BOARDING HOUSE AT 572 POPLAR WAS LOCATED BETWEEN HAMLIN PLACE AND HILL STREET, EAST OF DANNY THOMAS BOULEVARD. THE VACANT LOT IS ON THE NORTH SIDE OF THE STREET.

Vernon and Gladys
Courtesy of William Speer

185 Winchester Avenue
Apartment #328
Lauderdale Courts

In 1949, Vernon Presley, desperate to help his family escape 572 Poplar Avenue, applied for assistance with the Memphis Housing Authority. The Presleys were assigned to Mrs. Jane Richardson, who had to determine whether they met all of the requirements. Priority was given to families raising children, and residency in Lauderdale Courts was limited to white families making less than three thousand dollars per year, with rent adjusted to income. Mrs. Richardson examined Vernon's job status and moral character. To her the family seemed sincere and very nice, if a bit shy. She determined that they qualified to live in public housing, with rent set at thirty-five dollars a month.

On May 1, 1949, the Presley family moved into apartment 328 at 185 Winchester. It was a three-story, "I"-shaped building at the intersection of Third Street and Winchester Avenue. Their apartment was in the middle section of the building on the ground floor. A small flight of steps led to the building door; once inside, their apartment was the middle of the three.

Sometimes first impressions are lasting. Often, the Presleys are still depicted as loners and their son as a timid mama's boy. However, by most accounts the Presleys became friends with their neighbors in Lauderdale Courts. These people shared a lot in common: work, memories of hard times, and a desire to make a better life. The residents watched out for each other's children. The young Elvis was close to his parents, particularly his mother, but he soon found a group of boys his age and was busy growing up with them. Mrs. Richardson told biographer Jerry Hopkins that the Presley family was among her best tenants.

The one constant memory by everyone who knew the Presleys in Lauderdale Courts is that Elvis liked to sing and play guitar. Sometimes he played to his friends and elders in the apartment or on the front steps. He often wandered about the project; everywhere residents gathered, he played. One or two former residents of Lauderdale Courts claimed they taught Elvis how to entertain, but most are content to say they listened to and enjoyed his music. These people were some of his first audiences, and their appreciation of his talent gave him confidence to go on.

It was a confidence that built slowly. He used to practice in the laundry room in the basement of the building at 185 Winchester Avenue because he could be alone and practice different styles he heard on the radio. Jean Lazenby Foster, who lived in Lauderdale Courts with her twin, Joan, remembers her sister and she were about seven when they snuck into the laundry room and watched Elvis practice. They began giggling, and Elvis was so embarrassed he fled from the basement.

It is a memory that they cherish today. They were fortunate to know a young boy named Elvis Presley, a remembrance shared by many residents of Lauderdale Courts who never imagined that their boy would one day be king.

For Elvis, living in Lauderdale Courts provided a stability that he had never known before. His family had moved often, and the three years they spent there gave him plenty of time to set down roots.

Lauderdale Courts, though, was not meant to be a permanent residence for its tenants. Built in 1938 by the Public Works Administration of Roosevelt's New Deal, the Courts were meant to provide the poor with decent housing until they could provide for themselves. It had replaced a shantytown, where most of the residents lived without indoor plumbing or adequate heat. Life was almost luxurious compared to some circumstances, but it was not without cost, for residents had to comply with many regulations.

One of the requirements was that apartments were inspected monthly. Although Gladys was a conscientious housekeeper, she worried about having everything in perfect order for the inspection, especially as she juggled a job with family. Perhaps the most worrisome regulation was that tenants had to report a change in job or income, regardless of the permanence of the change. Among the many reasons a tenant could be forced to move was earning too much money, and this is what happened to the Presleys. In their case, a very nominal amount of temporary income cost them their residency at Lauderdale Courts.

DOWNTOWN. FROM POPLAR AVENUE, AT THE CORNER OF POP TUNES, TURN NORTH ON LAUDERDALE STREET. WINCHESTER IS THE SECOND LEFT. THIS IS A DEAD-END STREET THAT STOPS AT THE BUILDING WHERE ELVIS LIVED. LAUDERDALE COURTS IS WITHIN AN AREA BOUNDED BY EXCHANGE STREET TO THE SOUTH, THIRD AVENUE TO THE WEST, DANNY THOMAS BOULEVARD TO THE EAST, AND WINCHESTER AND ALABAMA TO THE NORTH. LAUDERDALE STREET SPLITS THE PROJECT ROUGHLY IN TWO.

698 Saffarans Avenue
"The Lost Address"

The Presleys' apartment at 698 Saffarans Avenue was only a step-ping stone for the family. Their time here was so short—just three months—that it's hard to imagine them fully unpacking, much less considering their residence here worth remembering. In fact, it nearly did fall into obscurity. For more than twenty-five years, this address was erroneously reported as 398 Cypress Avenue. The real address wasn't uncovered until 1991, when Joe Haertel, an astute Elvis fan, discov-ered the discrepancy and the true location of the Presley's 1953 apart-ment—a feat even the wire services considered newsworthy.

From a historical standpoint, this address is important because the Presleys moved here from the Lauderdale Courts housing project. In November of 1952, during Elvis's senior year of high school, Gladys went to work at St. Joseph's Hospital. The family's combined salaries exceeded the income limit allowed by public housing by a small, but enforceable, amount. Given ninety days in which to move, the Presleys didn't dare risk eviction.

On the day before Elvis's birthday, they moved into a two-room apartment at 698 Saffarans Avenue. The apartment was ten dollars a month more than the one they had left at Lauderdale Courts, and much smaller, so this was certainly a setback for the Presleys. Still, they must have been pleased by the location. Saffarans Avenue runs north and south adjacent to what was then Humes High School. The apartment, which has since been torn down, was directly across the street from Elvis's school.

How did the true address surface after all these years? This was the address listed on Elvis's draft card. He turned eighteen and regis-tered for the draft while living in this apartment.

DOWNTOWN. FROM POPLAR AVENUE, TURN NORTH ON MANASSAS STREET AND DRIVE ONE MILE, PAST THE NORTH PARKWAY AND JACKSON AVENUE INTERSECTIONS. SAFFARANS AVENUE IS JUST NORTH OF HUMES JUNIOR HIGH SCHOOL. TURN LEFT ON SAFFARANS AVENUE TO DRIVE PAST THE SITE. THE ADDRESS IS NOW A VACANT LOT.

462 Alabama Avenue

After he became famous, Elvis enjoyed driving his friends through downtown Memphis and showing them some of the places he remembered from his youth. He used to point to St. Jude Children's Research Hospital and say "I used to live there." In fact, Elvis lived in a house once located where the parking lot of St. Jude meets the interstate. This is the house where Elvis lived when he began recording at Sun Studio, then known as Memphis Recording Service.

The Presleys moved to the home at 462 Alabama Avenue in the spring of 1953. It was a well-kept, two-story brick house with a sweeping front porch. There were just two apartments in the house. The Presleys lived in the downstairs apartment, and Rabbi Alf Fruchter and his family lived above them. Vernon and Gladys occupied the only bedroom. Minnie Mae slept on a cot in the dining room. Elvis took the couch each night.

Mrs. Fruchter later told an interviewer, "They never had much. There wasn't even a decent chair to sit down in. About all they had was this cheap little radio."

Mrs. Fruchter remembered Saturday afternoons when Elvis and Vernon would polish Elvis's ten-year-old Lincoln. Others recalled seeing Elvis walk down the street with his guitar, his hair spilling over the collar of his pink shirt. And still others remembered him when he came back to visit the neighborhood, driving through the narrow streets with a carload of his friends packed into his fancy automobile, sometimes stopping to chat with his old neighbors.

Mrs. Anna Mae Bradley, who lived a block away on High Street, also recalled the Presleys' time at this address. Once, she was sitting on her front porch when Elvis stopped to visit with his guitar. He sat down next to her on the porch swing and began to play. "It seems like a hundred years ago now," she said. Though she couldn't remember what songs Elvis played, she laughed about how worn his shoes were. "You could see through them," she said.

Perhaps that's why Elvis's success was all the more sweet. In a matter of months, he went from being just a neighborhood kid to a local celebrity. Mrs. Bradley remembered the time he bought Gladys a pink Cadillac. Gladys's brother, Travis Smith, lived next to the Bradleys, and Gladys came over to show everyone her new car. "She pointed across the street and said, 'That's what Elvis bought me.' She was so proud of that car," Mrs. Bradley said.

Years later Mrs. Bradley had her picture taken standing by this car at the automobile museum at Graceland. Like many of those who knew Elvis when he lived on Alabama Street, she sometimes finds it hard to believe he did so well. Her memories of him were so simple.

DOWNTOWN. THIS ADDRESS ON ALABAMA AVENUE NO LONGER EXISTS. FROM POP-LAR AVENUE, TURN NORTH ON LAUDERDALE STREET. ALABAMA AVENUE IS THE SECOND RIGHT (WINCHESTER AVENUE IS THE SECOND LEFT, DIRECTLY OPPOSITE ALABAMA AV-ENUE). THE HOUSES THAT WERE ONCE ON THE LEFT, INCLUDING ELVIS'S HOME AT 462 ALABAMA AVENUE, WERE RAZED TO MAKE WAY FOR ST. JUDE CHILDREN'S RESEARCH HOSPITAL AND THE INTERSTATE.

Britlings Cafeteria where Gladys worked
Courtesy of the Memphis and Shelby County Room
Memphis/Shelby County Public Library and Information Center

PARENTS' EMPLOYMENT

United Paint Company
446 Concord Avenue

For whatever reasons, Vernon Presley has had his detractors, especially with regard to his work habits. Certain writers have been quick to point out that Vernon hopped from job to job. That may have been true in Tupelo, but not in Memphis where he held onto his job at United Paint Company for five years.

Vernon was hired at the company in February 1949. Though the job was mundane—packing paint cans into cardboard boxes—the company's location was appealing since it was within walking distance of the boarding house on Poplar Avenue. United Paint only paid a beginning wage of eighty-three cents an hour, but Vernon did not knock his good fortune of finding a job so near his home. When the Presleys moved to Lauderdale Courts, they moved even closer to Vernon's work. St. Joseph's Hospital was within sight of the company, and this would later prove convenient when Gladys started work there.

The site of the United Paint Company factory is nearly impossible to find because so many of the streets have changed. Concord Street is now North Parkway. Danny Thomas Boulevard and Interstate 40 have drastically changed the neighborhoods in this part of Memphis. Going back to the 1950s addresses, there are two listings for the United Paint Company factory, one at 446 Concord Avenue and one at 345 Jackson Avenue, depending on whether you look in the phone book or in the city directory. Concord and Jackson Avenues were parallel to each other so most likely these two addresses were part of the same complex facing two different streets.

DOWNTOWN. FROM POPLAR AVENUE, TRAVEL NORTH ON DANNY THOMAS BOULEVARD, PAST JACKSON AVENUE, TO NORTH PARKWAY. TURN LEFT ON NORTH PARKWAY. UNITED PAINT COMPANY WAS BETWEEN JACKSON AVENUE AND NORTH PARKWAY, EAST OF NORTH MAIN STREET. TODAY THERE IS NO RECOGNIZABLE PART OF THE COMPLEX.

St. Joseph's Hospital
264 Jackson Avenue

Gladys Presley always tried to shelter Elvis, so it distressed her when he began working at MARL Metal Company in 1952, while he was still attending high school. She thought his school work was more important. "It got so hard on him, he was so beat all the time, we made him quit and I went to work at St. Joseph's Hospital," she told an interviewer four years later.

Gladys had worked briefly at other jobs in Memphis. When she first came to the city, she worked as a seamstress at the Fashion Curtain Company (located at 284 Monroe Avenue), and she had done similar work in Tupelo. Later she worked at Britlings Cafeteria (located at 75 Union Avenue). Neither job suited her as well as her position at St. Joseph's Hospital, where she found her niche. She was a natural caregiver, and her patients adored her gentle manner. However, the job was too strenuous for Gladys, and she could only handle the work for a couple of years. Her health was never robust, and the long hours on her feet took their toll.

Mrs. Bramlett, who lived on Alabama Street and whose sons, John and Charlie, played football with Elvis, remembers that Elvis would meet his mother at the hospital at the end of her shift and drive her home. One day as they were leaving the hospital, Gladys told Elvis that she had seen a patient arrive in a pink Cadillac, and it was the most beautiful car she had ever seen. Elvis never forgot that conversation, nor the way her eyes lit up when she talked about that car.

DOWNTOWN. FROM POPLAR AVENUE, TURN NORTH ON THIRD STREET AND DRIVE PAST LAUDERDALE COURTS TO OVERTON AVENUE. TURN RIGHT ONTO OVERTON AVENUE. ST. JOSEPH'S HOSPITAL IS AT THE END OF THE STREET. ST. JUDE CHILDREN'S RESEARCH HOSPITAL IS LOCATED BEHIND AND TO THE RIGHT OF ST. JOSEPH'S.

L. C. Humes High School
Courtesy of the Memphis and Shelby County Room
Memphis/Shelby County Public Library and Information Center

SCHOOL

L.C. Humes High School
659 Manassas Street

There are some facts about Elvis's life that can never be proven, but where he went to school is not one of them. From 1948 to 1953, Elvis attended Humes High School—the only school that he attended in Memphis. Some writers have claimed that Elvis attended Christine School at 264 North Third, but a simple check of grade assignments lays to rest this argument. Christine School was an elementary school for grades one to six; Humes High School taught grades seven to twelve. When Elvis moved to Memphis, he was in the seventh grade.

Further proof is the fact that Vernon clearly remembered Elvis's first day at Humes. With over one thousand students, it was much larger than any school Elvis was familiar with in Tupelo. On his first day, the nervous and confused boy turned around and walked home. Vernon and Gladys allowed him to stay home for the rest of the day, but the next day, they insisted he walk into the school. They were determined that he receive the education which they lacked (when Elvis did graduate in 1953, he became the first in his family to complete high school). Stories of Gladys walking her teenage son to school probably originated during his first unsteady days in the seventh grade.

Mildred Scrivener was one of his last teachers at Humes High School, and one of his favorites. She believed Elvis thought of himself as an outsider, but he did not realize that a lot of the kids were just like him. In the families of many of Mildred Scrivener's students, both parents worked, and the kids carried a door key on a string around their necks. When they got home from school, they let themselves in the apartment. Door-key kids, she called them.

The first time Miss Scrivener noticed Elvis, he was eating an apple in the hallway, which was something he was not supposed to do. He was so nice and polite that she did not admonish him, and she remained charmed by him the rest of her life.

She first discovered Elvis could sing during a homeroom picnic. Elvis sat by himself playing guitar and singing ballad songs. Soon other students gathered around him, and he was encouraged to sing his heart out.

Slowly, Elvis asserted himself at school and made an impression on other students with his talent. He met George Klein at Mrs. Morman's music class in eighth grade. George still remembers Elvis performing the song "Cold, Cold Icy Fingers." Elvis would become one of George's best friends, but Mrs. Morman was not so enamored. She gave Elvis a "C" in the class, and at one point, she told him that he could not sing. Elvis replied, "You just don't like my kind of singing."

Elvis was an average student who did well in shop classes, less well in academics. He could have been a better student, but he also could have been a troublemaker. He was neither because he worked hard. He often fell asleep in Miss Scrivener's history class because he was working a factory job. She could have scolded him for sleeping in class, but she didn't. Sometimes it was necessary to enforce the rules, she believed, and sometimes it was necessary to look the other way.

Elvis came out of his shell during his senior year. Students soon noticed the sideburns he grew in defiance toward the other boys' crew cuts. Elvis also favored the unusual clothes he found at Lansky Brothers' Men's Store. He was growing handsome, and with his nice manners, the girls began to regard him as something special.

The teachers tolerated his unique style because he remained a polite, respectful young man, but many of the other boys considered him an oddball. A group once gave Elvis a collection of money and demanded he buy a haircut. On another occasion, Elvis was trapped in the bathroom with three boys looking for a fight. In walked Red West, a tough football player with musical aspirations of his own. Potential trouble was averted, and the two became friends. Elvis also befriended Marty Lacker, another student who rebelled from the status quo.

Humes was a tough working-class school, and the principal, Mr. T. C. Brindley, and his assistant, Miss Eleanor Richmond, worked hard for their students. Mr. Brindley maintained a revolving fund at the school for children who did not have money for some school activities. If students needed money to go to a school dance, they would quietly go to Mr. Brindley, and he gave them money from the fund. In turn, students supported school functions that raised money for this fund. Money collected at the annual variety show benefited that special student fund.

Elvis's first performance in front of a large audience was at the variety show for the special fund, where he sang in front of fifteen hundred people in the school auditorium. Miss Scrivener produced the show, and one of her duties was deciding who performed the encore. She had so many entrants that she decided the student who received the most applause would perform the encore. Mrs. Scrivener had to search for Elvis, who was nervously hiding behind a curtain, to tell him he had won. It was a defining moment for him—not only was he asked to go back onstage, but his performance brought the audience to an ovation. Perhaps it was that moment when he found the confidence to try a show business career, and to accept that such an outlandish idea was indeed possible.

Elvis as a library worker in 1951. He is in the back row, far right.
Courtesy of Anna Hamilton

*Elvis in speech class, 1951. He is in the third row, fourth from the left,
fourth from the right.*
Courtesy of Anna Hamilton

After he became famous, Elvis did not forget that moment at the
variety show and the teacher who encouraged him. He returned twice
to be a guest star on the show. Both shows sold out, raising money
for the school. Miss Scrivener recalled the story of Elvis's return to

Elvis's ROTC Company, 1951
Courtesy of the Memphis and Shelby County Room
Memphis/Shelby County Public Library and Information Center

Memphis in 1956, days before performing at the Tupelo Fair. Filming of his first film, *Love Me Tender*, was almost complete. Rather
than act the movie star, he chose to spend his time with students at
Humes High School, bringing along actor Nick Adams. Together they
talked to students in a class and answered their questions. At the
end Elvis went to his old homeroom and sat down at his old desk.
Miss Scrivener talked to Elvis, and as he left, he kissed her on the
cheek.

During one of his visits to Humes High School, Elvis gave a teacher
a television set to be used in the classroom. Then he gave the ROTC
department nine hundred dollars to buy new uniforms for a drill
team. Elvis felt that ROTC helped him overcome his teenage awk-
wardness during his school years.

The students at Humes were proud of him. Despite unprecedented
success, he remained one of the guys. Miss Scrivener was pleased
that Humes was still important to Elvis. Moreover, she felt that Elvis
was important to Humes' students. They saw him as an inspiration.
If he could make it, so could they.

Humes High School has been renamed Humes Junior High. The
auditorium where Elvis performed has been renamed in his honor.

DOWNTOWN. FROM POPLAR AVENUE, TURN NORTH ON MANASSAS STREET AND DRIVE
PAST THE NORTH PARKWAY AND JACKSON AVENUE INTERSECTIONS. HUMES JUNIOR
HIGH SCHOOL IS APPROXIMATELY A MILE FROM POPLAR AVENUE.

HIGH SCHOOL PROM

The Peabody Hotel
149 Union Avenue

In Memphis, the Peabody Hotel has long been the center of local traditions: viewing the twice daily parade of ducks through the lobby, sipping drinks by the fountain, dining and dancing in the Skyway, and attending weddings and receptions in the ballrooms. It's a place where Memphians celebrate birthdays, holidays, and many of the milestones of our lives; a place that goes back in our memory to childhood brunches on Mother's Day and to our first high school prom. The Peabody Hotel has remained one of the few constants in this city, and with the help of a successful renovation, it will undoubtedly continue to do so. Each spring the lobby and ballrooms fill with young adults in evening wear just as they did in 1953 when Elvis brought his date to the Humes High School Prom.

Her name was Regis Wilson, and she lived in Lauderdale Courts for six years before moving to nearby Merriweather Street. When they dated for three months during the spring of Elvis's senior year, she was fourteen and Elvis was eighteen.

Just three years later, many a teenage girl would swoon over the idea of going to the prom with Elvis, but it's doubtful anyone would have imagined it just as it happened. In reality Elvis was as awkward a teenager as many of us were.

Elvis rented a blue tuxedo and a shiny blue Chevrolet for the prom. When he picked up Regis at her house, he pinned a pink corsage on her. "It's hard to believe, but he did not know how to dance," Regis remembers. They sat and talked all evening. After the prom, he took her to a drive-in restaurant on Lamar Avenue where some of his friends said they would meet them. "We waited and waited, but his friends never showed up."

"At fourteen you can't really be in love with someone, but I liked him a lot," Regis said. They dated until she moved to Florida that May. When Elvis performed in Miami in 1956, she went to the show and tried to get backstage, but the security guard didn't believe her when she said she knew Elvis.

"I knew him at a time when his life was simple and he was sweet. I'd just have to say it was a special time," Regis said.

DOWNTOWN. THE PEABODY HOTEL IS LOCATED ON THE SOUTH SIDE OF UNION AVENUE, BETWEEN SECOND AND THIRD STREETS.

Market Mall, Lauderdale Courts
Courtesy of the Memphis and Shelby County Room
Memphis/Shelby County Public Library and Information Center

HANGOUTS

Market Mall
Lauderdale Courts

Lauderdale Courts covered such a large expanse that it was much like a small community, complete with its own facilities, parks, and recreation areas. In 1949 the twenty-six-acre project included sixty-six three- and two-story apartment buildings, with 449 apartments in all. The complex included a steam power plant at 243 Winchester Avenue and the headquarters of the Memphis Housing Authority at 264 North Lauderdale Street. Not surprisingly, the Court's residents adopted their own areas to socialize.

Market Mall was one such place. Before the construction of Lauderdale Courts, this was actually part of Market Street. Renamed

Market Mall when the street was blocked off, it is the east-to-west pedestrian walkway that begins at Third Avenue and ends at Lauderdale Street. On either side of Market Mall, apartments were built, with entrance doors facing the mall and a row of steps leading up to each door. The Market Mall and the doorsteps became informal gathering places for the young Lauderdale Courts residents. Many of these residents remember Elvis entertaining on Market Mall.

John Black, whose brother Bill was later Elvis's bass player, said, "We would play under the trees, underneath those big magnolia trees. It was just whoever would come, whoever showed up. We'd have a mandolin maybe, three or four guitars, and the people would gather. We weren't trying to impress the world, we were just playing to have a good time."

DOWNTOWN. FROM POPLAR AVENUE, DRIVE NORTH ON THIRD STREET; THE BEST VIEW OF MARKET MALL IS TO THE EAST OF THIRD STREET BETWEEN EXCHANGE AND WINCHESTER AVENUES. ST. MARY'S CATHOLIC CHURCH AND THE CONVENTION CENTER WILL BE TO THE WEST.

The Triangle
Lauderdale Courts

On the northern boundary of Lauderdale Courts was a grassy area that residents called "The Triangle." The Triangle was the home of many social gatherings at Lauderdale Courts—some of the kids played football here, some of the adults visited with each other, and sometimes the Courts' musicians played here.

Jean Lazenby Foster, a resident of Lauderdale Courts, said, "When we were coming up in the Courts, we used to sit out and have little groups all the time. Everybody singing and playing, and sometimes there's more than one guitar. There wasn't much on the TV back then so we stayed outside and played music, and it was the good old days."

Elvis was very shy then, John Black remembers. John and his buddies were older than Elvis, and when they played football in the

Triangle, Elvis would sit on the sidelines. John would eventually draw him into conversation. "I could make him talk. If you'd get him to talk to you, he would open up. Sometimes he was just lonesome and needed someone to talk to. He wasn't quite our age. I was into music and some of the same interests he had, so it made it easier for us to talk," John recalled.

Jean remembers a day when she was about fifteen and was sitting on the edge of the Triangle. Elvis was living at Graceland then. "Elvis came back to bring his mother and daddy to visit friends. I was playing the guitar facing the street, and the kids were facing me. They didn't see Elvis drive up, and I didn't tell them that he drove up. He gave me the high sign and the motion to be quiet, and he waved at me. When he came back out with them about thirty minutes later, he winked at me and waved good-bye and blew me a kiss."

Jean smiled at Elvis that day, but she didn't wave. Elvis deserved his privacy, and she knew that the kids would race toward him. She waited until his car had disappeared from view, and then she told the kids that Elvis had just left. "They almost killed me," she remembers.

DOWNTOWN. THE TRIANGLE WAS AT THE NORTHEAST CORNER OF LAUDERDALE STREET AND ALABAMA AVENUE. I-40 NOW COVERS THIS FIELD.

The Recreation Hall
Lauderdale Courts
Intersection of Winchester Avenue and Lauderdale Street

At the corner of Winchester Avenue and Lauderdale Street, near the boiler house, was the maintenance building of the Courts. It was in the basement of this building that the teenagers of Lauderdale Courts would hold parties, with the supervisor's permission. They were an enterprising lot, sending out invitations, setting up tables, decorating, and charging twenty-five cents per couple.

Elvis
Courtesy of Linda Everett

Buzzy Forbess, a friend of Elvis, remembers being teased by Elvis at one of these dances. Elvis asked the crowd to be quiet so that he could make an announcement. When he had everyone's attention, he declared that everyone except Buzzy had paid a quarter for admission. What Elvis neglected to say was that that afternoon, while horsing around, Elvis had talked Buzzy out of his quarter (his last quarter that he was saving for the dance) and lost it in a pinball machine. Of course, Buzzy was embarrassed.

When Elvis's friends organized these events, Elvis would often sing. However, other residents of the Courts also held parties in the hall, and Elvis wasn't always allowed to perform. An older, tougher group of aspiring musicians performed at many of these gatherings. One such group was made up of Johnny and Dorsey Burnette along with Paul Burlison, who would become the "Rock and Roll Trio." The Burnette brothers were Golden Glove boxers with a combative disposition to match. Elvis was four years younger than the Burnettes, and they refused to let Elvis grace the stage with them.

The Rock and Roll Trio would later record some of the most distinctive rockabilly of the era. Johnny and Dorsey both wrote songs and recorded as solo acts before their untimely deaths. Paul Burlison chose to give up life on the road and raise his family. He still performs an occasional show and chuckles over their impertinent treatment of Elvis.

DOWNTOWN. FROM POPLAR AVENUE, TURN NORTH ON LAUDERDALE STREET. WINCHESTER AVENUE IS THE SECOND LEFT. THE BUILDING ON THE SOUTHWEST CORNER OF THE INTERSECTION, WITH THE SIGN THAT SAYS "POLICE BOXING CLUB," WAS THE RECREATION HALL. IT IS NOT OPEN TO THE PUBLIC.

Odd Fellows Hall
Main Street and Court Avenue

During high school, Elvis frequently entertained at parties and gatherings. Elvis's high school friends claimed Elvis never learned the latest dances because he was too busy singing. "We were conforming to the dances of the time," Buzzy Forbess said. "The bop was big, and slow dances. Elvis, of course, had his own movements. At parties he was always playing and singing, so we learned to dance before he did."

One of the places where he often sang was at the Odd Fellows Hall, operated by a fraternal organization where several of his friends were members. The Odd Fellows held dances in the recreation room on the fourth floor of the Columbia Mutual Tower.

Although Elvis never joined the Odd Fellows, he often accompanied his friends when they hung out at the Odd Fellows Hall, shooting pool and occasionally playing ping-pong. The Odd Fellows sponsored various charities, and Elvis sometimes went with them on these charity outings. Elvis played for patients at Kennedy Veterans Hospital and the Home for Incurables during trips with the Odd Fellows.

DOWNTOWN. THE BUILDING IS AT THE NORTHEAST CORNER OF NORTH MAIN STREET (NOW A PEDESTRIAN MALL) AND COURT AVENUE. COURT SQUARE IS ADJACENT TO THE BUILDING. THE ODD FELLOWS NO LONGER MAINTAIN A CLUB ROOM AT THIS BUILDING, NOW CALLED THE LINCOLN AMERICAN TOWER.

Water Works
The Parkway Pumping Station
North Parkway and Dunlap Street

In the city there were no woods to explore, no backroads to meander, and no spacious yards in which to play. Nonetheless, there were patches of green where kids could play football or kick the can. On the corner of North Parkway and Dunlap Street, the city operated an artesian well and pumping station, and the surrounding property served as an unofficial park where Elvis and his friends often played.

Elvis's high school friend Buzzie Forbess remembers a particular football game there. During those days not only were the schools segregated, but their sports teams never played opponents of a dif-

Elvis playing football
Courtesy of Linda Everett

ferent color. One day, Elvis, Buzzie, and about ten of their buddies went over to the water works to toss around a football. When they got there, they found about forty black kids already at the park. They quickly organized teams, white against black, and began to play.

Elvis's team could generally hold their own, but this time they were no match. Maybe their hearts weren't quite in it, or maybe they were just silly. As their opponent's center would bend over the ball, the quarterback would shout, "Beans! Maters! Taters!" Rather than bracing for defense, Elvis's team would fall to the ground laughing just as the ball went flying over their heads towards a touchdown.

While Elvis normally took football seriously, on at least this one occasion, his humor overcame his competitive spirit. This time he and his friends were just being kids, playing on a vacant stretch of city land.

DOWNTOWN. FROM POPLAR AVENUE, TURN NORTH ON DUNLAP STREET AND DRIVE

Hall's Grocery
1588 Mississippi Boulevard

While Elvis was able to finish high school, his cousin Gene Smith (whose father was Gladys's brother, William Edward) dropped out so that he could help his parents. Gene ended up working full time for Hall's Grocery, delivering groceries by bicycle. In many families such a difference in circumstance could have driven the two boys farther apart. In the case of Elvis and Gene, it tended to draw them closer together, perhaps because there really was such a fine line separating their situations.

Elvis would visit Gene at the grocery nearly every afternoon after school. They would wander to the back of the store, to the dairy bar, and sip Purple Cows, a float made from grape soda and vanilla ice cream. Then they would talk about the things that were important to them.

Gene and Elvis had been close as children in Tupelo; only seven weeks separated their births. When Gene's family followed the Presleys to Memphis, the two boys continued their friendship. They could exchange some of their deepest thoughts, aspirations, and fears. As Gene entered the work force, Elvis didn't want his cousin to feel alone. He would listen to Gene talk about his hopes for simply finding a better job someday. In turn, Elvis would talk about his aspirations, how he wanted a career in music and was anxious to begin working as a gospel singer or musician. Instead, he ended up having to go to work after graduation himself.

SOUTH MEMPHIS. HALL'S GROCERY WAS RAZED TO MAKE WAY FOR THE I-240 LOOP. FROM I-240, HEADING DOWNTOWN FROM ELVIS PRESLEY BOULEVARD, TAKE THE SOUTH PARKWAY EXIT AND TURN WEST. TURN SOUTH ON MISSISSIPPI BOULEVARD AND DRIVE LESS THAN A MILE. THE APPROXIMATE LOCATION OF THE STORE IS BETWEEN SOUTH PARKWAY AND PERSON AVENUE.

Loew's State Theater and Planters Peanuts
Courtesy of the Memphis and Shelby County Room
Memphis/Shelby County Public Library and Information Center

ELVIS'S EMPLOYMENT

Loew's State Theater
152 South Main Street

From the time he was a young child, Elvis loved the movies. As a teenager, he could not have found a more ideal job than as usher at the Loew's State Theater. Unfortunately, this position was not long-lived. Still, it carried with it an odd bit of irony.

Elvis worked at the theater on two separate occasions, beginning in the fall of 1950. A sophomore in high school at the time, he would arrive home after 10:00 on school nights. After a few months, his mother asked him to quit because his grades were slipping. When school let out the following summer, Elvis was hired again.

For a young boy living in the housing project, the theater must have been another world. Built in 1920, no expense was spared in its construction, and it was designed as an opulent retreat from everyday life. One could enter the ornate lobby—decorated with grand columns, gold plating, and chandeliers—and experience a grandeur normally reserved for the upper class. In the 1930s, the theater became one of the first air-conditioned buildings in Memphis.

Elvis's friend George Klein remembers that as a movie usher, Elvis loved to watch the same movie again and again just to observe certain actors' movements and appearance. Elvis would ask himself, "How do they express themselves? How do they attract girls?" He saw that the girls were attracted to James Dean and Marlon Brando, young actors who never smiled on camera. Clark Gable always wore long-sleeve shirts with the top button undone. And Elvis noticed that Tony Curtis, a romantic young star, had black hair. Elvis's natural hair color was light brown, but for nearly all of his career, he dyed it jet black.

Elvis also noticed that all of these men—or at least the characters they portrayed—were men of action. They fought hard when the need arose, and they didn't stand for bullying or back stabbing.

Later that summer, Elvis became fond of a female coworker. Apparently another usher was sweet on her as well because when he learned the girl had given Elvis a candy bar from the concession stand he told the theater manager, Arthur Groom, that Elvis had stolen the candy. Elvis replied with his fists. Groom solved the dispute by firing both of them. Groom was probably the only person to ever fire Elvis Presley. This was not the only occasion Elvis fought an adversary, and the incident ought to put to rest the persistent rumor that the teenage Elvis was a helpless wimp.

Elvis, of course, was only a kid at the time, but here lies the irony: Six years later Elvis allowed his third movie, *Jailhouse Rock*, to premiere in that same theater. Arthur Groom, still the manager, had a good sense of humor about this incredible change of fortune. Three weeks before the premier, he posed with Elvis and an usher's uniform—presumably the same uniform that Elvis had worn—and told his story for the newspapers. Elvis was welcome to return to his job anytime, Groom said. In fact, he joked that he would especially like for Elvis to usher at the premiere. With a grin Elvis replied, "Sir, I don't believe I'm ready to go back to my old job yet." Even Mrs. Groom could not resist teasing her husband. "Well, all I can say, Arthur Groom, is that you'll work a long while before we own a car as tremendous as that one Elvis has out there," she chided.

Although the premier was a huge success—fans lined up the night before to insure their place in the theater—Elvis did not attend. He was traveling by rail to California for a series of concerts. This was not unusual for Elvis; he often didn't attend gala events. The premier of *Jailhouse Rock* was tinged with sadness, and this may have been another reason why he chose not to participate. His costar, Judy Tyler, had been killed in an automobile accident shortly after the completion of the movie. "I don't believe I can stand to see the movie we made together now," Elvis had said.

The theater was demolished some years ago. This neglected part of downtown is now being transformed into the Peabody Place office and shopping development.

DOWNTOWN, FROM UNION AVENUE, TURN SOUTH ON THE SOUTH MAIN STREET PEDESTRIAN MALL. THE LOEW'S STATE THEATER WAS LOCATED BETWEEN GAYOSO AVENUE AND PEABODY PLACE.

MARL Metal Manufacturing Company
208 West Georgia Avenue

Like many seventeen-year-olds, Elvis took an after-school job in the fall of 1952. He was, however, a bit overzealous. Working the second shift from 3:30 to 11:30 P.M. proved to be too difficult considering he was still a full-time student. He quit after two months.

Nonetheless, it was a valiant attempt to help his family. His application for employment, according to Vince Staten, an early biographer, listed five dependents, an astounding claim for a fresh-faced young kid.

Elvis had only one coworker because everyone else at MARL worked the first shift. By all accounts, Elvis got along well with his partner, and they took their breaks together. Elvis wasn't much of a conversationalist, though. It seems he was too busy playing his guitar.

DOWNTOWN. NO TRACE OF MARL METAL MANUFACTURING COMPANY REMAINS TODAY, AND THE SECTION OF WEST GEORGIA AVENUE WHERE THE BUILDING ONCE STOOD NO LONGER EXISTS. FOR A FEEL OF THE NEIGHBORHOOD, TURN EAST ON WEST GEORGIA AVENUE FROM RIVERSIDE DRIVE.

Tennessee Employment Security Office
122 Union Avenue

For Elvis, the milestone of his high school graduation did not offer the luxury of lazing about for the summer. He approached graduation with the determination to begin work (any kind of work) as soon as possible. On the very day of his commencement exercises, Elvis walked into the Tennessee Employment Security office.

He didn't have a trade and he didn't have much work experience. He was given the General Aptitude Test Battery to determine where it was best to try and place him. Although his scores were only average, he had his driver's license, and he seemed like a nice boy. He made an impression on his advisor, Mrs. Harris. She studied the files and came across a notice for temporary work at M.B. Parker Company. Elvis drove out there that afternoon and was hired for the summer.

However, Elvis didn't really care for the machine-shop work that he did at M.B. Parker. What he really wanted to do, he confided in Mrs. Harris when the job at MARL ended, was drive a truck. A few months later when Gladys Tipler called the employment office in search of a driver, Mrs. Harris remembered Elvis's request. "I've got the boy for you," she said. "But don't be fooled by his appearance."

M.B. Parker Company
1449 Thomas Street

The work was tedious at M.B. Parker, where Elvis worked during the summer of 1953. Nothing more than standing on an assembly line taking the heads off flame-throw regulators, replacing the "O" rings, and putting the heads back on. It wasn't particularly laborious work, but the shop was sweltering during the summer. Elvis, like all the guys, would pull off his T-shirt to try to stay cool.

Despite the tedium and the heat, the job suited Elvis just fine. In fact, this temporary job, found for him by the Tennessee Department of Employment Security, seemed ideal. He could earn an income while formulating his own plans and dreams. He could bide his time until something better came along.

It was a small company with an open-door policy. Before work one morning, more than a month after Elvis joined the company, he paid a visit to his supervisor Mr. Parker. Elvis was visibly upset, and he said that without an advance on his wages he wouldn't be able to make his payment on the Lincoln, and it would be repossessed. Mr. Parker explained that it was against company policy to make such a loan, but Elvis was so near tears that Mr. Parker agreed to write a personal check for thirty-three dollars. Two days later, Elvis promptly turned his paycheck over to Mr. Parker to repay the loan.

What is peculiar about this particular story is that Elvis's car was paid for. We will never know why Elvis so desperately needed an advance. However, it may have something to do with his desire to make a record at Memphis Recording Service, because sometime during that week of July 13, 1953, that's what Elvis did. Marion Keisker, the secretary at Memphis Recording Service, later remembered that Elvis was grimy when he came into the studio. He looked like a boy who had worked all day.

NORTH MEMPHIS. FROM POPLAR AVENUE, TURN NORTH ON DANNY THOMAS BOU-
LEVARD. THIS WILL BECOME THOMAS STREET. M.B. PARKER COMPANY IS NO LONGER IN
OPERATION. THE BUILDING WHICH ONCE HOUSED THIS BUSINESS IS NOW MID-SOUTH
MAINTENANCE, INC., LOCATED BETWEEN PLUM AND PEAR AVENUES ON THE WEST SIDE
OF THE STREET.

Precision Tool Company, Inc.
1132 Kansas Street

Elvis's employment at Precision Tool was a natural considering that
so many of his relatives worked there. Gladys's brothers, John and
Travis Smith, were working there when the Presleys moved to Memphis. Vernon joined them briefly, but quit when he was hired at United
Paint Company. Vernon's brother (and brother-in-law since he was
married to Gladys's sister), Vester, worked there for a number of years,
ending his employment when Elvis hired him to guard the gates at
Graceland. Elvis and his cousin, Gene Smith, were hired by the company at the same time in September 1953 to work the day shift.

Precision Tool made artillery shells for the federal government.
Working on the assembly line was exacting work, and every shell
was checked by government inspectors. At the same time, the workers were under pressure to meet production quotas. Vester and Gene
both claimed that Elvis was the fastest worker of them all.

It was also a dangerous job. One woman was hurt in 1959 when a
bomb simulator she was working on exploded. At the end of that
same year, the entire building was lost when another bomb exploded
and set off the ammunition in a chain reaction. The factory was rebuilt, along with its sister company, Dixie Chemical, but in 1963
another blast injured fifteen workers. Six years later, Gene's brother,
Robert, was killed when he slipped and fell into a vat of boiling
chemicals.

Given the dangers, perhaps it was just as well that Elvis left after a
few months employment.

SOUTH MEMPHIS. THIS LOCATION IS SOUTH OF DOWNTOWN IN AN INDUSTRIAL AREA.

Elvis's Precision Tool Company ID
Courtesy of Stephen Shutts

AREA. FROM CRUMP BOULEVARD, TURN SOUTH ON FLORIDA STREET, THEN WEST, OR LEFT, ON KANSAS STREET. PRECISION TOOL WAS HOUSED IN THE BUILDING NOW OCCUPIED BY VICKERS DISTRIBUTION AND TRANSFER COMPANY AT THE NORTHEAST CORNER OF KANSAS STREET AND MCLEMORE AVENUE.

Crown Electric Company
353 Poplar Avenue

When Elvis appeared on the *Ed Sullivan Show* in 1956, he said that if things didn't work out, he knew that he could go back to driving a truck. Back in Memphis, Gladys and James Tipler beamed as they heard those words because they knew that Elvis was talking about them. He had worked for them at Crown Electric Company, driving the delivery truck to the electricians on the jobs, and after he became famous, he often mentioned their company in interviews.

Elvis came to the Tiplers in November 1953, after leaving Precision Tool. Again he had turned to Mrs. Harris at the Tennessee Department of Employment Security in his search for a job. When she heard about the position at Crown, she thought it would be right for Elvis. She warned Mrs. Tipler not to judge Elvis by his appearance. "If she hadn't said that, I think I would have told him to take to the door," Mrs. Tipler later recalled. "His hair was long! Even though he was a clean-cut looking kid, I just wasn't used to that."

Mrs. Tipler grew to like Elvis. He was well mannered and a good employee. Elvis made a similar impression on all the workers. She wasn't happy, however, when she found out he carved his name on a wooden wall. When interviewed in 1956, she said "Now it's one of our proudest mementos of Elvis's stay with us. Funny how things happen sometime."

Although she always spoke of Elvis in glowing terms, in a later interview she remembered that Elvis was frequently late and always rushing to the mirror to comb his hair before doing anything else. This was especially true in the few months following the release of his first record, when he was trying to manage his full-time job and blossoming career. One day he had a flat tire. Without stopping to fix it, he raced into Crown Electric, leaving the broken-down truck and swinging his guitar on his shoulder as he walked back out the door. In frustration Mrs. Tipler said, "Elvis, put down that guitar. It's gonna be the ruination of you." Elvis just looked at her and laughed.

Elvis left the Tiplers' employ in November of 1954. Paul Burlison, an electrician with Crown and already a member of Johnny Burnette's Rock and Roll Trio, remembers that Elvis returned for a visit not long after he left Crown. "He pulled up to the front door in that pink Cadillac and blowed his horn. 'Come out here Gladys, I got something I want to show you. Look what that little ole guitar bought me,'" Burlison recalled.

Elvis stopped by to visit the Tiplers on several other occasions, once bringing along actor Nick Adams, who was staying with him at Graceland.

During Elvis's employment, Crown Electric Company was located near the intersection of Poplar Avenue and Lauderdale Street, which is now Danny Thomas Boulevard. It was a short walk south of 462 Alabama Avenue and Lauderdale Courts. The building was destroyed in 1983 to make way for a gas station.

Elvis had his own memento from his days at Crown Electric. He later bought an old pickup truck, much like the one he used to drive while working at Crown. At times he would drive around Memphis in that truck as secretly as he could.

As for the truck that he drove at Crown, the Tiplers sold it. Several years later, a man asked them if they'd be interested in buying an old truck with a bad motor. Mr. Tipler recognized it immediately—it was Elvis's old truck. The same dealer who bought it from Mr. Tipler had sold it to this man. Mrs. Tipler always wished her husband had bought it back, though they knew by then that Elvis would never have occasion to drive it again.

DOWNTOWN. CROWN ELECTRIC COMPANY WAS LOCATED ON THE SOUTHEAST CORNER OF POPLAR AVENUE AND DANNY THOMAS BOULEVARD. AN EXXON STATION NOW OCCUPIES THAT SITE.

CAREER INFLUENCES

Suzore #2 Theater
279 North Main Street

Unlike the opulent Loew's State Theater, the Suzore was a thread-bare operation. It had two old heaters down front in the winter, and in the summertime, two big fans didn't do much more than swirl the hot air. The roof leaked, and according to Elvis's friend John Bramlett, "We always took along two sticks—one to hold up our seats, the other to beat off the rats." But what the Suzore lacked in atmosphere, it made up for in its selection of movies. This is where the teenagers went to watch their favorite cliff-hangers, the serials that continued with an episode every week.

Elvis used to go to the Suzore nearly every week, sometimes with a group of ten or twelve guys, sometimes with just a friend or two. John Bramlett remembers going there with his brothers, Charlie and Odell, and Elvis. One night in particular stands out among the others.

They were in the middle of watching the movie when Gladys swept down the aisle looking for Elvis. When she spotted him she rushed over and began whispering excitedly to him. Dewey Phillips was playing his record "That's All Right," and he wanted Elvis to come to the radio station. "Elvis kept asking his mother, 'Are you serious?'" John remembered. Of course, Elvis hurriedly left the theater, and his appearance that night on WHBQ is legendary.

After leaving the Suzore Theater, Elvis's life would never be the same. Later, John Bramlett talked about the significant change that Elvis underwent that first night his music was played on the radio. "I knew he had been playing his guitar and singing on Alabama Street outside the Scotland Inn, a little beer joint. That first time people heard him and became excited by his voice was probably the last time anyone ever called a radio station to ask who he was."

The Suzore closed its doors a long time ago.

DOWNTOWN. THE SUZORE #2 THEATER ONCE STOOD ON NORTH MAIN STREET BE-TWEEN MARKET STREET AND WINCHESTER AVENUE, IN THE APPROXIMATE AREA OF THE I-40 OVERPASS. THE ENTIRE BLOCK WAS RAZED TO BUILD THE INTERSTATE.

The Green Owl
260 North Main Street

Despite segregation in the South, the working-class neighborhoods were for the most part racially mixed. Living in the inner city, Elvis was exposed to all of the music and culture the black community had to offer.

Charlie Bramlett, Elvis's boyhood friend who grew up at 573 Alabama Avenue, remembers a lot of black entertainers performing on different corners in the neighborhood. Near Winchester Park, at the bottom of the hill, were a lot of juke joints. "Going down there you'd hear really good black entertainment," Charlie said. "They'd play harmonicas and guitars and pitch washers. That's the way it was on Beale Street too. They would be out there singing and passing the hat."

Elvis and Memphis friends backstage at a nightclub
Courtesy of Anna Hamilton

The Green Owl was a beer joint located on North Main Street, not far from where W.C. Handy once operated his office and sheet-music shop. This is the club that Buzzy Forbess remembers most from his teenage days with Elvis. "Every now and then we would walk into the Green Owl, a beer joint for blacks. Elvis loved the Green Owl. They always had a crowd there, and people would spill over onto the sidewalk. He particularly liked one of the musicians in the Green Owl. This guy had fashioned a five-gallon bucket and a broom handle into a bass, and he was pretty good at playing it."

For most southern whites, the black culture was witnessed from afar, still separate by law and custom no matter how close they lived to one another. But Elvis's love of black music, played at places like the Green Owl, helped him to see past those barriers. As Vernon once said, "Elvis was more color blind than most."

DOWNTOWN. FROM UNION AVENUE, TURN NORTH ONTO NORTH MAIN STREET. THE GREEN OWL WAS LOCATED ON NORTH MAIN STREET BETWEEN MARKET AND WINCHESTER AVENUES. IT IS NOW DEMOLISHED.

Beale Street

Beale Street has been known to the world as a place of music since W. C. Handy began to publish blues songs in 1912, attracting musicians to the city. Patrons of nightclubs and other venues on Beale Street watched now legendary entertainers perform all night, while itinerant musicians worked for tips on the street. For the African-American community, Beale was much more than a place of good times. It was their refuge in a South that lived under the laws of segregation. Beale was the one place where blacks could go without experiencing any intimidation from whites. And it was a place where anything a person could want, from opportunity to pleasure, could be found.

Because of his love for music, Elvis Presley was one of the few whites who ventured to Beale Street. Blues legend B.B. King remembers Elvis at the pawn shops, watching the musicians who gathered there. The exposure obviously influenced the young Elvis because he was once heard thanking B.B. King for everything he had taught him. Other members of the Beale Street scene also claimed to have influenced Elvis. Calvin Newborn, a guitarist and the son of a local

Beale Street (Abe Schwab's)
Courtesy of the Memphis and Shelby County Room
Memphis/Shelby County Public Library and Information Center

bandleader, insists that he taught Elvis a few things on guitar. A promoter on Beale Street said he took Elvis into the Hotel Men's Improvement Club to watch the singers there. We may never know all the places that Elvis visited, especially in his formative years, but we can imagine where Elvis's curiosity led him.

Beale Street changed dramatically as the Civil Rights movement ended legal segregation, no longer remaining the focus of African-American Memphis. In 1968 the conflict over the garbage workers' strike and the assassination of Dr. Martin Luther King at the Lorraine Motel just blocks from Beale Street created a sense of fear about downtown Memphis that still exists. Much of the neighborhood around Beale was destroyed during an urban renewal project, but never rebuilt. The Beale Street commercial strip from Main to Fourth Streets looked like a ghost town until the 1980s when development began again.

B. B. King's and Willie Mitchell's are just two of the clubs on Beale Street that have given the area a new vitality. On weekend nights the street is alive with entertainers. Street musicians perform free for crowds gathering around them, and music blares outward from inside the clubs. All over is the sound of the blues as it's heard only in Memphis, just as Elvis might have heard it years ago.

DOWNTOWN. FROM UNION AVENUE, TURN SOUTH ON SECOND STREET AND CONTINUE FOR TWO BLOCKS TO REACH BEALE STREET. BEALE STREET TRAVELS WEST TO EAST, BEGINNING AT RIVERSIDE DRIVE. THE HISTORIC DISTRICT INCLUDES THE SECTION OF BEALE FROM SECOND TO FOURTH STREETS. THIS IS WHERE ALL THE ACTION IS; SEE THE APPENDIX FOR A SHORT DESCRIPTION OF WHAT TO SEE ON BEALE. DRIVING ON BEALE STREET IS NOT PERMITTED ON THE WEEKENDS AND OTHER FESTIVE OCCASIONS.

Palace Theater
324 Beale Street

Professor Nat D. Williams hosted Amateur Night talent contests in the Palace Theater on Beale Street. His fellow host was Rufus Thomas, a showman of multiple talents who won fame in the 1960s for his funky dance tunes. On Amateur Night anyone could get on the stage, but they were at the mercy of the audience. If the audience didn't like the act, the performer was run off the stage under a hail of rotten tomatoes, or "shot" with a toy pistol by the "Lord High Executioner." The audience's favorites, on the other hand, were rewarded with prize money of up to five dollars.

Ambitious and talented performers competed for the chance to be heard by the right people. Isaac Hayes, David Porter, and Carla Thomas, Rufus's daughter, were among the soul music stars who got their start at the Palace Theater's Amateur Nights.

Although there's no proof that Elvis performed at these shows, some people recall that he did. Part of the mystery of Elvis is finding when and where he performed before "celebrity" caused his every move to be watched, and memory sometimes has a tricky way of rearranging the precise order of events. At the end of his life, Nat Williams recalled that Elvis did perform at the Amateur Night shows many times when he was starting his career. Nat admired the way Elvis sang the blues. "We had a boast that if you made it on Beale Street, you could make it anywhere. And Elvis Presley made it on Beale Street," he said.

Elvis may well have sung in the talent show competition, although the date is anyone's guess. Did he come here as a high school student or a recent graduate? More likely, he may have appeared shortly after July 1954, when he began to pal around with Dewey Phillips who loved to hang out on Beale. The truth may never be known.

The Palace Theater was also the place for the famed Midnight Rambles, a variety show open only to a white audience. These shows were known for the bawdy performances of the dancing girls and the rowdy behavior of the patrons. Sadly, the theater did not survive the decline of Beale Street. Historic markers were placed on the site, now a vacant lot. Only its neon sign has been saved, used today by another nightclub bearing that same name.

DOWNTOWN. THE PALACE THEATER WAS LOCATED IN THE BEALE STREET HISTORIC DISTRICT AT HERNANDO STREET, BETWEEN THIRD AND FOURTH STREETS. NOW DEMOLISHED, HISTORIC MARKERS FOR NAT D. WILLIAMS AND RUFUS THOMAS MARK THE LOCATION.

Home of the Blues Record Shop
107 Beale Street
Corner of Main and Beale Streets

There was scarcely a musician in town who didn't know the Home of the Blues Record Shop. The shop's proprietor, Ruben Cherry, didn't load the racks with new releases or dump his inventory when an artist's star began to fall. Instead he tried to carry one of everything, figuring that every record had a buyer somewhere.

It was an archives of sorts, and part of a Memphis musician's education was gleaned from standing in front of the old wooden bins flipping through records. At the same time, it was like a giant song factory, because every song there had the potential of becoming a hit. Copyright and ownership were ill-defined in those days, and any musician looking for a song to cut might start with an older record.

Home of the Blues
Courtesy of the Memphis and Shelby County Room
Memphis/Shelby County Public Library and Information Center

When the Rock and Roll Trio, made up of Johnny and Dorsey Burnette and Paul Burlison, stopped in Memphis before a Nashville recording session, the newspaper reported that they were going to the Home of the Blues Record Shop to pick out songs to record. "If you liked it you could always change it into rockabilly if it just had good words and a melody," Paul Burlison said. "You could always put a beat to it if you wanted to. You could take an old country song and put a beat to it like Elvis did with 'Blue Moon of Kentucky.'"

Johnny Burnette once told an interviewer that after school he used to hang out in the Home of the Blues. He used to run into Elvis quite frequently there, he said.

When "That's Alright" was released, Ruben Cherry was the first to stock it. In fact, many Memphians remember buying their first Elvis records at Home of the Blues. Ruben was such a strong supporter of Elvis that he even loaned Elvis money to get to his early concerts.

In 1976, upon learning that his old friend was ill, Elvis wrote a letter to Ruben thanking him for his early support. The letter was read at Ruben's burial service.

DOWNTOWN. THE MEMPHIS LIGHT, GAS AND WATER BUILDING NOW STANDS AT THIS SITE ON THE CORNER OF MAIN AND BEALE STREETS, WITHIN THE BEALE STREET HISTORIC DISTRICT. IRONICALLY, THE POWER COMPANY DONATED PART OF THIS PROPERTY ON THE SOUTH SIDE OF BEALE STREET FOR PLACEMENT OF THE ELVIS PRESLEY STATUE IN 1980. WHILE THE STATUE IS NO LONGER AT THIS SITE, IT IS STILL A POPULAR PLACE FOR ELVIS FANS. A NEW STATUE WILL BE DEDICATED AT THIS SITE ON AUGUST 15, 1997.

The Blues Shop
286 North Main Street

Where was Elvis's very first recording—"My Happiness" and "That's Where Your Heartaches Begin"—played? Probably not at the Presley home. Although Elvis told Memphis Recording Service receptionist Marion Keisker that he was making a record to give to his mother, the Presleys did not own a record player.

He may have taken his acetate to The Blues Shop, a little record store across the street from the Suzore #2 Theater where the young men would gather to listen to the inventory. The shop played an unheralded role in Elvis's music education, introducing him to different styles of blues, gospel, and jazz. For years this favorite hangout has been referred to as "Charlie's," simply because everyone called it by the owner's name. Charlie was quick to play the latest offerings for anyone who stopped in at the store.

Buzzy Forbess, Elvis's high school friend, remembers that Elvis persuaded Charlie to play his acetate. Elvis was so proud of that record he wanted everyone to hear it.

Later he took it to his classmate Ed Leek's house to play on the family record player. For whatever reason he left it there, and the acetate disappeared until Ed offered it for sale some thirty plus years later. RCA/BMG purchased it and released it as part of the *Elvis Presley, The King of Rock and Roll: The Complete 50s Masters* boxed set in 1992. But before Ed Leek stored it away, Elvis may have played the acetate in a forgotten record store on North Main.

DOWNTOWN. FROM UNION AVENUE, TURN NORTH ON NORTH MAIN STREET. THE BLUES SHOP WAS LOCATED ON NORTH MAIN STREET BETWEEN MARKET AND WINCHESTER AVENUES. THE STORE IS NOW DEMOLISHED.

Pop (Poplar) Tunes
306 Poplar Avenue

Founded by Joe Cuoghi and John Novarese in 1946, Pop Tunes has come to symbolize the very best in Memphis music. Indeed, Cuoghi went on to found Hi Records, which recorded the Bill Black Combo, Willie Mitchell, and Al Green. It was a natural venture for Coughi, given the friendships and influence he established as a record retailer.

Sam Phillips of Sun Records would visit the store, sometimes bringing a new recording artist to introduce to Coughi. Jerry Lee Lewis was one such young man. B.B. King came into the store on his own one evening and played his guitar. Coughi liked King so much that he called a friend of his who worked at a radio station, supposedly giving B.B. King his first real break. Dewey Phillips used to stop by the store on the way to his afternoon radio show, and he often came by after the show when the store was closed. After hours, Coughi and his other music-business friends would sit around spinning records and filling each other in on the latest industry gossip.

Whether Elvis knew of Coughi's influence when he first started hanging around the record store is debatable. Located a short walk from Lauderdale Courts, Elvis spent so much time in the store that Cuoghi came to know him as a shy, polite kid. Years later Cuoghi remembered a very young Elvis coming into the store just to see if his records were selling. Whenever a young girl came in to ask for one of his records, Elvis would start to grin, but he would never come forward. Cuoghi would tell the girl, "Elvis Presley? Why that's him right over there." After the girl left, Elvis would say, "Mr. Cuoghi, don't do that. It embarrasses me."

Even after Elvis became a big star, recording for RCA, he occasionally stopped by Pop Tunes for the evening record-playing sessions. Somehow Elvis's fans always found out about his visits and would line up against the windows with their noses pressed to the glass.

Joe Cuoghi died in 1970, and it's hard to determine the last time Elvis visited the store. However, when Elvis died, *Time* magazine printed a photograph of Pop Tunes. The message on the old neon sign in front of the store read simply, "Elvis, we miss you."

DOWNTOWN. ON POPLAR AVENUE BETWEEN LAUDERDALE STREET AND DANNY THOMAS BOULEVARD. TODAY, POP TUNES IS STILL THE BEST SOURCE FOR MEMPHIS MUSIC AND HAS SEVEN STORES. THE POPLAR AVENUE LOCATION HAS CHANGED ONLY SLIGHTLY. IN 1960, THE STORE WAS MOVED FROM 306 POPLAR AVENUE TO A NEW BUILDING AT 308 POPLAR AVENUE BECAUSE OF A STREET-WIDENING PROJECT.

GOSPEL AND RELIGIOUS INFLUENCES

Blackwood Brothers' Record Shop and Offices
186 Jefferson Avenue

During the 1950s, an office and shop located at 186 Jefferson Avenue served as the headquarters for the Blackwood Brothers, a gospel quartet that had a profound effect on Elvis. Not only were they friends of Elvis, attending the same church as he did, but they were also leaders in the gospel music field. The Blackwood Brothers helped create today's gospel music business. Their many "firsts" in the business included: the first gospel music group to sell their own records; the first to contract with a national record label, RCA; the first gospel group to appear on network television, the *Arthur Godfrey Show* in 1954; and the first quartet to tour with their own bus and airplane.

The Blackwood Brothers created the National Quartet Convention

The Blackwood Brothers' Record Shop
Courtesy of James Blackwood

in 1957. From that organization came the Gospel Music Association and its annual "Dove" awards. The Blackwood Brothers also initiated several style changes in the music, bringing black gospel and pop music influences into the "four-singers-and-a-piano" format. They were not afraid to add a little banter and showmanship to their performances. Gospel music was entertainment, and it was a way to convey the message.

The original quartet consisted of Roy, Doyle, James, and R.W., Roy's son. Born in Mississippi, they moved about the country where radio opportunities took them before settling in Memphis in 1950. Radio station WMPS gave them an hour slot on the radio show, *High Noon Roundup*. With that air-time exposure, the quartet was able to book appearances in churches and auditoriums on tour. The Blackwood Brothers even created their own events, including the gospel sings at Ellis Auditorium that brought in other gospel quartets and singers to perform with them.

Their impact on Elvis Presley was subtle, but crucial and long-lasting. The young boy wanted to be a gospel singer. Were it not for a twist of fate, he may well have been. When he was still in high school, the Blackwood Brothers created a junior group, the

Songfellows. They were young singers whom the quartet believed had promise as future members. Elvis practiced with this group often and hoped to join. But Elvis was told he could not sing, that is, sing in a quartet. He was devastated, and he certainly could not imagine the twist of fate just around the horizon.

On June 30, 1954, the Blackwood Brothers' plane crashed, killing quartet members R. W. and Bill Lyles along with a third passenger. The news shattered everyone close to the quartet. Despite their grief, the surviving members felt compelled to continue. Cecil Blackwood, a younger brother of R. W., and J. D. Sumner, a bass singer, were chosen to fill the void left by the accident.

Elvis was asked to join the Songfellows when Cecil moved up to join the senior group, but he had already signed with Sun Records. Also, the sting of the earlier rejection had not yet healed. Years later, Elvis would still comment about that rejection.

Through it all Elvis remained a respectful friend of the Blackwood family. Their paths would not cross often on those many tours, but they did on at least one occasion. At a concert date in Texas, after a long conversation with the quartet, Elvis announced that he would only sing gospel that night.

The influence of the Blackwood Brothers was perhaps at its strongest during Elvis's later performances. When he began touring again in the 1970s, Elvis had gospel singers accompany him on vocals. The first male quartet Elvis employed was the Imperials, which included Terry Blackwood, a son of Doyle. In 1972, Elvis hired J. D. Sumner and the Stamps Quartet to perform with him.

In times of their greatest need, the Presley family called upon the Blackwood family. Elvis paid for their flight back to Memphis so they could sing at his mother's funeral. Less than twenty years later, Vernon Presley asked James Blackwood (who then sang with the Masters Five) to sing at Elvis's funeral.

Today the Blackwood family continues to sing gospel music around the country. Only James Blackwood remains from the original family quartet.

The shop at 186 Jefferson provided office space for their various enterprises and a retail outlet for their recordings. Doyle Blackwood stopped performing with the group to manage this shop. It was open for business in the early 1950s, so it is likely that Elvis did visit the site. In 1960, the Blackwoods moved their shop to 209 North Lauderdale Street, just around the corner from Pop Tunes. This shop had room for their own recording studio and coincided with the creation of Skylite Records, their record label.

DOWNTOWN. THE BLACKWOOD BROTHERS' RECORD SHOP AND OFFICES WERE LOCATED ON THE NORTHWEST CORNER OF THE INTERSECTION OF JEFFERSON AVENUE AND THIRD STREETS. THE BUILDING HAS BEEN REPLACED BY THE ONE MEMPHIS PLACE OFFICE TOWER. THE BLACKWOOD BROTHERS' SHOP AT 209 NORTH LAUDERDALE STREET IS STILL VISIBLE. FROM POPLAR AVENUE, TURN LEFT ON LAUDERDALE STREET. THE SHOP IS ON THE WEST SIDE, JUST SOUTH OF EXCHANGE STREET AND LAUDERDALE COURTS.

The Blackwood Brothers in concert
Courtesy of James Blackwood

First Assembly of God Church
1084 East McLemore Avenue

The Presleys were very involved in their Assembly of God church in their hometown of Tupelo, so upon their move to Memphis, it seemed

First Assembly of God Church
Courtesy of the Mississippi Valley Collection

reasonable that they would join another Assembly of God congregation. However, for whatever reasons, neither Elvis or his parents officially became members of the First Assembly of God Church in Memphis, although they often attended services.

Reverend James E. Hamill, pastor of the First Assembly of God Church, was a strong leader. By the time he retired in 1981, his congregation had grown from ninety to three thousand. He was determined to reach as many souls as he possibly could, and he was creative in his mission. He was the first minister to offer a service on local television. And when his four-year-old church moved to 1084 East McLemore Avenue in 1949, Reverend Hamill created a bus service to bring his congregation to the church on Sunday. That bus service is how Elvis, a boy without his own transportation, could attend a church two miles from his home, although years later various members would try to claim credit for introducing Elvis to the church.

Even as a young boy, Elvis enjoyed the church, and he attended more frequently than his parents did. Elvis attended Sunday school in the mornings and the worship service afterwards. He was a good student of the Bible, but a little shy. He chose not to sing in the church choir.

The Blackwood Brothers gospel quartet and their families joined the church in 1950. In the basement of the church, the Blackwood family sometimes practiced gospel singing, with Elvis participating and watching. Late in 1953, Elvis met Dixie Locke at Sunday school, and they would date for nearly two years. She witnessed his change from a young man who made a demo record to a budding star.

As Elvis's fame rose, he continued to go to Sunday services, though his fans soon followed him to First Assembly. When Opal Walker, one of Elvis's first fans, learned from Dewey Phillips which church Elvis attended, she and her friend got a sudden interest in religion. She remembers flirting with Elvis after the services.

Eventually Elvis stopped attending because he did not want his fame to disrupt the services, but he would remain close to the congregation and especially the Blackwoods. When Gladys Presley died, the family called Reverend Hamill to preach at her funeral.

Although Elvis voraciously read books on a number of religious and philosophical topics in his later years, he never forgot his roots in the Assembly of God church.

In 1962 the First Assembly of God Church moved to 255 North Highland Street. Today Dixie Locke Emmons is the church secretary.

SOUTH MEMPHIS. FROM BELLEVUE BOULEVARD (ELVIS PRESLEY BOULEVARD), TURN WEST ON MCLEMORE AVENUE AND DRIVE ABOUT A HALF MILE. THE CHURCH BUILDING IS NOW OCCUPIED BY THE ALPHA CHURCH CONGREGATION OF THE TEMPLES OF THE LIVING GOD.

Centenary A.M.E. Church
878 Mississippi Boulevard

Elvis loved nothing better than listening to the rising power of a gospel choir as it moved the congregation closer to the spirit.

According to his cousin Gene Smith, Elvis particularly enjoyed the choir at the Centenary African Methodist Episcopal Church, and the two teenagers often sat in on Sunday morning services.

It is difficult to imagine the two boys as the only white faces in the otherwise all-black congregation, yet they were always welcomed. Out of courtesy Elvis and Gene sat in the balcony, as blacks were required to do when they visited white churches and social events. "Elvis would be swept up by the singing," Gene said, "and although he couldn't sing along with the choir down on the ground floor because we had to be respectful and keep quiet, he continually wanted us to go there on Sundays so we could sit and listen to the hymns being sung and partake of the spiritual power of that particular gospel group."

SOUTH MEMPHIS. FROM CRUMP BOULEVARD, TURN SOUTH ON MISSISSIPPI STREET. THE BIBLE DAYS REVIVAL CHURCH NOW OCCUPIES THIS BUILDING.

East Trigg Baptist Church
1189 East Trigg Avenue

Reverend Harper Brewster had a favorite saying, "When grace is in, race is out." The doors of his black church in South Memphis were open to everyone, and the number of white visitors who sat in his congregation during the years before desegregation were testimony to his ministerial gift. One of those white visitors was Elvis Presley.

Brewster knew that the challenge of any minister is to get people's attention. "It's a funny thing," Reverend Brewster once said, "So many people will listen to a song when they won't listen to a sermon." Once when he was criticized by a group of ministers for putting "all that jubilation" into his services, Reverend Brewster said, "You want to catch fish, you got to fish with the kind of bait they'll come to. If singing a song too slow rocks them to sleep, pick it up."

He was thrilled that so many people would come to his church to hear his music. Brewster recalled, "There'd be as many white faces—

and sometimes more—than black faces at evening services. Elvis Presley was just a casual boy who came for the singing."

Reverend Brewster used the power of music to fill the thirty-two pews of his small church. His radio show on WDIA, called *Old Camp Meeting of the Air*, was one of the first gospel shows on radio, and through it he was introduced to a white audience who eventually came to the church to hear his powerfully delivered message. He had the gift of "whooping"—the ability to tell a story in a melodious style. His sermons were lyrical and dramatically delivered in his rich, mellifluent voice. And the music, well, everyone came to hear the music. The choir, one of the best in the city, was nationally acclaimed, and Reverend Brewster himself wrote many of their songs. Mahalia Jackson recorded Reverend Brewster's song "Move On Up a Little Higher," but because Brewster did not concern himself with copyrights and royalties, he was not credited. "My music has never been to make money," he would say. A gospel song was simply a sermon set to music, he felt, and a good sermon has the power to influence.

Today East Trigg Baptist Church is still active, although the congregation is now predominately black. After the turmoil surrounding Dr. Martin Luther King's assasination in Memphis in 1968, many white people avoided places that they considered to be predominantly black, such as the East Trigg neighborhood. Before his death in 1987, Reverend Brewster commented, "Once integration started in a big way, the (white) people were afraid to come down here, and attendance fell off. But way back in the late 1940s and 1950s my church was integrated."

SOUTH MEMPHIS. FROM BELLEVUE BOULEVARD (ELVIS PRESLEY BOULEVARD), TURN WEST ON TRIGG AVENUE AND DRIVE TWO BLOCKS.

Elvis at the Model Sandwich Shop on Adam Street.
Courtesy of Anna Hamilton

RESTAURANTS

Culpepper's Chicken Shack
204 Hernando Street

When Mr. Culpepper's Chicken Shack opened in 1932, its clientele was mostly drunks and gamblers, but that soon changed. His
belief that everyone deserved the best of service, not to mention his
tasty barbecue chicken, made his restaurant a favorite of Beale Street
entertainers and patrons. What's more, it attracted the attention of
Boss Crump, the political leader of Memphis, and he spread the word
to the white community, many of whom daringly ventured to Beale
to visit Culpepper's.

Elvis was one of many young white men who ate at Culpepper's.
At any given time at Culpepper's, one might see men in their work-
ing clothes sitting next to a couple in a tuxedo and evening gown.
And one never knew what celebrity might walk into Culpepper's.
Cab Calloway and Bing Crosby dined there, as did William Holden

and Mae West. Bobby Blue Bland and B.B. King were regulars. What appealed to celebrities and working class alike is that Mr. Culpepper always treated everyone the same, regardless of their dress or position in life.

Of course, Elvis felt this way too. Once, someone asked Elvis why he referred to Mr. Culpepper, a black man, as "Mister." Elvis replied, "I've been calling him Mister all along, why would I change now?"

DOWNTOWN. BEFORE URBAN RENEWAL, HERNANDO STREET RAN NORTH TO SOUTH AND CROSSED BEALE. MUCH OF THIS STREET, INCLUDING THE RESTAURANT SITE, WAS DEMOLISHED AND IS NOW A VACANT LOT WITHIN THE BEALE STREET HISTORIC DISTRICT.

K's Drive-In (now K's Restaurant)
166 Crump Boulevard

K's Drive-In was a favorite hangout in Memphis. It was the sort of place where you could ease your car into the parking slot with your date beside you and call your order into the intercom conveniently located at window level. In a few minutes, a carhop would deliver your food, securing the tray to your window. When Elvis was a teenager, the restaurant did a big business, employing twenty-one carhops at one time.

Gene Smith remembers that he and Elvis would often double-date during the time when Elvis was dating Dixie Locke. The couples would pile into Elvis's old Lincoln and head to K's for cheeseburgers and milk shakes. Sometimes Elvis would bring along his guitar and entertain the group.

It's been years since K's stopped their drive-in business and renamed themselves K's Restaurant. When the neighborhood began to decline, they shortened their hours, closing at 2:00 each afternoon. Still, the restaurant is operated by the same family and has kept the menu the same, and it still serves some of the best home cooking in the city.

Earl's Hot Biscuits
179 Crump Boulevard

Across the street from K's Drive-In was Earl's, another Memphis landmark known as the "King of the Homemade Hot Biscuits." The restaurant's huge neon sign, towering thirty-five feet in the air above the restaurant and drive-in area, featured a cook rolling biscuits. Though the restaurant was busy serving country cooking at all hours, it was busiest late at night, when it became a hangout for young people.

After shows at the Eagle's Nest, Elvis would join his band members and their wives at Earl's and order up hamburgers, fries, and milk shakes.

One of the carhops who waited on Elvis during that period in the early '50s was W. W. Herenton, a future mayor of Memphis. "He looked different," Mayor Herenton said as he recalled Elvis during those days. "He dressed different. He cut his hair different. He was a unique, fun-loving guy. He hadn't become famous yet, but I remember him clearly."

Whether Elvis continued to go to Earl's in the '60s is anyone's guess. In 1964 a second Earl's opened in West Memphis. Though the original restaurant has closed, the second location still draws a crowd.

DOWNTOWN. FROM BELLEVUE BOULEVARD (ELVIS PRESLEY BOULEVARD), TURN WEST ON CRUMP BOULEVARD. EARL'S ONCE STOOD ON THE SOUTH SIDE OF THE STREET WHERE A CAPTAIN D'S RESTAURANT IS NOW LOCATED, VIRTUALLY OPPO-SITE K'S DRIVE-IN.

THE PRESENT-DAY SITE OF EARL'S CAN BE REACHED BY TAKING I-55 OR I-40 ACROSS THE MISSISSIPPI RIVER TO WEST MEMPHIS. TAKE THE INGRAM BOULEVARD EXIT AND TURN RIGHT TO CROSS OVER THE INTERSTATE. TURN RIGHT ON THE SERVICE ROAD BEHIND THE HAMPTON INN HOTEL. FOLLOW THAT ROAD TO THE NEXT PARKING LOT, WHICH

The Peanut Shop
134 and 24 South Main Street

In the '50s and '60s, there were three Peanut Shops in the city, two
on South Main Street and one on Summer Avenue. As shoppers hurried past the downtown stores, "Mr. Peanut," an iron statue of the
familiar peanut wearing a monocle and top hat, would tap his cane
against the window to attract their attention. To protect the window,
a coin was glued to it at precisely the point where Mr. Peanut's cane
met the glass.

Justin Adler, who bought the stores from Planters Peanuts, would
come in early every morning to polish the windows and clean the
store thoroughly before opening for the day. "I kept that place spar-
kling," he said.

Mr. Adler remembers the times Elvis would come into the store.
The store at 134 South Main Street was near the Loew's State Theater, and when Elvis worked as an usher there, he often stopped in
this Peanut Shop. "You know how he used to loll around things?"
Mr. Adler said. "He used to loll around on those showcases and talk
to the sales ladies. I'd walk in the customer's aisle and just slip my
hand under the back of his usher's coat, grab him by the belt, and
escort him out."

Given Elvis's fondness for peanut-butter-and-banana sandwiches,
it stands to reason that he was drawn to the smell of freshly roasted
peanuts.

DOWNTOWN. THE STORE AT 134 SOUTH MAIN STREET NO LONGER EXISTS. THE LO-
CATION IS PART OF THE PEABODY PLACE OFFICE COMPLEX. THE STORE AT 24 SOUTH
MAIN STREET IS STILL IN BUSINESS, WITH "MR. PEANUT" TAPPING AWAY ON THE WIN-
DOW. FROM MADISON AVENUE, TURN SOUTH ON THE MAIN STREET PEDESTRIAN MALL.

Taylor's Cafe menu
Courtesy of Stephen Shutts

Taylor's Cafe (now Sun Studio Cafe)
710 Union Avenue

Jack Clement, an alumni of Sun Studio and a talented Nashville producer, once said of Taylor's Cafe, "That's where all the guys did their writing and talking, and that's where the Sun sound was really born." Sam Phillips, who boasted of not having a desk at his Memphis Recording Service, had his own booth at Taylor's, and it was here that he would pore over paperwork with a fresh cup of coffee at hand. Musicians would often grab a bite to eat here, some while taking a much-deserved session break. If they were especially tired, they might spend the night in one of Miss Taylor's upstairs rooms. Johnny Cash, Roy Orbison, and Jerry Lee Lewis all rented rooms in her second-floor boarding house above the cafe.

With so many professionals congregating at the cafe, it became a popular hangout for those who dreamed of a career in music, a place where they could eavesdrop on conversations about the industry and occasionally even hear the muffled music being created next door. Many people recall that Elvis often came into Taylor's before he got his break at Sun. There, he could sit just a few feet from Sam Phillips, sip a coke, and go over the many ways he might draw attention to himself. He could plan and he could dream, all the while trying to find the courage to make his dreams come true.

Eventually Elvis did find a way to introduce himself to Sam. Not long after their introduction, Sam invited his friend Scotty Moore to sit down with him in his booth at Taylor's Cafe. Over a cup of coffee, Sam told Scotty about a young man who had come in to record a song for his mother. It was at Taylor's that the idea of pairing Scotty and Bill Black with Elvis was born.

Taylor's Cafe has been closed for many years, however Sun Studio operates their cafe in the same location. The restaurant's tin ceiling and checkered-tiled floor are from the original restaurant.

DOWNTOWN. THE SUN STUDIO CAFE (TAYLOR'S CAFE) IS IN THE SAME BUILDING AS SUN STUDIO AT THE INTERSECTION OF UNION AND MARSHALL AVENUES, SEVEN BLOCKS FROM THE MISSISSIPPI RIVER. ALTHOUGH SUN STUDIO HAS A UNION AVENUE ADDRESS (THE CORNER OF THE BUILDING FACES UNION), TO PARK YOU WILL NEED TO VEER TO THE NORTH ONTO MARSHALL AVENUE. CALL 521-0664 FOR RESTAURANT HOURS.

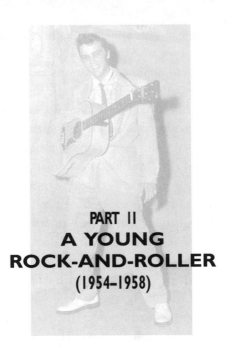

PART II
A YOUNG
ROCK-AND-ROLLER
(1954–1958)

RECORDING
STUDIO

Memphis Recording Service/Sun Records
706 Union Avenue

Out of this little storefront at Union and Marshall Avenues came music that would change the world. By nurturing the talent of Elvis Presley, Sam Phillips, the founder of both Sun Records and the Memphis Recording Service, helped create rock-and-roll.

Once when he was asked how he discovered Elvis, Sam replied, "I didn't discover Elvis. Elvis discovered me."

Sometime in the summer of 1953, Elvis walked into the office, then marked by the sign, "Memphis Recording Service." For a small fee, anyone could make a record at the company. When Elvis walked in, either Marion Keisker, the company's receptionist, or Sam (depending on who told the story) asked him what he wanted to do. Then they asked him what kind of music he could sing. All kinds, he answered. Who do you sound like? was the next question. He replied, I don't sound like nobody. Elvis went on to record a couple of songs, and they thought enough of his ability to capture at least some of them on tape and take his name and phone number.

Earlier, Sam had created Sun Records for the purpose of finding unknown, raw talent who would not have a chance at a major record label. Above all else, Sam prized individuality, especially in the blues singers of the South. But he had come to the conclusion that the only way to gain commercial success was to find a white singer who had that black feeling in his voice.

From our perspective today, it seems as if Elvis jumped into stardom overnight. In reality Elvis waited almost a year before Sam felt the time was right for a true recording session. Finally Sam asked him to sit in the recording studio and play what he knew. The shy young man began playing an assortment of songs. In between the romantic ballads and hillbilly tunes, he sang a gospel number.

After that session, there were many practice sessions with Scotty Moore and Bill Black. In one studio session Elvis sang the song "That's Alright" as an afterthought. Elvis's rendition of the song had the sound that Sam was looking for. Following that historic moment was months of touring the South and all-night recording sessions.

Just as he had in later years, Elvis had his own unique recording style even then. Inspiration found him in the middle of the session, usually after hours of playing whatever caught his interest. Marion Keisker told one interviewer, "He never came to a session ready. He never rehearsed like Johnny (Cash) and some of the others would. They'd rehearse until they thought they had something presentable, and then go to Sam. But Elvis never had anything ready."

In all, Sam only released ten songs performed by Elvis on his Sun label. At the end of 1955, he sold Elvis's recording contract to RCA Victor. The forty thousand dollars Sam received was the most money he had ever made. By then Carl Perkins and Johnny Cash had already recorded for Sam. Jerry Lee Lewis, Warren Smith, Roy Orbison, Billy Lee Riley, and Charlie Rich followed. All of them recorded hit songs that defined rock-and-roll. Soon, all these artists also would

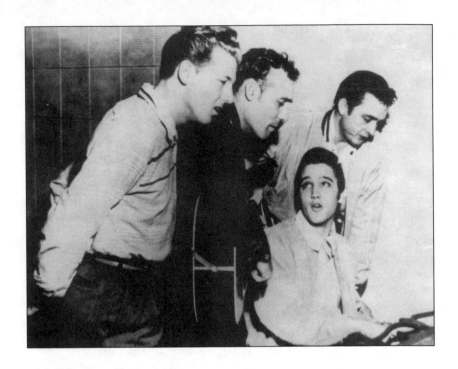

The Million Dollar Quartet
Elvis with Jerry Lee Lewis, Carl Perkins, and Johnny Cash at Sun Studio
Courtesy of Mark Bell, Sun Studio

leave Sam for other recording deals. Sam produced hit songs for less than ten years. But his place in history is secure.

How Sam accomplished that feat is remarkable, though it cannot be told fully here. Sam was a creative recording engineer, wheedling a distinctive sound out of mostly second-hand equipment that he installed by himself. More importantly, he was a producer of untrained musicians, coaxing their hidden talent from within. His recording sessions were often all-night, spontaneous events. There was no time clock and no pressure to succeed. He made it all fun, and they responded by recording music that has lasted for the ages.

DOWNTOWN. SUN STUDIO IS LOCATED AT THE INTERSECTION OF UNION AND MARSHALL AVENUES. MARSHALL AVENUE INTERSECTS UNION AVENUE AT A SHARP

ANGLE. ALTHOUGH SUN STUDIO HAS A UNION AVENUE ADDRESS (THE CORNER OF THE BUILDING FACES UNION), THE REST OF THE BUILDING ACTUALLY FRONTS MARSHALL AVENUE. TO PARK AND ENTER THE STUDIO, ONE SHOULD TURN ONTO MARSHALL AVENUE. BE CAREFUL NOT TO STOP YOUR CAR OR WALK ONTO UNION AVENUE TO VIEW OR PHOTOGRAPH THE STUDIO. THAT IS ONE OF THE CITY'S BUSIEST THOROUGH-FARES, AND IT IS DANGEROUS FOR PEDESTRIANS.

TODAY SUN STUDIO IS OPEN FOR TOURS. VISITORS ASSEMBLE IN THE CAFE AND THEN ARE LED INTO THE RECORDING ROOM. THE TOUR ITSELF IS AN AUDIO PRESEN-TATION OF THE SUN RECORDS STORY AMIDST SOME OF THE ORIGINAL RECORDING EQUIPMENT AND MUSICAL INSTRUMENTS. ABOVE THE CAFE IS AN EXHIBIT GALLERY OF PHOTOGRAPHS AND ARTIFACTS. SUN STUDIO ALSO OFFERS RECORDING SERVICES IN A ROOM OFF LIMITS TO THE TOURS. CALL 901-521-0664 FOR DETAILS.

Chisca Hotel, home of WHBQ radio
Courtesy of Memphis and Shelby County Room
Memphis/Shelby County Public Library
and Information Center

RADIO STATIONS

WHBQ Radio
Lobby of the Hotel Chisca
272 South Main Street

Dewey Phillips of WHBQ Radio was another Memphian who shared in the creation of rock-and-roll with his late-night radio show *Red, Hot and Blue*. Sadly though, he did not enjoy his success for long. His show was as unpredictable as he was. He played whatever struck his fancy, interspersing outrageous litanies like this between each record: "Get your wheelbarrow full of whatever, roll it up through the front door and dump it out and tell 'em Phillips sentcha." In an age of sedate and polished disc jockeys, Dewey was out of place. Yet it was precisely his unique style that made his show so popular. Teen-agers across the mid-South tuned in faithfully, and while his ratings were high, station managers tolerated his eccentricities. Even they didn't know what he would do next, so they assigned another worker to keep him from destroying the equipment.

Dewey Phillips
Courtesy of the Mississippi Valley Collection

It wasn't just Dewey's banter that attracted his listeners. Dewey "heard something in records before other people heard it," said his friend newspaper writer Robert Johnson. He had a knack for picking hits. Songs with the "big beat" were Dewey's favorites, especially black rhythm-and-blues.

On July 10, 1954, Dewey's friend Sam Phillips (who was no relation, though Dewey claimed he was) brought in a new pressing from his Sun Records label, and Dewey played it on his show that night. The phone started ringing immediately, and Dewey played Elvis's "That's Alright" and "Blue Moon Of Kentucky" again. "I played the record thirty times, fifteen times each side," Dewey later said. "When the phone calls and telegrams started to come in, I got a hold of Elvis's daddy, Vernon."

Elvis, who was nervous about his record's radio debut, sat watching a movie at the Suzore #2 Theater. His mother and father discovered him there and sent him to WHBQ. "Mr. Phillips, I don't know nothing about being interviewed," he said nervously when he arrived at the studio.

"Just don't say nothing dirty," Dewey replied as he discretely turned on the microphone. He began asking questions, and Elvis, who thought he was still waiting for the interview to begin, answered them confidently. One of the questions Dewey asked was which high school Elvis attended because he wanted the radio audience to understand that Elvis was white, not black as some might have guessed by the singer's style.

From that moment Dewey's life was intertwined with the rising career of Elvis Presley. Elvis joined him on the air several times, though every appearance was fraught with security problems. Once Dewey announced that Elvis and the band were tuning up inside the radio station. Soon a crowd of teenagers rushed through the hotel entrance and up the stairs to the radio station on the mezzanine floor. Only a glass wall separated the musicians from the excited crowd, and the police were called to restore order. Elvis and the band had to escape through a back exit.

Situated at the corner of Linden Avenue and South Main Street, the Hotel Chisca had two entrances. The disc jockeys and musicians preferred to use the Linden Avenue, or side entrance, into the hotel lobby. They would walk up a flight of stairs to the mezzanine floor, turn left down the hallway, and walk through the two glass doors into the station. In the back left portion of the station was Dewey's small room, filled with records and the endangered equipment. The room usually was crowded during show time because of Dewey's large entourage. Visitors to Dewey's show would also gather at the gravel parking lot across Linden Avenue (now part of the Memphis Light Gas and Water Building). Like everyone else, Elvis would lean against a car and chat.

Soon all the new rockabilly artists asked for a few minutes on Dewey's shows, hoping for their own big break like the one Elvis received. As rock-and-roll became a national craze, Dewey Phillips received star treatment in Memphis. He was even given his own television show by WHBQ.

Initially, Elvis relied on Dewey for advice. Dewey said that Elvis even asked him to manage him, but Dewey refused the offer. Elvis and Dewey remained friends for several years, until Dewey's losing battle with alcohol became apparent. Sam Phillips always said that Dewey never drank on the air. Nonetheless, he grew increasingly irreverent, and as radio moved toward structured play lists and smooth-voiced disc jockeys, Dewey couldn't adapt. He lost his job at WHBQ. Elvis, saddened by his mentor's decline, often sent money to Dewey's family. In 1968, at the age of forty-two, Dewey Phillips died.

Elvis's link to WHBQ continued when his friend George Klein hosted both a radio and television show for the station. George remained one of the top-rated disc jockeys in Memphis for many years. Elvis helped him by allowing George to play new songs and by making an occasional on-air visit. George regaled his listeners with behind-the-scenes stories of Elvis on movie sets, in recording studios, and on concert tours. Today George Klein hosts his *Elvis Hour* radio show on WHBQ radio.

WHBQ moved from the Hotel Chisca to a new facility at 462 South Highland in 1962. The Hotel Chisca is now the headquarters of the Church of God in Christ and is not open to the public.

DOWNTOWN. FROM UNION AVENUE, TURN SOUTH ON FRONT STREET TO LINDEN AVENUE, THEN TURN EAST ON SOUTH MAIN STREET. THE HOTEL BUILDING OCCUPIES THE SOUTHEAST CORNER OF THIS INTERSECTION.

Elvis and George Klein
Courtesy of the Mississippi Valley Collection

WDIA Radio
2074 Union Avenue

In 1948 a failing radio station made a decision that would make history. WDIA Radio hired Nat D. Williams, an educator and writer, as the first black disc jockey in America. Williams was so successful that the station decided to program entirely for blacks. The effect on the station was immediate. It became one of the most popular radio stations in the country. When the station increased to fifty thousand watts, it literally had the majority of the region's black population as its listening audience. Through its revolutionary format, WDIA became a symbol, another small step towards the end of segregation.

WDIA broadcast rhythm-and-blues as well as gospel music. B.B. King got his start in show business when he walked into the station and asked for a job as an announcer. Soul music legend Rufus Thomas, who worked with Nat Williams on talent shows at the Palace Theater, was also hired as a disc jockey, a job he still holds today.

WDIA was so prominent that musicians and their promoters would court the station's disc jockeys. It was not unusual to hear performers on the air talking with the jock or playing their latest song. A favorable reaction by WDIA could make a song a rhythm-and-blues hit.

For Elvis, WDIA opened possibilities to black music that might not have existed otherwise. The nightclubs on Beale were usually off-limits to white teenagers. But WDIA, station 1070, "the 'I' on your radio dial," was on the air almost whenever he wanted to listen.

In December 1956, Elvis showed his appreciation by making an appearance at a WDIA charity show. By that time, the station was known as the Goodwill Station for the wide variety of charities it sponsored. Its chief fund-raiser was the Goodwill Revue, and it was held that year at the Ellis Auditorium. Demand for tickets was exceptionally high, with the final attendance at nine thousand people. The entertainment was provided by Ray Charles, B.B. King, and the WDIA announcers in a comedy skit. Elvis was only supposed to show up and take a bow. Backstage he mingled and told everyone how much he benefited from listening to the station. When Elvis was announced, he wiggled his legs and was besieged by teenage girls. Order was restored, and Elvis was led away to safety.

Nat D. Williams voiced his amazement at the teenagers' reaction in a column published in the *Pittsburgh Courier*. "How come cullud girls would take on so over a Memphis white boy," he asked, "when they hardly let out a squeak over B. B. King, a Memphis cullud boy?"

Today the station and its FM counterpart, K-97, are still the market leaders in Memphis radio. The station broadcasts now from an office at 112 Union Avenue, the former home of WMPS.

MIDTOWN. THE ORIGINAL LOCATION, NOW DEMOLISHED, WAS ON UNION AVENUE, TWO BLOCKS EAST OF FLORENCE AVENUE. A MEDICAL CLINIC IS NOW AT THE SITE. TODAY WDIA IS LOCATED DOWNTOWN, A FEW DOORS WEST OF THE PEABODY HOTEL ON UNION AVENUE ON THE NORTH SIDE OF THE STREET.

WMPS Radio
112 Union Avenue

In 1949 Robert Hopgood took a job as a disc jockey at WMPS. Under the moniker of Bob Neal, he hosted two shows, the *WMPS Farm Report* beginning at 5:00 A.M., and the *High Noon Roundup* at 12:00 P.M. Both shows combined farm information with Bob's hillbilly humor, spiritual messages, and music. It was an odd mix, but WMPS gave Bob complete leeway to program his show as long as he gained an audience and did not offend anyone. Live performances by country-and-western artists, Smiling Ed Hill and the Louvin Brothers among them, were also part of the shows. Beginning in 1950, the Blackwood Brothers performed live on radio during half of the *High Noon Roundup*.

At that time an audience could watch the disc jockey and the performers, and were encouraged to do so, through plate-glass windows outside of the station. One frequent member of the audience for Bob Neal's show was a young boy from Humes High School named Elvis Presley.

On December 29, 1954, Bob Neal became Elvis Presley's manager. He would hold that position until November 20, 1955, when Elvis signed a management contract with Colonel Tom Parker. At the same time, Elvis's recording contract with Sun Records was sold to RCA Victor. During that one year, Bob Neal would book Elvis as part of package tours of country-and-western artists in small towns across the South.

Bob would continue to perform on his radio shows until the station switched to a Top Forty format in 1958 or 1959. Without the freedom to play the music he liked, Bob quit radio. By that time, having managed Elvis, he had established his own roster of country music stars to represent.

WMPS is no longer in operation. WDIA is now at this address.

DOWNTOWN. THE RADIO STATION'S FORMER LOCATION IS ON UNION AVENUE, A FEW DOORS WEST OF THE PEABODY HOTEL. THE BUILDING IS ON THE NORTH SIDE OF THE STREET.

LOCAL
PERFORMANCES

The Bon-Air Night Club
4862 Summer Avenue

With a forty-year perspective, Elvis's success seems instantaneous. During the summer and fall of 1954, as his career was unfolding day by day, it must not have seemed that way to Elvis. He was happy for any chance to perform, and the idea of being given top billing was light years away.

The Bon-Air Club was host to Elvis's first public appearance following the release of "That's Alright." The club was a small, nondescript place located at the edge of town on the highway to Nashville. Inside were tables and chairs for maybe fifty patrons, a bar, and a platform for the musicians.

Elvis performed here several other times in the few weeks following the release of his first hit as a guest artist of Doug Poindexter's Starlight Wranglers. Scotty Moore and Bill Black, members of the Starlight Wranglers, had convinced the group to let Elvis perform a

Elvis on stage at the Bon-Air Club
Courtesy of Mary Greer

few songs. The other musicians would step aside while Scotty and Bill backed Elvis.

Elvis's music was quite a diversion from the Starlight Wrangler's hillbilly style. The audience, which was accustomed to Hank Williams–type ballads, didn't react very warmly to Elvis. Scotty later said, "There was a little response, but it was more like 'What's he doing?' "

Nonetheless, at that first performance at the Bon-Air, Elvis danced with a few of the ladies and visited with some of his friends who had come to support him. The Tiplers, Elvis's employers, were there to cheer him on. "Elvis was really proud that we would go with him and support him like we did," Mrs. Tipler recalled.

The Bon-Air Night Club has since been demolished.

NORTHEAST MEMPHIS. FOLLOW SUMMER AVENUE, PAST PERKINS, STRATFORD, AND AVON ROADS. THE MARKET BASKET PRODUCE STAND IS NOW LOCATED ON THE FORMER SITE OF THE BON-AIR NIGHT CLUB. THE PRODUCE STAND IS ON THE NORTH SIDE OF THE STREET, JUST BEFORE MENDENHALL ROAD.

The Bel-Air Night Club
1850 South Bellevue Boulevard

The Bel-Air Night Club was also the site of several of Elvis's early appearances. Like the Bon-Air Night Club, it was a small place on a highway just outside the city. The Bel-Air was located on the opposite side of town from the Bon-Air in South Memphis on Highway 51. It was part of a tourist-court motel by the same name.

The Starlight Wranglers had been performing at the club for many months in 1954. In August, when Elvis appeared with them at the Bel-Air, he was beginning to develop a following. His record was getting a lot of air play, and his appearances at the Overton Park Shell, the Bon-Air, and the Eagle's Nest had audiences talking and spreading the word.

For the Starlight Wranglers hosting Elvis was becoming uncomfortable. They were finding themselves playing to crowds who preferred a different type of music, Elvis's music, to their steel-guitared country. Not surprisingly, the Wranglers told Scotty and Bill that they had to leave the band. Scotty later said, "There weren't any hard feelings or anything. It just came as a parting of the ways."

As if to give the Wranglers some relief, and certainly to gain more exposure, Elvis started performing with the Jack Clement Band at the Bel-Air and the Eagle's Nest. Clement, who was an engineer at Memphis Recording Service, was most likely granting Sam a favor in letting Elvis perform with him. It may have been a favor he regretted. Years later Jack remembered that while he was on stage, Elvis was trying to pick up his girlfriend.

The Bel-Air Club is no longer open. A sign for the Bel-Air Motel still exists on Bellevue Boulevard. Behind a new strip shopping center is the old, abandoned motel and club. Access is denied to visitors by a chain-link fence.

SOUTH MEMPHIS. FROM GRACELAND, DRIVE NORTH ABOUT THREE MILES ON ELVIS PRESLEY BOULEVARD. AT THE SOUTHEAST CORNER OF ELVIS PRESLEY BOULEVARD AND VALSE STREET, A LARGE SIGN MARKS THE SITE OF THE BEL-AIR MOTEL. THE SURROUNDING COMMERCIAL

The Eagle's Nest
Intersection of Lamar Avenue and Winchester Road

Where Elvis Presley first sang for pay is a question that may never be answered. The Overton Park Shell performance on July 30, 1954, is often considered the first paid performance, and it may well be. But other shows are sometimes mentioned as the "first" Elvis Presley performance. One place where this show may have taken place was the Eagle's Nest, a nightclub located within the Clearpool entertainment complex.

According to accounts, the performance occurred while Elvis was still working for Precision Tool, and he is said to have been paid five dollars. As the story goes, the house entertainment was the Johnny Long Band, and during their intermission, Elvis sang and played guitar alone.

One witness, John Bruce, vividly remembers that Elvis performed in October 1953 because the month coincided with a new car purchase. According to Bruce, Dewey Phillips introduced Elvis as the "poor man's Liberace" because Phillips believed Elvis was going to play the piano. Bruce recalled that he felt sorry for Elvis because it was apparent that he was poor. Even worse was the reaction that Elvis received. Scarcely anyone paid attention to him as he strummed his guitar singing Dean Martin's hit "That's Amore."

Because this story is undocumented, its truth may be in doubt. However, what is certain is that Elvis performed at the Eagle's Nest in the fall of 1954 in a show headlined by "Sleepy Eyed" John Lepley, a country-and-western disc jockey at WHHM. In the club's advertisements for Elvis's shows, Lepley's name appeared prominently. Even the backing band (Scotty and Bill, and probably the Starlight Wranglers) is listed before Elvis. Lepley, who favored more traditional country-and-western artists, was not involved with Elvis Presley very long.

The Eagle's Nest was named in honor of Delta airlines pilots who drank here; it was close to the municipal airport. The nightclub was upstairs above the Clearpool Room, the large ballroom and restaurant within the Clearpool entertainment complex. The complex was named for the large swimming pool on the property. The Pieraccini family owned and operated Clearpool, which was three miles southeast of Rainbow Lake, their second entertainment center on Lamar Avenue. Members of the Pieraccini family are among those who remember a very young and shy Elvis Presley taking the stage before a fidgeting crowd and crooning a Dean Martin ballad.

Today the Lamar and Winchester intersection is in an industrial and warehouse district in Memphis. Little remains of the Clearpool entertainment complex, except for the Americana Club at 4090 Winchester Avenue. This club promotes its connection to Elvis and the fabled Eagle's Nest, and often hosts live country-and-western music.

SOUTHEAST MEMPHIS. FROM ELVIS PRESLEY BOULEVARD, TURN EAST ON WINCHESTER ROAD. FOLLOW WINCHESTER ROAD PAST THE AIRPORT TO THE INTERSECTION OF WINCHESTER ROAD AND LAMAR AVENUE.

Elvis and Maureen Hunter at the Eagle's Nest
Courtesy of Dana Blake

Elvis at the opening of the Lamar-Airways Shopping Center
Courtesy of Opal Walker

Lamar-Airways Shopping Center
Lamar Avenue between Airways Boulevard
and South Parkway

A part of the Elvis Presley lore is the story of how he once played on the flatbed of a truck with Scotty and Bill for an insignificant amount of money. Unlike some of the legends that surround Elvis's rise to stardom, this performance did occur. Elvis, Scotty, and Bill played for the opening of the Lamar-Airways Shopping Center. Sometimes this performance has been called his first paid gig, although the date, September 9, 1954, makes that statement incorrect. It also has been titled the Katz Drug Store grand opening, but the Katz Drug Store was only one of twenty-two stores in Memphis's first shopping center.

The lineup at the three-day festivities included an Indian band, the WDIA band, the Air Force marching band, and Elvis Presley performing with Scotty and Bill, who were dubbed Sleepy-Eyed John's Eagle's Nest Band. On the first day of the grand opening, Elvis arrived with Scotty and Bill. Opal Walker, who liked Elvis's music after listening to Dewey Phillips's radio show, snapped a couple of pictures as the band stood near their car. Elvis wore black pants with a pink stripe down the side of each leg and a pink shirt. He had a very faint mustache. She remembers how little fanfare there was before the show. "Nobody knew who he was," she said.

That changed once he stepped onto the flatbed truck that served as a stage, she recalls. George Klein was the emcee who introduced Elvis. During the show, Bill rode his bass across the stage. She doesn't remember exactly what Elvis sang, or for how long, but she does remember that everybody crowded around him after the show.

Scotty later said, "An entire parking lot full of teenagers just went crazy." The show was the beginning of a new era for Elvis, Scotty, and Bill, one in which they would need to learn to protect themselves from the crowds. "When we see it begin to start, Elvis goes one way and we go the other," Scotty said just two years later. "We call it being foxy. We scatter like quail." Perhaps it was here, at the opening of the Lamar-Airways Shopping Center, that Scotty and Bill first caught a glimmer of what the months ahead would bring.

Today the shopping center is still in existence, though it will undoubtedly never experience a moment as electrifying as Elvis's performance that day.

MIDTOWN. FROM GRACELAND, DRIVE NORTH ON ELVIS PRESLEY BOULEVARD AND TURN EAST ON LAMAR AVENUE. DRIVE ONE MILE ON LAMAR AVENUE TO THE INTERSECTION WITH AIRWAYS BOULEVARD. JUST BEFORE REACHING AIRWAYS BOULEVARD, PARK AVENUE BEGINS AS LAMAR AVENUE TURNS TO THE SOUTHEAST. THESE THREE ROADS— LAMAR AVENUE, PARK AVENUE, AND AIRWAYS BOULEVARD—FORM A TRIANGLE PATTERN ON THE MAP. WITHIN THAT TRIANGLE, ON THE NORTH SIDE OF LAMAR AVENUE, IS THE SHOPPING CENTER.

Overton Park Shell
1928 Poplar Avenue in Overton Park

Since 1936 this outdoor concert shell has provided an entertainment venue in the center of the largest city park in Memphis. At first, the summer programs included light operas, symphony concerts, and plays. Ever the musical student, Elvis claimed that as a teenager he would come to the shell and listen to the operas. He particularly enjoyed Mario Lanza songs.

Beginning in the 1950s, Bob Neal used the shell for his country-music shows. Seven or eight acts would entertain the patrons. Before one show in July 1954, Sam Phillips asked Neal if he would let his new Sun artist, Elvis Presley, perform. Neal agreed and placed the young singer at the bottom of the advertisement playbill, misspelling Elvis's name as "Ellis."

With such an inauspicious start, Elvis Presley's entertainment career was launched. That show, held on July 30, featured Slim Whitman singing "Indian Love Call" as the headliner.

Marion Keisker remembered talking with a woman in the audience before Elvis's show. "Who did you come to hear?" the woman asked.

"Elvis Presley," Marion answered.

"Who?" the woman said.

"After this show you won't ask me again," Marion confidently replied. Even at that early stage in his career—his first commercial show in front of a large audience—Marion Keisker thought Elvis had a lot of charisma.

Obviously raw as a performer, Elvis did not set young hearts afire on that day until he began to move with the rhythm of the song. Then the girls screamed. Between sets Elvis asked his manager why the girls were screaming. He was told, "It's you. Go out there and do it again."

Two weeks later, on August 10, Elvis again appeared at the Overton Park Shell, this time as an unbilled artist. However, this is the show that people remembered as the beginning of the "Elvis wiggle."

On August 5, 1955, Elvis performed at the Shell for the last time,

Elvis backstage at the Overton Park Shell
Courtesy of Joel Hurley, Secretary of Save Our Shell

now as the star of Bob Neal's playbill. Elvis was still accessible then, and there are pictures of him backstage looking young and ready to play.

Today the amphitheater is officially called the Rauoll Wallenberg Shell in honor of the Swedish diplomat who rescued Jews during World War II. Although it is still owned by the city, a volunteer, nonprofit group called Save Our Shell is the manager. This organization restored the shell after it fell into disrepair in the '70s, and it hosts a variety of shows each summer. While certain officials would prefer to simply tear down the shell, Save Our Shell is committed to seeing that this doesn't happen, and they struggle to insure that the amphitheater is preserved for future generations.

MIDTOWN. OVERTON PARK IS ON THE NORTH SIDE OF POPLAR AVENUE, BETWEEN MCLEAN BOULEVARD AND EAST PARKWAY. IF TRAVELING EAST, TURN LEFT AT THE MAIN

Ellis Auditorium
Cook Convention Center
225 North Main Street

Everyone has a place in their life that holds bittersweet memories. Ellis Auditorium was such a place for Elvis, for it was here that he experienced some of the most significant moments in his life, both joyous and sad. In his youth, he spent childhood evenings dreaming of success in the building, and later he savored the fulfillment of his dreams as he performed in concert on this very stage. In 1971, he was presented his dearest honor at the auditorium when he was awarded a trophy for being named one of the "Ten Outstanding Young Men of America" by the Jaycees. But it was here, too, where he deeply mourned the loss of close friends.

Elvis's acquaintance with Ellis Auditorium began as a teenager, when he attended the gospel sings that were later so influential to his music. Gospel quartets filled the auditorium, and it was rare when Elvis wasn't sitting in the audience. Occasionally he worked selling soft drinks, a job that was given to a select few chosen from among the teenagers gathered outside the door just before show time. According to Guy Coffey who hired him, he sometimes had to coax Elvis out of the building after the show because Elvis liked to linger on the empty stage.

That kind of work was far from regular though, and Elvis couldn't always afford admission to the gospel shows. Through the graces of members of the Blackwood Brothers gospel group, who were members of the First Assembly of God Church which Elvis attended, he was sometimes able to come in the back door.

When two members of the Blackwood Brothers were killed in a

Elvis at Ellis Auditorium, February 25, 1961
Courtesy of the Library of Congress

plane crash, Elvis grieved for his own loss and for the suffering of their families in a funeral held at Ellis Auditorium with a crowd of five thousand mourners. Beyond admiring the Blackwood Brothers' talent, Elvis valued their friendship. Elvis was so shaken by this event that for many years he refused to fly. Coincidentally, just a week after the tragedy, he recorded his first hit, "That's Alright," at Memphis Recording Service. And not long after the tragedy, he began traveling across country.

Ellis Auditorium was the site of many of Elvis's triumphs. Just a year earlier, on June 3, 1953, he had walked across the stage at Ellis Auditorium for his high school graduation, becoming the first in his family to complete high school.

On May 15, 1956, Elvis performed on the stage during the Memphis Cotton Carnival. Elvis shared top billing with Hank Snow, but the crowd obviously came to see Elvis. In an unprecedented move, both sides of the auditorium were opened, forcing Elvis to play to audiences at both his front and back. Uncomfortable with this arrangement, Elvis spent most of his time standing sideways or turning to face both audiences.

February 25, 1961, marked Elvis's return to this stage, and his first appearance in Memphis after returning from the army. The occasion was a benefit for local charities. The two shows raised $51,607, which was donated to thirty-seven Memphis organizations and the Elvis Presley Youth Center in Tupelo.

Throughout the '60s, the Blackwood Brothers sponsored a gospel convention in the city, the highlight of which was the presentation of the prestigious Dove Award to a gospel quartet. Elvis quietly attended these events; his fame so distracted the crowd that he would silently enter after the ceremonies began and leave before they ended. More than once the Blackwood Brothers asked him to perform at the convention, however Elvis's contract did not allow him to do so.

Elvis's connection to Ellis Auditorium was renewed because the Elvis Reunion Concert was held there for years. The concert, which was a tribute to Elvis's love of sacred music, was held annually during Elvis Week in August. Many of the performers Elvis worked with sang a variety of his hits and favorite gospel songs at the show. The headliner for the show was J. D. Sumner, who was once a member of the Blackwood Brothers and later sang as a background vocalist with Elvis as a member of the Stamps Quartet.

In 1997 the city of Memphis plans to demolish Ellis Auditorium and replace it with a more modern concert hall.

DOWNTOWN. FROM POPLAR AVENUE, TURN NORTH ON THIRD STREET, A ONE-WAY

Russwood Park
Courtesy of the Memphis and Shelby County Room
Memphis/Shelby County Public Library and Information Center

Russwood Park
914 Madison Avenue

It was a steamy day when Elvis headlined the July 4, 1956, show at Russwood Park. The concert was scheduled directly after Elvis's appearance on *The Steve Allen Show* in New York, and his return to Memphis filled the city's teenagers with excitement. They began camping out at the gate at Russwood Park, the city's baseball stadium, early that morning, despite the ninety-seven-degree temperature.

A concert at Russwood Park was a rare event. The evening's show, which was to benefit local charities, was billed as the "Elvis Presley Jamboree." Elvis was the last of a long line of performers, and he didn't disappoint, though he spent just twenty legendary minutes on stage. Elvis was joined by the Jordanaires, who were flown in by

Colonel Parker. His appearance, immortalized in the video "Elvis '56," brought the crowd rushing toward the stage. "He shimmied, squirmed and wriggled the mob into a panic which took efforts of police, sailors, and firemen to restrain," *The Commercial Appeal* reported.

Though Elvis had appeared in Memphis just two months earlier, his hometown fans obviously had not lost their enthusiasm for him. Nor did his other admirers. Standing backstage was Mrs. Hank Williams, who had driven down from Nashville to see Elvis's show.

Elvis got caught up in the spirit of charity for the event. Aside from his time and energy, Elvis donated his diamond horseshoe ring as the door prize. The ticket number was called, and as Elvis waited on stage for the winner to appear, he was surprised to see his old friend from Alabama Street, Charlie Bramlett, escorting the winner to the stage. Elvis's face lit up when he saw Charlie, and he grabbed his hand and pulled him on stage.

Russwood Park burned in 1960, and the site is now part of the Baptist Memorial Hospital complex.

DOWNTOWN. FROM UNION AVENUE, THEN TURN NORTH ON PAULINE STREET, JUST BEFORE BAPTIST HOSPITAL. TURN LEFT AT MADISON AVENUE, WHICH IS THE NEXT INTERSECTION. THE BAPTIST MEMORIAL HOSPITAL MEDICAL CENTER PLAZA COMPLEX IS NOW WHERE RUSSWOOD PARK ONCE STOOD.

HOMES

2414 Lamar Avenue

It was a small brick house on Lamar Avenue, the midtown stretch of U.S. 78. The highway traffic robbed the neighborhood of any quaintness it might have possessed, and just a few blocks away, Lamar Avenue met Airways Boulevard, the home of used-car lots and other assorted businesses. For all practical purposes, it was a very ordinary house in a working-class neighborhood, and not at all the sort of home that might attract a burgeoning rock star. But this is where Elvis moved his family in late 1954.

Although the home was rented, it marked a new era in the Presleys' Memphis existence. This is the first time while living in the city that the family had a house to themselves. Moreover, it was all due to Elvis's success. For once Gladys and Vernon didn't have to worry about meeting the week's bills. At the same time, Elvis's career was just beginning, and no one knew how long it might last or where it might go. It was an exciting time, but full of uncertainty. Especially for Gladys, who was keenly aware that while their lifestyles were improving her son was rarely at home anymore. Elvis was tearing up the road with Scotty, Bill, and their new drummer D.J. Fontana.

The home at 2414 Lamar Avenue was a transitory residence, though in a different sense than their earlier moves. They no longer had to worry about irate landlords and bureaucratic regulations. They could move now because they wanted to, and just six months after settling into this house, they did just that.

MIDTOWN. FROM I-240 TAKE THE LAMAR EAST EXIT. DRIVE ABOUT TWO MILES. THE HOUSE IS BETWEEN BARRON AVENUE AND KEATING STREET, ON YOUR RIGHT. TODAY THE HOME IS MUCH LARGER THAN IT WAS IN ELVIS'S DAY. IT IS COMMERCIAL PROPERTY, HOUSING THE OFFICES OF MADISON AND BRITTON PUBLIC ACCOUNTANTS.

1414 Getwell Road

In June of 1955, the Presleys traded accommodations on busy Lamar Avenue for a home on another busy thoroughfare, Getwell Road, but in the bargain they moved into a larger house. Beyond that, one may wonder what drew Elvis to this part of town. However, the answer is simple. Sam Phillips lived just a few blocks away on McEvers Road, and Elvis probably became familiar with the neighborhood while visiting Sam.

Of all the places where Elvis lived, the most significant events in his career may have occurred while living in this house. Just two months after moving in, he signed a contract with Colonel Tom Parker, a decision that propelled him into the national spotlight. One of Colonel Parker's first duties as Elvis's manager was to sign Elvis with a major recording label. Then Parker structured a seven-year contract with Paramount Pictures.

"Heartbreak Hotel," "Money Honey," "Blue Suede Shoes," and "Lawdy, Miss Clawdy," were among the songs Elvis recorded while his family lived in this house. Also during this time, he appeared on six episodes of Jimmy and Tommy Dorsey's *Stage Show* and on his first episode of *The Milton Berle Show.*

Elvis didn't spend much time in Memphis or at 1414 Getwell during the eleven months the family lived there. At the most, he would come home for a few days and then rush out again. The neighbors would see him outside playing with the family's white spitz while he unwound from the frenzied pace of his career.

In 1989 the house was moved to make way for a Chief Auto Parts Store. For a few years, the house was kept in a vacant lot a few blocks west of this address while the owner tried to restore it as a tourist attraction, but all attempts to preserve the house failed when it burned in 1994.

SOUTHEAST MEMPHIS. FROM ELVIS PRESLEY BOULEVARD, TAKE I-55 NORTH. TURN ON THE I-240 EAST EXIT. FOLLOW I-240 EAST PAST THE LAMAR AVENUE EXIT, THEN TURN NORTH ON GETWELL ROAD. ELVIS'S HOME WAS LOCATED ON THE NORTHEAST CORNER OF GETWELL AND KIMBALL ROADS.

1034 Audubon Drive

On May 11, 1956, Elvis used his first royalty checks from RCA to buy the ranch-style home at this address. He paid forty thousand dollars cash for the three-bedroom, two-bath house with carport. The Presleys kept the front and back yards well manicured, and Elvis added a swimming pool and change house in the back yard.

The house is typical of this nice, upper-middle-class neighborhood. The other property owners in the neighborhood were successful businessmen or professionals. They were accustomed to a community where everyone quietly tended to their home and yard. For the Presleys, this house represented a tremendous leap in status. Only three years before, they had lived in public housing. Now they resided in one of the best areas of Memphis. From the beginning the Presleys shared their new success with relatives and friends. Their house was usually filled with guests, many of whom still lived downtown.

Most of the adult neighbors were skeptical about the newcomers at first, and then appalled by them. Elvis's family was pleasant, but

Elvis outside his house on Audubon Drive
Courtesy of Linda Everett

they just did not fit in. Gladys liked to hang her laundry out back to dry. She wanted to keep chickens out in the back, but there was not enough room. Worst of all from the neighbors' viewpoint was the constant noise surrounding the house.

For Memphis teenagers, 1034 Audubon Drive was the place to be. Everyone could tell when Elvis was home by the crowd in and around the house, and Elvis encouraged their presence. He signed all autographs, gave rides on his motorcycles, and let them in on his plans.

Paul Burlison remembers when he and Johnny Burnette came to visit Elvis. Burlison and Burnette had known Elvis from the Lauderdale Court days and were now members of The Rock and Roll Trio. When Elvis learned they were looking for some new songs to cut, he invited them to come over and listen to some of the demos he had been given. He had more than enough to share.

When they arrived, there were cars parked way down the street and people lined up on both sides of the guarded gate. "The guard said he (Elvis) wasn't going to be seeing anyone until around 1:00, so we said we'll come back later on in the afternoon. We started back across the street, got about halfway, and we heard this big roar go up. We turned around and looked and he had come out on the porch. He just had his pants on, didn't have a shirt on. I think he had on house shoes," Paul recalled.

Elvis saw them, invited them in, and led them to the kitchen. Paul continued, "His mama had some tea cakes. She made them big old country type tea cakes, big old sugar cookies. She had a bunch of them on the table. Bill Black was out there. Nick Adams and Natalie Wood was there. So we went into the dining room and sat down and talked. She fixed us some coffee and we ate those cakes." Eventually they listened to some of the demos, but Burlison and Burnette didn't find any they liked.

The house was not set far from the street, and the constant crowd of fans and curiosity seekers must have become tiresome for the Presleys. It certainly did for the neighbors. They banded together and offered to buy the Presleys' home until they discovered that Elvis was the only homeowner without a mortgage. Finally, the family did decide to move. The crowds had become too much. Even when Elvis was away, fans would come to the house, and Gladys was unable to rest. In March 1957, they bought the home which had the space they needed for privacy.

EAST MEMPHIS. FROM POPLAR AVENUE, TURN SOUTH ON GOODLETT ROAD. FROM GOODLETT ROAD, TURN LEFT ON PARK AVENUE, THEN TURN RIGHT ON AUDUBON DRIVE, WHICH IS THE FOURTH STREET ON THE RIGHT. FOLLOW AUDUBON DRIVE AS IT VEERS TO THE RIGHT PAST HAVERHILL ROAD. ELVIS'S HOUSE WILL BE ON THE LEFT.

Graceland
3764 Elvis Presley Boulevard (U.S. 51 South)

For Elvis, Graceland became a refuge in a storm of celebrity constraints. The fans could crowd around the gate at the bottom of the hill. Colonel Parker, from his home in Madison, Tennessee, could plan the next movie contract or tour. RCA could schedule the next recording sessions. At Graceland Elvis could relax, and it was a constant sanctuary for the next twenty years of his life. At the same time, it changed as Elvis did.

Elvis purchased the twenty-room mansion on March 19, 1957. Vernon and Gladys discovered the home while on a Sunday drive in the Whitehaven community south of Memphis. They noticed the "For Sale" sign and went up the driveway. As they approached the house, they could hear a church service inside. The house was not occupied at the time, and it was rented to a congregation. Impressed by what they saw, they informed Elvis, who was out of town, that they had found the right house. Elvis paid half of the $100,000 purchase price by trading his Audubon Drive home, then he paid the balance in cash.

At the time the estate had no fencing or gate. A gravel driveway led from the road to the house, which was at the top of a hill. The highway, then the principle route from Chicago to New Orleans, was two lanes. The area around Graceland was for the most part pasture and woods, which gave the Presley family the feeling that they had moved out of the city and into the country. Gladys could raise chickens again, feeding them from her apron.

Although Graceland does resemble historic Southern plantation homes, it was not constructed until 1939. The property was once part of the Toof family plantation, and it was named after Grace Toof, daughter-in-law of the estate's founder. Mrs. Ruth Brown, a niece of Mrs. Toof, sold the home to Elvis.

Elvis had elaborate plans to redecorate. "I want the darkest blue there ever was for my room—with a mirror that will cover one side of the room," he said. "I probably will have a black bedroom suite, trimmed in white leather, with a white rug."

He ordered purple walls with gold trim for the living room, dining room, and sun rooms, and white corduroy drapes. However, Gladys said that she wasn't fond of purple walls. "Elvis, like most young people, likes dark, cozy colors," she told a *Memphis Press-Scimitar* reporter. She eventually persuaded Elvis to tone down his color scheme.

Gladys was looking forward to the privacy of the new estate, but

Elvis at Graceland shortly after he purchased the mansion
Courtesy of Jean Lazenby Foster

soon even the relatively remote location of the home was not enough. Graceland rapidly became the top tourist attraction in Memphis, with as many as fifty fans gathering on a given day. The now famous stone wall and wrought-iron front gates were installed for privacy. Elvis hired some of his relatives to guard the gate and keep order among his admirers. He would still come down to visit on occasion, and sometimes he would invite his fans inside the house, though that happened more frequently in the early days.

Graceland was quiet during Elvis's service in Germany. When he returned, the house was somehow different. Gladys's death and Vernon's remarriage had taken their toll.

In time Priscilla Beaulieu would live here with Elvis, and she would redecorate in the more formal style that is currently on display in the mansion. She was the one who chose the fifteen-foot white sofa, white carpet, and the royal blue drapes in the living room. Eventually Elvis and Priscilla married and had Lisa Marie, and Graceland was blessed with a family again. One of the things people remember most about that era is the pair of friendly, but enormous, great danes who seemed to own the place.

After Elvis's divorce from Priscilla, he became involved with Linda Thompson, and Graceland's style changed again. She introduced thick shag carpeting and velvet drapes, all in a crimson red.

Although Elvis let the women in his life decorate, there were times when he had firm opinions about how Graceland should look. He often acted on a whim, whether remodeling or decorating. On one occasion he tired of a building in the back and rented a bulldozer so that he could tear it down himself. When he decided to incorporate a bit of Hawaii in his decor, he bought all of the furnishings for the "jungle room" in less than thirty minutes.

When Elvis decided he wanted company, he invited a host of friends and family. Guests often even included friends of friends, and it wasn't unusual for fifty to a hundred people to be at the estate.

James Godsey, who started going to Graceland in 1968, remembers how much fun it all was. "At home he would just cut up and enjoy himself. He had a great sense of humor. If he knew you real well, you had to be careful because he would do about anything to get the upper hand. He loved to play practical jokes, and he wasn't one to give up. He had to be the best at everything. Even when around the house, he was always very meticulous about the way he looked. He was always doing something for attention.

"It was always a lot of fun, but there were always a lot of people around who were more impressed with the fact that they were at Graceland than they were interested in knowing him. What impressed me most about Graceland was the way each room had something that meant something to him.

"He was very proud of his accomplishments and real proud of his piano. If you wanted him to play something he would, but what he would play would depend on his mood."

Often, in solitary and quiet moods, Elvis would play the piano. It is said that on his last night on earth he played "Unchained Melody" and "Blue Eyes Crying In The Rain."

By the time of Elvis's death in 1977, Whitehaven had changed dramatically. Suburban development forever changed the rural character of the community. Subdivisions were built around Graceland until Whitehaven became one of the largest residential areas of Memphis. The city annexed Whitehaven in 1969. Strip shopping centers opened

Elvis inside Graceland, 1957
Courtesy of Henrik Knudsen

along the highway, which was then widened to six lanes. Traffic became so heavy that it was dangerous for fans to stop in front of
Graceland. Elvis helped the city finance an additional lane for visitors
to stop without obstructing traffic on the highway. In 1971, the Memphis city council voted to rename U.S. 51 South in honor of Elvis Presley,
an honor that Elvis neither encouraged nor disapproved of.

WHITEHAVEN. ONE OF THE MOST VISIBLE SYMBOLS OF MEMPHIS, GRACELAND IS WELL
MARKED FROM THE INTERSTATES. FROM I-55, TAKE EXIT 5B FOR ELVIS PRESLEY BOULE-
VARD AND DRIVE SOUTH ABOUT A HALF MILE. GRACELAND IS OPEN FOR TOURS; SEE
THE APPENDIX FOR A SHORT DESCRIPTION OF WHAT TO SEE AND DO AT GRACELAND.

MUSICIANS
AND FRIENDS

Scotty Moore's Homes
983 Belz Avenue and 1248 Meda Street

In 1954, Scotty Moore was living at 983 Belz Avenue when Sam
Phillips asked him to audition a young singer Sam believed had potential. At that time, Scotty played guitar for Doug Poindexter and
the Starlight Wranglers, a country-and-western band. His friend Bill
Black played bass fiddle in this band, and they had done some recording at Sun Records, Sam Phillips's record label. Scotty and Sam
began to talk during those sessions, and the two men found they
shared ambitions in music that were not being met. Both men wanted
to find ways to do something different and important in the music
business. As a result of these conversations, Sam hired Scotty to scout
out new talent.

When Scotty called Elvis at Sam's request, he said that he worked
for Sam Phillips and would like Elvis to audition for him. Would
you be interested? Scotty asked Elvis. The next day, July 4, Elvis
arrived at Scotty's house. Dressed in a black shirt, pink pants with a
black stripe, and white shoes, Elvis was intent on making an impres-

sion. He picked up his guitar and began playing some of his favorite ballads by Hank Snow, Billy Eckstine, Eddy Arnold, and Jo Stafford. Eventually Bill Black arrived—Scotty's wife Bobbie had gone down to get him when Elvis arrived—and the three of them, Scotty, Bill, and Elvis, kicked some songs around. All in all, it was the most informal of auditions. Elvis was noticeably shy, and Scotty and Bill weren't overly impressed.

Scotty duly reported to Sam Phillips what he thought. "Elvis had a good voice, though he didn't really knock me out," Scotty recalled. That was enough to encourage Sam to give Elvis a try. Elvis, Scotty, and Bill would go into the studio the next night with Sam engineering.

By 1956, Scotty was living at 1248 Meda Street in midtown, between South Parkway and Lamar Avenue. A year later, Scotty and Bill, unhappy with their salaries, quit working for Elvis full-time. For a while after that, they joined Elvis for various concerts or recording sessions in a per diem arrangement.

Both Scotty and Bill tried a hand at producing after working with Elvis. Scotty became a part-owner of the Fernwood record label, which unfortunately had only one hit song, "Tragedy" by Thomas Wayne. The label folded by 1961, and Scotty went back to Sun as a production manager for the Memphis studio. When Sun opened a studio in Nashville, Scotty moved there. The Nashville branch did not remain open long, but Scotty found a new home, and he is still a part of the Nashville recording business.

983 BELZ AVENUE: NORTH MEMPHIS. BELZ AVENUE NO LONGER EXISTS. IN ITS PLACE IS A DECAYED INDUSTRIAL AREA. TO GAIN AN IMPRESSION OF THIS OLD WORKING-CLASS AREA, TAKE THOMAS STREET NORTH TO CHELSEA AVENUE. TURN RIGHT ON CHELSEA AVENUE AND DRIVE TO MOREHEAD STREET. TURN LEFT ON MOREHEAD STREET AND DRIVE TO FIRESTONE AVENUE, THEN TURN RIGHT AND CONTINUE TO BREEDLOVE STREET. TURN RIGHT AGAIN ON CHELSEA AVENUE TO COMPLETE THE TOUR.

1248 MEDA STREET: MIDTOWN. FROM ELVIS PRESLEY BOULEVARD, TURN EAST ON SOUTH PARKWAY. MEDA STREET IS THE FIRST STREET TO THE RIGHT PAST LAMAR AVENUE. SCOTTY'S FORMER HOME WILL BE ON YOUR RIGHT. IT IS NOW A PRIVATE RESIDENCE.

Bill Black's Homes
971 Belz Avenue, 4188 Pike's Peak,
and 3890 North Watkins Street in Frayser

Memphians think of their city as a small town. In many ways it is, and it was even more so in the 1950s, when it seemed that everyone knew each other, especially those interested in music. In 1954, when Bill Black and Scotty Moore first began playing with Elvis, Bill lived just three doors away from Scotty on Belz Avenue.

The most popular account of Elvis's first meeting with Scotty Moore and Bill Black is that Sam Phillips arranged their introduction. However, Bill Black's mother lived at 209 Market Mall in Lauderdale Courts and knew Gladys Presley. Elvis knew Bill's brother Johnny, and he sometimes hung around when Johnny played music with the Burnette brothers in the Market Mall. It's possible that Elvis and Bill met long before Sam Phillips arranged their introduction, although Bill was several years older than the teenaged Elvis and might not have given him much thought. Even their first jam session didn't seem very memorable at the time. "I don't think any of us was very impressed with the others the first time we got together," Bill said.

In the beginning, Bill was working with Scotty in the Starlight Wranglers. Bill played bass and was also the band's comedian. Country-and-western bands always had one band member dress as a hillbilly clown and perform stage antics to amuse the audience.

By 1956, Bill Black was living at 4188 Pike's Peak in the northeast section of Memphis. In the late 1950s, Bill formed his own band, The Bill Black Combo, which had several hits on the Hi label, including their best-known song, "Smokie-Part 2." He also founded Lyn-Lou Music Publishing Company, which worked with Billy Swan (of "I Can Help" fame), among other songwriters. With his new success, Bill built a home at 3890 North Watkins Street in Frayser, a suburb north of Memphis. Today it is still recognizable because not only is it the only home of its size in the surrounding neighborhood, it is the only home with a tennis court and swimming pool.

Unfortunately, Bill Black did not enjoy his success for long. He died of a cerebral hemorrhage on October 21, 1965.

971 BELZ AVENUE: NORTH MEMPHIS. BELZ AVENUE NO LONGER EXISTS; SEE THE PRE-
VIOUS ENTRY FOR DIRECTIONS TO THIS NEIGHBORHOOD.

4188 PIKE'S PEAK: NORTHEAST MEMPHIS. FROM I-240 NORTH, TAKE EXIT 8 TO JACK-
SON AVENUE. DRIVE SOUTH LESS THAN A MILE TO WALES AVENUE. TURN LEFT ON WALES
AVENUE AND DRIVE TO TANT ROAD. TURN RIGHT ON TANT ROAD AND DRIVE TO THE
FIRST INTERSECTION, PIKE'S PEAK. TURN LEFT ON PIKE'S PEAK. BILL BLACK'S FORMER HOME
WILL BE ON THE LEFT.

3890 NORTH WATKINS STREET: NORTH MEMPHIS/FRAYSER. FROM THOMAS AVENUE
(U.S. 51 NORTH), TURN EAST ON WATKINS STREET AND DRIVE A FEW BLOCKS. THE HOME
IS ON A CURVE JUST BEFORE THE INTERSECTION WITH ST. ELMO ROAD.

BILL BLACK'S FORMER HOMES ARE PRIVATE RESIDENCES; PLEASE RESPECT THE OWN-
ERS' PRIVACY.

Sam Phillips's Homes
1028 McEvers Road and 79 South Mendenhall Road

For Sam Phillips, becoming a recording industry legend was a
struggle. "I was starving to death financially," Sam said about his
early Sun days. When he founded Memphis Recording Service in
1950, he didn't have the luxury of buying the new equipment he
needed. Instead he had to put it together himself, adapting, rework-
ing, and fixing whatever pieces he could salvage. He was forced to
continue working as an engineer for WREC Radio until 1951, and
the bread and butter of his business was the recordings of weddings,
funerals, birthdays, and other personal events he made for a fee.
Though he was proud of his recordings by B.B. King, Howling Wolf,
Ike Turner, Jackie Brenston, and the Prisonaires, none of those efforts earned much money, and Sam became keenly aware of the financial burdens of running his own business.

To add to his sense of responsibility, Sam was the father of two
very young children, Knox and Jerry. In those early years, the family
lived in a small house at 1028 McEvers Road, in what was a quiet
neighborhood. Knox Phillips remembers that Elvis stopped by the
house at this address to visit the Phillips family.

After Sun Records became a success, Sam bought the house at 79 South Mendenhall Road where he still lives today. His home is unmistakable, surrounded by a stone-and-wrought-iron fence decorated with music notes.

1028 MCEVERS ROAD: SOUTHEAST MEMPHIS. FROM ELVIS PRESLEY BOULEVARD, TAKE I-55 NORTH TO THE I-240 EAST EXIT. FOLLOW I-240 EAST PAST THE LAMAR AVENUE EXIT. EXIT ONTO GETWELL ROAD AND DRIVE NORTH. MCEVERS ROAD WILL BE TO YOUR LEFT, PAST QUINCE ROAD. SAM PHILLIPS'S FORMER HOUSE IS ON THE CORNER OF MCEVERS ROAD AND MCEVERS CIRCLE.

79 SOUTH MENDENHALL ROAD: EAST MEMPHIS. FROM ELVIS PRESLEY BOULEVARD, TAKE I-55 NORTH TO THE I-240 EAST EXIT. FROM I-240 EAST, TAKE EXIT 15 FOR POPLAR AVENUE WEST. FROM POPLAR AVENUE, TURN NORTH ON MENDENHALL ROAD. THE HOUSE WILL BE ON YOUR RIGHT. BOTH HOMES ARE PRIVATE RESIDENCES. PLEASE RESPECT THE OWNERS' PRIVACY.

Ace Appliance Company
3431 Summer Avenue

By the early 1950s, when he was a member of the Starlight Wranglers, Bill Black was already a father. He was older than Scotty Moore, and with family obligations weighing heavily on him, he could no more imagine full-time work with the Wranglers than could Scotty. Bill resigned himself to working at Ace Appliance Company, all the while hoping for some sort of a break with his musical career.

In the summer and fall of 1954, he took to the road with Scotty and Elvis, and for awhile it looked as though he might never look back. Splitting the gate with Elvis on tour was yielding some decent pay, which was increasing as Elvis became known. Once Elvis signed with Colonel Parker and began recording with RCA, Bill and Scotty were placed on salary: two hundred dollars a week while Elvis was on tour, and a one-hundred-dollar weekly retainer when Elvis was not on tour. For Christmas, Elvis gave them each a thousand dollars.

It was a good income, but eventually Bill and Scotty began to resent the fact that their salaries were not increasing. "He promised that the more he made, the more we would make," Scotty said in September of 1957, but the two did not feel this was the case. They resigned that month.

We may never know if Elvis was fully aware of Scotty and Bill's unhappiness. Part of the problem may have been that Scotty and Bill could no longer talk to Elvis. Colonel Parker made all of the financial decisions, including how much Elvis would pay his musicians.

At the time of his departure from Elvis, Bill said, "I don't believe Scotty and I could raise more than fifty dollars between us. I didn't expect to get rich, but I did expect to do better than I have and to make a good living for my family."

To make ends meet, Bill went back to work in the service department at Ace Appliance Company, which is still in business today. Soon after leaving Elvis, he founded the Bill Black Combo, which had its big hit, "Smokie," in 1959.

EAST MEMPHIS. ACE APPLIANCE COMPANY IS ON SUMMER AVENUE EAST OF HIGH-LAND ROAD.

University Park Cleaners
613 North McLean Boulevard

When Scotty Moore came to Memphis in 1952, his goal was to make it in the music business. But with a wife to support, he couldn't follow his dream without some other way to pay the bills. He was forced to work full time and pursue his musical aspirations after hours.

He went to work for his brother who owned the University Park Cleaners, a business that is still in operation at the same location. Scotty's job was to clean hats, an ideal position because he was finished with his work by two o'clock every afternoon.

If he had relied on the success of the Starlight Wranglers, Scotty might have worked at the shop until he retired, or he might have gone into business for himself with his own dry cleaner. As it turned out, he held this job less than two years.

"I figured you had to pay your dues," Scotty told one interviewer. "Over a period of time, you'd get your break. But what happened to us, well, I think it was a fluke."

MIDTOWN. FROM POPLAR AVENUE, TURN NORTH ON MCLEAN BOULEVARD. UNIVERSITY PARK CLEANERS IS LOCATED ON THE WEST SIDE OF MCLEAN BOULEVARD, PAST JACKSON AVENUE.

Anita Wood's Home
2186 Monroe Avenue

When Anita Wood won the Mid-South Youth Talent Contest, she was offered a job on WHBQ's television show *Dance Party*, hosted by Wink Martindale. The move to Memphis was a little frightening for the young girl from Jackson, Tennessee, who was not accustomed to the big city. She moved in with Miss Patty, a kindly woman who took Anita under her wing.

She was living with Miss Patty at 2186 Monroe Avenue when Elvis's friend Lamar Fike called to find out if she would like to go on a date with Elvis. Anita found herself having to refuse Elvis's offer because she already a date for the evening and didn't think it would be fair to break it.

A couple of weeks later, Elvis asked Anita for another date. This time Anita accepted, and on the night of the date, Elvis's long limousine pulled up in front of Miss Patty's door. It was the first date in a five-year relationship, and the first of many times Elvis would arrive at Miss Patty's.

After Elvis and Anita had been dating for awhile, Elvis began to wonder why a reporter from the *Memphis Press-Scimitar* was waiting to take pictures of him every time he came to pick up Anita. It puzzled him for a long time, and though he continued asking the reporter how he knew he was going to be there, Elvis couldn't get an honest answer. Finally the reporter slipped and admitted that Anita had been tipping him off. He was never tipped off again.

Elvis and Anita's relationship continued until 1962. In 1964 Anita married the professional football player, Johnny Brewer.

MIDTOWN. FROM UNION AVENUE, TURN NORTH ON COOPER STREET, THEN TURN RIGHT ON MONROE AVENUE. THE WHITE-FRAME HOME IS ON THE NORTH SIDE OF THE STREET, ONE HOUSE FROM THE CORNER OF NORTH COX STREET AND MONROE AVENUE.

Elvis and Anita Wood leaving a Union Avenue Plymouth Dealership
Courtesy of Linda Everett

Anita Wood
Courtesy of Stephen Shutts

Bob Neal
Courtesy of the Mississippi Valley Collection

PUBLICITY AND PROMOTION

Bob Neal's Office
160 Union Avenue

Bob Neal promoted country-music shows in and around Memphis, drawing upon his popularity with country-music fans as a disc jockey at WMPS. Neal met Elvis when Elvis appeared at one of the shows he was promoting at the Overton Park Shell. In December 1954, Neal became Elvis's manager. Neal was obviously impressed with Elvis because up to that time the promoter/disc jockey had never been involved in artist management.

Neal agreed to arrange all the bookings and handle publicity for Elvis in exchange for fifteen percent of the earnings. Bob's wife Helen became the first fan club liaison for Elvis, mailing out information to fans from the office at 160 Union Avenue. Both husband and wife took it upon themselves to make Elvis a part of their large family, and Elvis became an older brother to their five children. All the Neals were impressed with Elvis's polite ambition.

Bob knew that for Elvis to make it, he had to perform away from the South. Yet it was hard for Bob to juggle long journeys to concert dates with his job at WMPS and his family obligations. Bob contracted Jamboree Attractions, a Nashville talent agency managed by Colonel Tom Parker, to help arrange concert tours.

One year after it began, Bob's management deal with Elvis came to an end when Elvis signed with Parker and RCA. As Elvis and Parker went on to make millions, people would often ask Bob if he regretted missing a percentage of that success. For Bob, the choice was simple. Either sacrifice your family to meet the demands of Elvis's career, or stay in Memphis. He chose to stay.

For the next few years, Bob continued to divide his time between WMPS and his new passion for artist management. He went on to create a partnership with Sam Phillips called Stars, Inc. that handled tours for Sam's roster of Sun artists. He also tried his hand at managing a record shop called Bob Neal's, which was located at 50 South Main, but he sold it to Poplar Tunes. The end of his partnership with Sam coincided with programming changes at WMPS. He quit the station and entered the artist management business on his own. For the rest of his life, Bob Neal managed country-and-western artists. He died in 1983.

DOWNTOWN. BOB NEAL'S OFFICE WAS LOCATED ON UNION AVENUE AT SECOND STREET, ACROSS FROM THE PEABODY HOTEL. A HOLIDAY INN SELECT NOW OCCUPIES THIS LOCATION.

Blue Light Studio
130 Beale Street

At the corner of Second and Beale Streets, next to Lansky Brothers' Men's Store, stood a small photographer's studio. For a small fee one could walk into the Blue Light Studio and have a studio portrait made. In January 1956, just before Elvis's first television appearance on *Stage Show*, he had a professional portrait made there. It was not his first portrait, if you count the unflattering photograph taken by a *Memphis Press-Scimitar* photographer just before his appearance at the opening of the Lamar-Airways Shopping Center. But the crew cut and bow tie he sported in that photograph could hardly have been the look he was going for then.

He trusted the Blue Light Studio because he had passed by the shop and looked at the pictures on display for years. On this particular day, Mrs. Margaret Sutton took Elvis's photograph. His hair is neatly combed in a pompadour, and his clothing has a bit of flash, evident even in the black-and-white image. His expression is wistful.

Little did he know the studio would soon hang his picture on display. And roughly ten years later, Priscilla Beaulieu had her own portrait made at the Blue Light, her first hopeful step towards a modeling career.

The Blue Light Studio survived the decline of downtown Memphis. In the 1970s when Beale Street was abandoned, the studio simply moved a few blocks away to 145 South Main Street. In 1994 the studio moved again to 115 Union Avenue. Today one can still walk in to have a portrait taken, and one can still see the portraits of Elvis and Priscilla.

DOWNTOWN. TO REACH THE ORIGINAL LOCATION FROM UNION AVENUE, TURN SOUTH ON SECOND STREET AND CONTINUE UNTIL REACHING BEALE STREET. THE ORIGINAL LOCATION WAS ON THE NORTHWEST CORNER OF BEALE AND SECOND STREETS. TODAY THE BLUE LIGHT STUDIO IS ON UNION AVENUE BETWEEN MAIN AND SECOND STREETS, WEST OF THE PEABODY HOTEL.

Blue Light Studio
Courtesy of Mississippi Valley Collection

Speer Photography
1330 Linden Avenue

Out of the millions of photographs of Elvis Presley, William and Vancil Speer created twelve of the most compelling. These head-and-shoulder portraits, taken in 1955, have been reproduced countless times for publicity or for publication.

In his younger days, William Speer dreamed of working with his camera in Hollywood. Speer was able to indulge his passion by making portraits of visiting entertainers. One day, Elvis came to Speer's shop with his then-manager, Bob Neal. The young singer, still unknown outside of the South, wanted professional stills made to impress Hollywood studios. Immediately Speer knew that Elvis had it—the special ability to shine for the camera that makes one a movie star.

William's wife, Vancil, was attracted to Elvis in a more feminine way. Her role in the portrait shoot was wardrobe and set design. She persuaded Elvis to take off his shirt for some of the portraits by convincing him the two shirts he had brought were not enough for the number of pictures they wanted to take. A sheepish Elvis complied to her requests.

The Speers usually shot two or three portraits, but Vancil pushed for twelve. Perhaps Elvis was more relaxed knowing that the photographer was across the room from him, instead of at close range. Speer had to shoot at a distance because he used an unusually large camera for portraits—a rare German Goerzdader lens that weighed more than twenty pounds. Instead of f-stops, the camera had "waterhouse stops," where one drops different apertures into the lens. Because Elvis moved around so much, Speer shot him with the apertures wide open.

A few years later, Elvis brought Anita Wood to have her professional still made. This time Elvis was a distraction, not the subject. After Speer told him to be quiet or go away, Elvis stopped visiting their studio.

Though they rarely saw Elvis again, they frequently saw one of their famous photographs of him. Colonel Parker used it for the glossy

Elvis
Courtesy of William Speer

pictures sold to millions of Elvis fans in the '50s. Parker did not bother to compensate Speer for the use of that photo.

Nonetheless, the Speers, especially Vancil, remained fans of Elvis. The couple is retired now and lives in one of the most unusual homes in Memphis, which is devoted to their artistry.

MIDTOWN. FROM UNION AVENUE, TURN SOUTH ON CLEVELAND STREET AND DRIVE TO LINDEN AVENUE. WILLIAM SPEER'S STUDIO WAS AT THE CORNER OF CLEVELAND STREET AND LINDEN AVENUE. ITS FORMER LOCATION IS NOW THE METHODIST HOSPITAL PARKING GARAGE, LOCATED DIRECTLY ACROSS THE STREET FROM CRUMP STADIUM.

TRAIN STOPS
AND STATIONS

White Station Train Stop
Poplar Avenue between Colonial and Mendenhall Roads

There is a scene in the video *Elvis '56* that captures an especially poignant moment in Elvis's career. The scene occurs just after a trip to New York during which Elvis appeared on *The Steve Allen Show* and was forced to sing "Hound Dog" to a basset hound. After the *Steve Allen Show*, he was interviewed by Hy Gardner for the show *Hy Gardner Calling*. The next morning he walked into RCA studios and recorded two of his biggest hits, "Hound Dog" and "Don't Be Cruel." The following day he boarded a train for Memphis.

Twenty-eight hours later, he got off at White Station on the outskirts of Memphis. Still wearing his suit and tie, he left the Colonel and others on the train, and he walked home alone to Audubon Drive. Met without fanfare, it seemed like an ordinary moment, except that we are witness to it. Alfred Wertheimer's photographs, seen on the video, captured Elvis at that rare point in his career when he was seemingly famous and unknown all at once, when he could walk home unrecognized but be followed by a New York photographer; when he could leave the television and recording studios and return to his mama's home cooking. Perhaps that's why the moment is so poignant, because it was so short-lived.

EAST MEMPHIS. FROM ELVIS PRESLEY BOULEVARD, TAKE I-55 NORTH TO I-240 EAST. FROM I-240 EAST, TAKE EXIT 15 FOR POPLAR AVENUE WEST. FROM POPLAR AVENUE, TURN RIGHT ON MENDENHALL ROAD AND LOOK FOR THE TRAIN TRACKS. ELVIS GOT OFF SOMEWHERE BETWEEN MENDENHALL AND COLONIAL ROADS. THERE WAS NO TRAIN STATION IN 1956, NOR IS THERE ONE TODAY, SO IT IS IMPOSSIBLE TO DETERMINE THE EXACT LOCATION. TODAY THERE ARE NO LONGER PASSENGER TRAINS ALONG THIS LINE, BUT THE TRACK IS USED QUITE OFTEN BY THE FREIGHT LINES, WHICH OFTEN BLOCK TRAFFIC IN THIS BUSY COMMERCIAL DISTRICT.

STORES

Harry Levitch Jewelers
176 South Main Street

One of Elvis's finest traits was his loyalty. He never forgot those who helped him or his friends, and he especially liked to do business with those who treated him well during his youth.

Harry Levitch impressed Elvis at an early age. Having grown up poor, Levitch vowed that if he were ever successful he would help young people get through high school. One of Elvis's friends, Red West, was a benefactor of Harry's kindness. Shortly after Elvis graduated from Humes High School, he visited Harry's store and introduced himself. "You helped my friend, and I'll never forget it," Elvis said.

During the Christmas season of 1954, Elvis went to Harry's store and bought an electric mixer for his mother's Christmas gift. Harry was surprised when Elvis returned a few days later and asked for another electric mixer. It too was for his mother, Elvis explained. She had never owned one before, and now that he could afford it, he wanted her to have one for each end of the kitchen so that she wouldn't have to walk back and forth. From that time on, Elvis was

Harry Levitch
Courtesy of the Mississippi Valley Collection

a frequent customer, although as his fame increased, he was unable to visit Harry's shop and would require Harry to come to Graceland.

Years later Elvis commissioned Harry to make the engagement ring he gave to Priscilla. Then he flew Harry to Las Vegas for the wedding ceremony to personally deliver custom wedding rings. Harry and Elvis's friend George Klein were the only non-family members invited to the ceremony.

Elvis purchased many items from Harry over the years, the last in December of 1976, when Elvis asked Harry to bring an assortment from his store to Graceland so that Elvis could pick out Christmas gifts.

One can still shop at Harry Levitch Jewelers, just as Elvis did years ago. The store is now located at 5100 Poplar Avenue.

DOWNTOWN. THE ORIGINAL BUILDING NO LONGER EXISTS, BUT IT WAS LOCATED ON THE EAST SIDE OF SOUTH MAIN STREET, BETWEEN GAYOSO AVENUE AND PEABODY PLACE. THIS PART OF MAIN STREET IS UNDERGOING EXTENSIVE REBUILDING. THE STORE IS NOW LOCATED IN EAST MEMPHIS AT 5100 POPLAR AVENUE. FROM ELVIS PRESLEY BOULEVARD, TAKE I-55 NORTH TO I-240 EAST. FROM I-240 EAST, TAKE EXIT 15 TO POPLAR AVENUE WEST. THE SHOP IS ON THE NORTH SIDE OF POPLAR AVENUE, JUST EAST OF MENDENHALL ROAD.

Lansky Brothers' Men's Store
126 Beale Street

After World War II, Guy and Bernard Lansky opened a clothing store at this address on Beale Street. They worked long hours selling to a mostly black clientele. Their stock included flashy, bold-colored items favored by musicians. One day they noticed a young white kid peering through the shop window. The Lanskys were, and are today, aggressive salesmen. One of them walked outside in order to persuade the curious lad to come inside and buy something. The boy could not afford to buy anything that day, but promised that someday he would buy them out. Don't buy us out, Lansky asked, just buy from us.

That he did. The young boy was, of course, Elvis, and he would remain friends with the Lanskys for the rest of his life. Elvis bought many of his first stage clothes, including the pink-and-black suits, from the Lanskys. As fashions changed over time, Elvis would change his tastes. But he always wore something spectacular and bold.

A shopping visit by Elvis was a merchant's dream, especially when Elvis brought his friends to the store to buy them gifts. The Lanskys happily accommodated their famous customer on many such shopping excursions. They made deliveries to Graceland whenever Elvis requested an order, and they brought back special items for him from New York. They once traded a buying spree with Elvis for a three-wheel Messerschmidt motorcycle, which they still own.

In turn Elvis always told everyone where he bought his clothes, and many people shopped at Lansky Brothers' simply because Elvis did. After Elvis's death in 1977, the Lanskys displayed pictures of him taken in the shop, as well as articles of his clothing they possessed (Elvis was prone to give away or trade clothes on a whim). They continued to sell clothes on Beale Street until 1991, when declining sales forced them to close.

In the summer of 1997 the new Elvis Presley's nightclub will open inside the renovated Lansky building. This club will be the first of several themed nightclubs conceived by Elvis Presley Enterprises. Entertainment will feature blues, rock, and country acts that Elvis would have enjoyed. Southern food will be served in the restaurant. Elvis memorabilia will be on display.

DOWNTOWN. FROM UNION AVENUE, TURN SOUTH ON SECOND STREET AND FOLLOW IT TO BEALE STREET. LANSKY BROTHERS' MEN'S STORE OCCUPIED THE BUILDING AT THE SOUTHWEST CORNER OF SECOND AND BEALE STREETS.

O.K. Houck & Company Music Shop
121 Union Avenue

With many of Elvis's personal possessions, what was once worth a few dollars is now worth a fortune. Such is the fate of one of his first guitars. At the beginning of 1956, Elvis traded in his used 1942 Martin D-18 guitar for a new guitar at the O.K. Houck & Company Music Shop. Elvis had used the guitar in recording his first professional releases at Sun and in some of his early concert performances. However, the guitar held no sentimental attachment for him. He was recording for RCA then and wanted no more used equipment.

For a number of years, the guitar was kept in the attic of an Elvis fan. He eventually loaned it to the Country Music Hall of Fame, where it was on display in their museum. In 1991, it was sold at auction to a British collector. In 1993, it was sold at auction again, this time to a Seattle music entrepreneur who called the guitar the "Holy Grail of Rock-and-Roll." He claimed to have paid $151,000 for it, though some sources say the dollar amount was over $200,000.

O.K. Houck & Company began selling pianos and sheet music in Memphis in 1901. When Elvis traded in his guitar there, the company's main product was still pianos. The company moved east to 4966 Poplar Avenue during the 1960s. Recently, O.K. Houck & Company went out of business.

DOWNTOWN. THE ORIGINAL LOCATION WAS ON UNION AVENUE BETWEEN MAIN AND SECOND STREETS, ON THE SOUTH SIDE OF THE AVENUE. THE PEABODY HOTEL IS NEARBY.

Krystal
Courtesy of the Memphis and Shelby County Room
Memphis/Shelby County Public Library and Information Center

RESTAURANTS

Krystal
135 Union Avenue

In the 1950s, fast food was a relatively new concept. While McDonald's was capturing the northern market, Krystal was establishing a presence in the South. Competing against established, sit-down-and-eat restaurants, Krystal's difference was the size and shape of its hamburgers. They were square, and so small that no one ever ordered just one Krystal burger; instead people would order a half dozen or a dozen. Like barbecue and pork rinds, Krystal's burgers have become a part of Southern food culture, and Elvis loved them.

It's hardly the sort of meal you would serve to a first date, but then again, Elvis's dating style was unconventional. The first time he took out Anita Wood, he picked her up in his Cadillac limousine. She was surprised to see his friends George Klein and Cliff Gleaves in the car, and even more astonished when they immediately went to the Krystal. Elvis bought dozens of the hamburgers, which Anita didn't care for, and the guys started eating them as they rode back to Graceland.

George Klein remembers Elvis would come into WHBQ to visit Dewey Phillips. Since George worked at WHBQ too, Elvis would ask him to come along for a bite to eat. He and George usually would go get a sack of Krystals.

The Krystal that Elvis used to frequent, the one at Union Avenue and Second Street across from the Peabody Hotel, was torn down years ago, but there are still a lot of the restaurants in Memphis. And you still can order the classic Krystal burger that Elvis loved. The Krystal location nearest to that original location is at 1377 Union Avenue.

DOWNTOWN. THE KRYSTAL WHERE ELVIS BOUGHT HAMBURGERS WAS LOCATED JUST WEST OF THE PEABODY HOTEL ON THE SOUTHWEST CORNER OF UNION AVENUE AND SECOND STREET. HUEY'S RESTAURANT IS LOCATED THERE NOW.

State Café
84 Beale Street

When Elvis returned to Memphis in October of 1956 after a frantic Texas tour, he found his hometown anything but restful. The week of October 14 was marred by his participation in a gas station fight and a subsequent court appearance. A few days later, an ordinary visit to a movie theater ended in mayhem when four hundred girls destroyed his Cadillac. That week, the full impact of his fame must have hit Elvis with spinning force, and it all began with an incident at the State Café.

Elvis and his friend Dewey Phillips met for a quiet, late-night dinner in this small restaurant near Dewey's studio at WHBQ. Just before the food arrived, Elvis discretely removed his dental caps, wrapped them in a handkerchief, and set them aside on the table.

The caps, designed by a Hollywood dentist, were created to improve the appearance of Elvis's teeth for the movies. Elvis had fallen into the habit of wearing them, although they had to be removed before meals.

As Elvis and Dewey were chatting and enjoying their food, Elvis was spotted by a group of girls. They rushed toward the table and clamored around him. Elvis and Dewey got up, and in the commotion of well-wishers and autograph seekers, the handkerchief was knocked to the floor and the caps rolled away. Dewey and Elvis dropped to their knees trying to find them, but it was too late. One of the caps had already been stepped on and shattered into tiny pieces. Dewey later told a newspaper reporter that Elvis said he had paid $150 apiece for them.

DOWNTOWN. FROM UNION AVENUE, TURN SOUTH ON SECOND STREET AND DRIVE TO BEALE STREET. TURN RIGHT ON BEALE STREET. THE STATE CAFÉ IS NO LONGER IN BUSINESS, AND THE BUILDING IS DEMOLISHED. THE RESTAURANT WAS LOCATED ON THE NORTH SIDE OF BEALE STREET AT THE CORNER OF MAIN STREET; THE HEADQUARTERS FOR THE TRI-STATE BANK NOW OCCUPIES THE SITE. ACROSS BEALE STREET IS ELVIS PRESLEY PLAZA, WHERE THE STATUE OF ELVIS STOOD FROM 1980 TO 1994.

COURT
APPEARANCE

Shelby County Courthouse
Adams Avenue Between Second and Third Streets

It was a scene fitting any of Elvis's movies: A handsome young man is driving alone when he notices something wrong with his automobile. Pulling into the nearest gas station, he hopes to get the car fixed. Instead, he is promptly surrounded by girls asking him for his autograph. He's polite and accommodating. In the background, the station manager is seething because of all the feminine attention the young man is receiving. The manager bluntly tells the young man to move out of the way. Hot words are exchanged. The driver makes his way to the automobile, but the manager approaches him from behind, reaches in the car, and hits the unsuspecting young man.

This was the situation in which Elvis found himself at the Gulf Station at the corner of Second Street and Gayoso Avenue on October 18, 1956. Like the hero on the big screen, Elvis leapt from the car, swinging at his attacker. His fist blackened the other man's eye just as another gas station employee rushed toward him. Elvis punched that man too, before the police intervened and separated the men.

Elvis and the other two men, Edd Hopper and Aubrey Brown, were charged with assault and battery, as well as disorderly conduct. Hopper, the man who had instigated the whole melee, insisted that he did not know who Elvis was. Elvis contended that Hopper had pulled a knife on him as he stepped from the car. Elvis claimed, "I'll take ridicule and slander, but when a guy hits me, that's too much." Slowly, Elvis regained a bit of his humor. When the police began writing his ticket and asked him his name, he quipped, "Well, maybe you'd better put down Carl Perkins," referring to the Sun Records artist.

The next day, Elvis and his father arrived at the Shelby County Courthouse to find over two hundred girls sitting in the courtroom waiting for him. He took a seat in the last row and waited patiently while the judge tried several public drunkenness charges. Finally, he called Elvis's case. Judge Sam Friedman ruled that the gas station attendants had behaved inappropriately and fined them. He dismissed the charges against Elvis. When he announced his decision, a roar erupted from the audience—girls shrieked and flashbulbs popped. "Stop the applause," the judge cried. "This is a courtroom, not a show!" Newsreel coverage of the trial made national and international news.

Though Elvis was vindicated, it was a defining moment for him. Judge Friedman acquitted him of any wrongdoing, but he did give

Elvis at the Shelby County Courthouse, October 19, 1956
Courtesy of the Library of Congress

Elvis some serious advice. "I realize your position and that crowds follow you wherever you go. In the future try to be considerate and cooperate with businessmen. Avoid crowds where business will be interrupted."

This advice, and the incident that preceded it, made Elvis even more aware of the cost of celebrity. That it occurred during a week of fan disruption made it all the more meaningful. Just a few days earlier, Elvis's dental cap had been destroyed at the State Café when he was besieged by fans who inadvertently knocked it from the table. The day after his court appearance, his Cadillac would be damaged at the Plaza Cinema when several hundred fans beset it. It was a week wrought with conflict, and undoubtedly one in which he realized that his life could never again be ordinary.

DOWNTOWN. FROM UNION AVENUE, TURN NORTH ON THIRD STREET AND DRIVE FIVE BLOCKS TO ADAMS AVENUE. THE SHELBY COUNTY COURTHOUSE IS TO YOUR LEFT ON THE CORNER OF THIRD STREET AND ADAMS AVENUE. THE INFAMOUS GAS STATION AT SECOND STREET AND GAYOSO AVENUE IS NOW PART OF THE PEABODY HOTEL PARKING LOTS.

MOVIE
THEATERS

Plaza Cinema
3402 Poplar Avenue

The Plaza Cinema was nestled in the heart of Poplar Plaza, one of the city's premier shopping centers. Built in 1952, the theater featured a sleek, modern design and offered the ultimate in customer comfort: in addition to spacious rows, there was a party room with space to entertain several guests and enclosed balconies for those who desired more privacy.

On October 21, 1956, Elvis learned a valuable lesson about privacy at the Plaza Cinema. That night, Elvis arrived at the theater around 9:30 P.M. accompanied by his girlfriend, Barbara Hearn, and another girl, identified only as Jane. As Elvis was buying their tickets, he looked up to see a group of teenagers rushing toward him. "He gave me a five dollar bill, grabbed the tickets, and before he could pick up his change the girls were on him," the ticket seller said.

The theater manager, who was watching the whole affair, quickly escorted Elvis to a private, reserved balcony, while Barbara stayed behind long enough to get his change. Though their real reason for visiting the theater was to see the newsreels of Elvis's Tupelo appearance, they watched part of the movie, Walk the Proud Land. Then, they decided to leave before the feature's end so they could avoid the crowd. They were shown the side entrance.

Elvis couldn't leave as quickly as he would have liked. About four hundred girls had his car surrounded; some were even poised on top of the hood. One glance and Elvis darted back into the theater. He reappeared only after the police arrived, jumping into the back of a police cruiser with his two female friends right behind him. With red lights flashing and sirens screaming, the car sped off.

The next day, Elvis graciously told a newspaper reporter that the girls did not hurt his Cadillac. The cracked windshield and nicks happened on his Texas tour, he said. In truth, his car was horribly damaged that night. Paint was scraped, upholstery was torn, and the fenders were dented. But the brunt of the assault was eventually washed away—hundreds of love messages written in lipstick.

EAST MEMPHIS. THE PLAZA CINEMA WAS LOCATED IN THE POPLAR PLAZA SHOPPING CENTER ON POPLAR AVENUE BETWEEN PRESCOTT STREET AND HIGHLAND AVENUE. THE THEATER WAS CLOSED IN 1987; BOOKSTAR, A RETAIL BOOKSTORE, NOW OCCUPIES THE SITE.

Strand Theater
138 South Main Street

When the world premier of Elvis's second movie, Loving You, was held at the Strand Theater in Memphis on July 9, 1957, there was none of the glamour associated with typical movie premiers. Elvis and his costars did not arrive by limousine, step onto a plush red carpet into the glare of a thousand flashbulbs, and smile at the pressing crowds as they made their way to the theater door. That simply wasn't Elvis's style; he wouldn't officially be a part of the movie's debut.

Instead, the premier passed as unobtrusively as the opening of any movie, except that in this case the crowds were much larger. Elvis's fans began arriving in the wee hours of the morning, starting a line that eventually reached halfway to Beale Street hours before the ticket office opened at 9:00 A.M. Eight showings that day drew capacity crowds, a fact that delighted Hal Wallis, the film's producer. He phoned from Hollywood three times to ask the theater's manager, Alex Thompson, about the movie's attendance.

"We've had some good movies here, but I've never seen anything like this," Lloyd Bailey, another manager, told a reporter. Talking about Elvis's fans, Bailey said, "They finally finished ripping off all my billboard displays including a cardboard cutout of Elvis."

Elvis was more reluctant to speak to reporters. He insisted that the newspapers not be informed of his own plans to attend the theater. At a private, midnight showing, Elvis brought his parents, girlfriend Anita Wood, and cousin Gene Smith, to see his movie. At the end, Gladys gushed, telling Alex Thompson that she thought it was terrific and would probably come back to see it again. Of course, this was her screen debut—she and Vernon cheer from the fourth row while Elvis sings "Got A Lot Of Living To Do."

DOWNTOWN. FROM UNION AVENUE, TRAVEL ONE BLOCK SOUTH ON SOUTH MAIN STREET. THE STRAND WAS LOCATED ON SOUTH MAIN STREET BETWEEN GAYOSO AVENUE AND BEALE STREET, ONE STOREFRONT NORTH OF THE LOEW'S STATE THEATER. THIS SECTION OF MAIN STREET IS NOW A PEDESTRIAN MALL. THE BUILDING WAS DEMOLISHED AND IS NOW PART OF THE NEW PEABODY PLACE DEVELOPMENT.

MOTORCYCLES

Tommy Taylor's Memphis Harley-Davidson
235 Poplar Avenue

There is no telling how many times the young Elvis drove past
Tommy Taylor's Memphis Harley-Davidson dealership and imagined
himself driving one of the big bikes. To Elvis, motorcycles were more
than a symbol of rebellious freedom. "Everyone looked up to bik-
ers," Elvis's friend George Klein remembered. "If you rode a Harley,
you were like a cowboy of the city, a guy who had a lot of moxie."

Although he had undoubtedly wanted a Harley for a long time,
Elvis bought his first motorcycle on a whim. He was twenty-one years
old and had recently completed filming his first movie, *Love Me Tender*. At the time, movie stars Natalie Wood and Nick Adams were
visiting Elvis from Hollywood. Almost on a lark, Elvis walked into
Tommy Taylor's Memphis Harley-Davidson and picked out a magnificent bike. Natalie sat on the back seat, wrapping her arms around
him as they roared off. Nick, on another bike, sped after them.

That first night, they rode all over the city for more than three hours. They continued to ride the motorcycles throughout the city several more times before Natalie and Nick left Memphis. They were spotted so frequently that when a rumor began that Elvis had been injured in a traffic accident, it was assumed that Natalie was with him on his doomed bike. Newspaper reporters were hot on the story, checking hospital emergency rooms and police stations. They soon discovered the story was false; Elvis had left earlier that day for an appearance in Las Vegas.

Aside from Gladys, no one was more relieved that Elvis temporarily set aside his motorcycle than the executives at Warner Brothers. Studio officials, it was reported, were frantic at the thought of their rising stars speeding along on motorcycles, risking the same fate as James Dean.

DOWNTOWN. TOMMY TAYLOR'S MEMPHIS HARLEY-DAVIDSON WAS LOCATED ON POPLAR AVENUE BETWEEN THIRD AND FOURTH STREETS, ON THE SOUTH SIDE OF THE STREET. THERE IS NO TRACE OF THE FORMER BUSINESS. THE SHELBY COUNTY JUSTICE CENTER OCCUPIES THE BLOCK WHERE TOMMY TAYLOR'S MEMPHIS HARLEY-DAVIDSON WAS LOCATED. LAUDERDALE COURTS HOUSING PROJECT IS LOCATED ONE BLOCK NORTH.

FOOTBALL

Crump Stadium
Linden Avenue at Cleveland Street

Elvis wanted to play football for his high school team at Humes but had to work after school. Instead, Elvis watched the team play on Friday nights during the fall season. Many of the Humes games were played at Crump Stadium, which was adjacent to their archrival school, Central High.

In Memphis, the last high school footbal game of the year was a special match-up between the city's two best teams. The game was called the E. H. Crump Memorial Football Game for the Blind, with proceeds from the game donated to the Lions Club's charitable activities for the blind. Both the stadium and the game were named for Edward Hull Crump, the longtime political leader of Memphis who died in 1954.

Even after his fame reached a level that made him recognizable everywhere, Elvis still wanted to attend events like the Crump game. However, he soon realized he could not. Fans rioted with joy when they saw Elvis at the stadium for the game on December 1, 1956. The crowd was contained by eighty-five policemen, and Elvis quickly left the stadium. The following year, Elvis made a presentation to the Lions Club before the game. He had purchased fourteen hundred game tickets, enough for every student at Humes High School, and at the presentation he talked of the days not so long before when he wanted to play himself. This time, he did not try to attend the game.

Until 1965, when the Memphis Memorial Stadium (now the Liberty Bowl) opened, Crump Stadium was the largest arena in Memphis, used by both colleges and high schools. Today, it is still in use as a high school football stadium, with seating for twenty thousand.

MIDTOWN. FROM UNION AVENUE, TURN SOUTH ON CLEVELAND STREET, THEN TAKE THE SECOND RIGHT ONTO LINDEN AVENUE AT CENTRAL HIGH. METHODIST HOSPITAL IS IN THE VICINITY.

Elvis on stage at the Mid-South Fair, September 1956
Courtesy of Linda Everett

PLAYGROUNDS

Mid-South Fairgrounds
Libertyland
940 Early Maxwell Boulevard

One night, either in 1956 or 1957, Elvis and his friends were look-ing for something to do. Remembering the fun they had as kids, Elvis turned to his buddy George Klein and said, "I wonder how much it would cost to rent the whole damn fairgrounds?" Though he now had enough wealth to pursue any interest—he could have traveled the globe if he cared to—what he really wanted was to ride a roller coaster and play a few games on the midway. George called the manager of the Fairgrounds Amusement Park, who gave Elvis a reasonable price, and a pastime was born that Elvis enjoyed until his death.

Elvis's trips to the fairgrounds usually proceeded something like this: Shortly before midnight, Elvis's car would roll out of the gates of Graceland, past whatever fans were gathered there, and speed towards midtown Memphis. He would always be followed by several other cars filled with friends. The caravan would arrive at the fairgrounds to find an even bigger crowd of acquaintances waiting for them. Usually, a night at the fairgrounds was an event attended by no less than a hundred people.

Elvis's favorite ride was the Zippin Pippin, a rickety wooden roller coaster that is still in operation today. He always rode in either the first or the last car because, he said, there was no thrill in the others. God help those in the other seats, because the ride lasted until Elvis had enough. It would scarcely come to a stop when Elvis would yell "Hit it!" Then the cars would rapidly accelerate, careening down the track, without allowing the passengers to catch their breath before the wild ride began again. A ride with Elvis sometimes meant the equivalent of twenty ordinary rides.

Elvis also liked the Dodgem Cars, which appealed to his competitive nature. Here, too, he had his favorite car, one he thought was faster than any of the others. Elvis and his cohorts formed one team, playing against a team of their guests for hours at a time.

Meanwhile, the other rides carried some guests, while other folks lined up at the concession stand and ordered corn dogs or soft drinks.

Libertyland's Zippin Pippin
Courtesy of the Mississippi Valley Collection

The fairgrounds were as full of life as on an ordinary spring day. At the end of the night, Elvis would pick up the tab for everyone.

These occasions were the only way Elvis could enjoy the amusement park. In the early years, he had nearly caused chaos when he attended the Mid-South Fair, which was held at the same fairgrounds. One night in 1957, he spent six hundred dollars at two booths, winning 125 dolls in little more than an hour. Surrounded by a huge crowd, he kept tossing his winnings to the people behind him.

Marian Keisker, who worked for Memphis Recording Service, recalled a similar incident. She ran into Elvis at the fair in 1956, and they chatted as they walked down the midway. "The crowd grew like sugar candy on a cone," she said. "One girl was clinging to him and had to be pulled off. We went to the booth where the teddy bears were, and of course he won a teddy bear the first throw. He drops it in my arms and all of a sudden it's gone; a little girl had snatched it. So he won me another one. By now the crowd was closing in and pressing me so hard to the booth my shin bones were about to crack. Finally the crowd was about to push the whole booth over, so we went over the booth and under the canvas in the back, and raced madly to the front gate where we got into a police car and they drove us away. I was bruised and battered for days."

Elvis never lost his enthusiasm for the carnival, though in later years he began to avoid the fair altogether and invited smaller crowds. He last visited the amusement park on August 8, 1977, just a few days before his death. That night, he treated his daughter, Lisa Marie, to an evening of fun. He brought about twenty guests with him.

In 1975, the city rebuilt the amusement park and created a theme name, Libertyland, in honor of the nation's bicentennial. Today, one can still ride the Dodgem Cars and Zippin Pippin, just as Elvis did. Libertyland also offers live entertainment, including an Elvis tribute show during August. Call 901-274-1776 for hours and admission information.

MIDTOWN. FROM UNION AVENUE, DRIVE SOUTH ON EAST PARKWAY. THE MID-SOUTH FAIRGROUNDS, WHERE THE MID-SOUTH FAIR IS NOW HELD EVERY SEPTEMBER, ARE ON EAST PARKWAY BETWEEN CENTRAL AND SOUTHERN AVENUES.

Elvis at the Rainbow Roller Skating Rink
Courtesy of Linda Everett

Rainbow Roller Skating Rink
2881 Lamar Avenue

The Pieraccini family had two entertainment businesses on Lamar Avenue: Clearpool, which contained the Eagle's Nest nightclub (see page 74), and Rainbow Lake, an amusement complex that included the Rainbow Roller Skating Rink. Before stardom, Elvis frequented the skating rink, sometimes with his girlfriend Dixie Locke. At that time, he was just another teenager, although the late Joe Pieraccini remembered Elvis asking to play his acetate (the song is unknown) in the skating rink jukebox.

After stardom, Elvis often rented the facility for all-night parties. Mrs. Doris Pieraccini, wife of Joe, remembers charging Elvis just thirty-five dollars. She provided rollerskates, food, and drink for everyone in his party and helped keep out those not invited. Sometimes a crowd would bang on the windows and doors when it was known that Elvis was skating. Often, Elvis arrived at the rink in a nondescript truck instead of one of his famous cars in order to keep his party a secret. In spite of all the chaos, Elvis remained a cheerful, pleasant guest. When a friend of Doris brought her daughter to the rink, Elvis spent time skating with the child.

Elvis loved to skate—the physical activity was his antidote for stress and nervous energy. The skating often became a rough battle among the men, a sort of football game on wheels. One employee of the rink, Will McDaniel, earned a name for himself by knocking Elvis down. Because McDaniel was wearing a shirt with the moniker "Bardahl" on the label, he has been known by that name ever since.

Occasionally, Elvis would tear his shirt or pants, and one of the entourage was sent to find a replacement. After Elvis threw away the torn clothing, Doris would retrieve it from the trash. To this day, she has remnants of two pairs of pants, as well as a shirt worn in *Love Me Tender*.

In times of great stress, Elvis would use the skating rink frequently. Elvis skated with large parties of friends for nine days before his induction into the army in March of 1958. The second night after his mother's death in August of that year, Elvis skated again. This time there was no party, and very few people were with him. He simply skated around the rink until dawn. That marked the end of the skating parties. Doris never saw him again after 1958. She still remembers him as a sweet young man.

FROM I-240, TURN WEST ON LAMAR AVENUE. THE RAINBOW ROLLER SKATING RINK WAS ON THE LEFT SIDE OF LAMAR AVENUE BETWEEN SEMMES AND KIMBALL AVENUES. PANCHOS INCORPORATED NOW OPERATES A TORTILLA CHIP FACTORY ON THE SITE.

Rainbow Roller Skating Rink
Courtesy of the
Mississippi Valley Collection

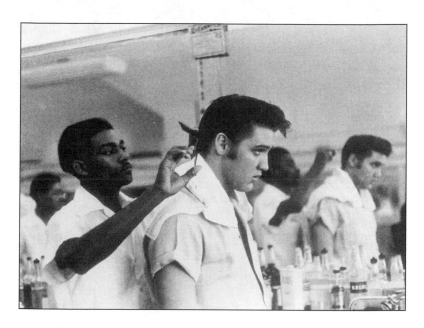

Elvis at Jim's Barber Shop
Courtesy of Linda Everett

HAIR CUTS

Jim's Barber Shop
7 North Third Street

In 1957, the *Memphis Press-Scimitar* reported the following: "Girls, Elvis has his hair cut at Jim's Barber Shop at 201 South Main. But don't rush down to the place. Elvis never has enough sheared off to make many souvenirs." Thus began the rush of fans anxious to take home a bit of Elvis's hair.

Albert Gale, who had been cutting the rock star's hair since Elvis was a young teenager, remembers those days well. "Girls used to come in and collect Elvis's hair off the hair cloths. It was really embarrassing," he said. Eventually, Elvis hired his own barber to come to Graceland and travel with him. Vernon remained a client of Jim's until his death.

At that time, Jim's Barber Shop was located at 201 South Main

Street, where it occupied the southeast corner of the Malco Theater. In the 1980s, the theater was renovated and renamed the Orpheum. As part of the theater's transformation into a cultural center, Jim's was asked to move.

Today, the barber shop is located on North Third Street within the heart of the downtown business district. You can still get a haircut, shave, or a special facial massage at Jim's.

DOWNTOWN. FROM UNION AVENUE, TURN NORTH ON NORTH THIRD STREET. JIM'S IS ON NORTH THIRD STREET BETWEEN MADISON AND COURT AVENUES, ON THE WEST SIDE OF THE STREET.

THE ORIGINAL LOCATION IS ON SOUTH MAIN STREET AT THE SOUTHWEST CORNER OF BEALE STREET. THE ORPHEUM THEATER IS THE SITE OF BROADWAY PRODUCTIONS AND MANY OTHER ENTERTAINMENT ACTS.

DEPARTURE
FOR THE ARMY

Local Draft Board 86
Merchants and Manufacturers Building
198 Beale Street

Nothing shocked the world of rock-and-roll-loving teenagers as much as the news of Elvis's draft notice, issued from the office of Local Draft Board 86. Letters flooded the draft board begging the army to release Elvis from his impending two-year hitch. However, the draft board would not relent, saying that Elvis was no different from any other young man. The board did give Elvis a six-month extension to film the movie *King Creole*, a move that irritated certain veterans' groups.

At 6:35 A.M. on March 24, 1958, Elvis arrived at the draft-board office on Beale Street to be sworn into the United States Army. Surprisingly, all was calm when he finally reported for military duty. Perhaps the combination of a cold, drizzling rain and the early hour led to a manageable crowd. Elvis was met by a swarm of newsman and photographers, but there was only a sprinkling of die-hard fans. Colonel Parker, not one to miss any sort of publicity opportunity, was already present and handing out balloons advertising *King Creole*.

With several months to prepare for this day, Elvis was resigned. He looked tired, having arrived after an all-night open house at Graceland, but he still quipped with reporters, asking if any cared to join him. His parents, who accompanied him, were less cheerful; his mother appeared on the verge of tears. After a few moments outside, he stepped into the draft-board office to be inducted with eleven other draftees. Elvis took part in the brief ceremony and then boarded the bus which would carry the new recruits to Kennedy Hospital for their physical.

DOWNTOWN. FROM UNION AVENUE, TURN SOUTH ON SECOND STREET AND CONTINUE TO BEALE STREET. TURN RIGHT ON BEALE STREET. THE BUILDING WAS LOCATED AT THE SOUTHEAST CORNER OF MAIN AND BEALE STREETS, ACROSS THE STREET FROM THE ORPHEUM THEATER. THE MEMPHIS LIGHT GAS AND WATER BUILDING NOW OCCUPIES THE SITE.

Kennedy Veterans Hospital
Getwell Road at Park Avenue

Though Elvis was accustomed to cameras by 1958, he may not have been prepared for the continual flash of bulbs as photographers documented every single part of his induction into the army. Certainly he didn't mind the photographers while he filled out the seemingly endless array of forms, but he probably felt differently when he had to strip to his shorts. The cameras flashed as he followed the yellow lines on the tile floor, stopping at several points in the examination center to be measured, poked, and prodded. His fellow inductees blinked against the glare of the cameras as they moved with him; but the photographers had no concern for their modesty. Elvis, the symbol of teenage rebellion, was meeting Uncle Sam, and this historic occasion was to be duly recorded.

The defining moment, at least for the media, was the cutting of Elvis's hair. As if wishing to make this moment less dramatic, Elvis had visited his barber twice during the previous week, getting a small amount cut each time. By the time the army barber had his way,

Elvis was already sporting a modest flattop. Of course, the final result was measurably shorter than Elvis would have liked.

Nonetheless, Elvis accepted this ritual of conformity with extraordinary grace and dignity. Although he spent a long day under intense scrutiny, he remained outwardly respectful and even cheerful. He never once complained that joining the army was not what he wanted to do. Whenever questioned, he said, "I'll do what they ask," or "it's a duty I'm going to fill." Only once did he comment that a soldier's life would be an adjustment for him. "Those fellows are getting up about the time I go to bed," he said.

Finally, late that afternoon, he took the solemn oath and became a soldier. At 5:00 P.M., he kissed his mother, said goodbye to his family and friends, and boarded the bus which would carry him to Fort Chafee and basic training.

EAST MEMPHIS. FROM I-240, EXIT NORTH ONTO GETWELL ROAD. DRIVE NORTH ON GETWELL ROAD FOR ABOUT TWO MILES. THE HOSPITAL SITE IS PART OF THE UNIVERSITY OF MEMPHIS SOUTH CAMPUS. THE UNIVERSITY ENTRANCE IS ON THE RIGHT AS YOU APPROACH PARK AVENUE.

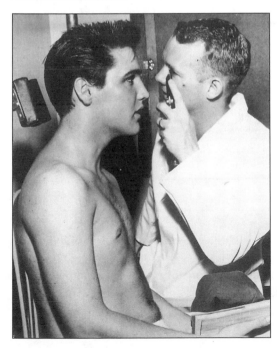

Elvis undergoing his Army physical at Kennedy Veterans Hospital, March 24, 1958
Courtesy of the Library of Congress

Elvis stopping in the corridor of Methodist Hospital to admire a young fan's pin. His mother died the day after this picture was taken.
Courtesy of the Library of Congress

ELVIS'S MOTHER'S DEATH

Methodist Hospital
1265 Union Avenue

In Elvis's life, there was one grief that stood above all others. For Elvis, the death of his mother at Methodist Hospital was a tragedy of immense proportions, both in its immediacy and in its implications. Upon her death, Elvis lamented, "Everything that I have now is gone." It was a powerful statement for a twenty-three-year-old to make, but in all of his life, he would never again feel such despair. Their bond went beyond that of mother and son—she was the source of his strength and his guiding voice.

That he was in the army then and living away from Memphis only added to his sadness. Gladys and Vernon had followed Elvis to Texas, where he was in basic training, but Gladys's health was failing. On Friday, August 8, 1958, she and Vernon boarded a train for Memphis so that her own doctor could care for her. She was hospitalized immediately at Methodist Hospital with a diagnosis of hepatitis. On Tuesday, Elvis flew home on emergency leave (only the second time he had ever flown). Upon arrival in Memphis, he remained by her bedside. Alert but weakening, Gladys finally persuaded Elvis that he should return to Graceland. Elvis left the hospital about 9:00 on Wednesday evening. She died at 3:15 the next morning. Vernon called Elvis to rush to the hospital, but he arrived too late. When she died, Gladys was just forty-six.

MIDTOWN. THE HOSPITAL IS NOW CALLED METHODIST HOSPITAL CENTRAL AND IS JUST ONE BRANCH OF THE METHODIST HOSPITAL SYSTEM. THE HOSPITAL IS LOCATED ON THE SOUTH SIDE OF UNION AVENUE, JUST EAST OF THE I-240 EXITS.

Forest Hill Cemetery
1661 Elvis Presley Boulevard

On August 15, 1958, one day after her death, Gladys Presley was laid to rest in the Forest Hill Cemetery. Her body had lain in state at Graceland until nine that morning, then it was transported to National Funeral Home (later renamed Memphis Funeral Home) for public services. More than three thousand people, mostly women and young girls hoping for a glimpse of the grief-stricken Elvis, filed past her body. Colonel Parker told a reporter for the *Memphis Press-Scimitar* that Elvis said his mother loved all of his fans, and he wanted them to have a last chance to see her. Reverend Hamill officiated at the chapel service.

A one-hundred-car procession traveled from the funeral home to the cemetery. Hundreds of people lined Bellevue Boulevard to watch the procession drive past. Sixty-five law-enforcement officers helped guide the procession.

The burial at Forest Hill Cemetery was a scene that would be repeated nineteen years later, when Elvis would be buried in a mausoleum at Forest Hill. An estimated fifty thousand bystanders watched his final journey. More than twenty-two hundred floral arrangements covered the lawn in front of the mausoleum. By the next day, every flower had been taken by fans as a souvenir.

Because of continuing crowds and security threats, the bodies of Elvis and his mother were moved to the Meditation Garden at Graceland six weeks after his interment.

SOUTH MEMPHIS. FROM GRACELAND, TRAVEL THREE MILES NORTH ON ELVIS PRESLEY BOULEVARD. THE CEMETERY IS ON THE WEST SIDE OF THE STREET. THE MAUSOLEUM WHERE ELVIS WAS ENTOMBED BRIEFLY IS STILL VISITED BY ELVIS FANS. ALSO BURIED HERE IS BASSIST BILL BLACK, WHO DIED IN 1965.

Burke's Florist
1609 Elvis Presley Boulevard

Burke's Florist was conveniently located just a couple of blocks north of Forest Hill Cemetery. Most likely, Elvis stopped in one day on his way to visit his mother's grave and bought flowers to take with him. He became a regular customer, frequently buying flowers for his visits to the cemetery, and for other occasions as well.

In a lot of ways, Elvis was a considerate Southern gentleman. If he heard that a friend or acquaintance was ill or suffered a death in the family, he would arrange for flowers to be sent on his behalf. Often, that meant a call to Burke's Florist.

SOUTH MEMPHIS. FROM FOREST HILL CEMETERY, TRAVEL NORTH ON ELVIS PRESLEY BOULEVARD PAST THE CALVARY CEMETERY. BURKE'S WAS ON THE SAME SIDE OF THE STREET AS BOTH CEMETERIES. BURKE'S IS NO LONGER IN BUSINESS. ANOTHER FLORIST, LOVE'S UNLIMITED FLORIST, NOW OCCUPIES THIS SITE.

Union Station
Courtesy of the Mississippi Valley Collection

A GRAND WELCOME

Union Station
199 East Calhoun Avenue

For years, Union Station was considered the hub around which much of Memphis revolved. Trains bearing such memorable names as the Panama Limited chugged into the station and deposited cars full of travelers, while in the giant, marble lobby, other people rushed to meet their parties or to embark on their own journey. Day or night, the station bustled as if it was a small city. It was in this busy world that Elvis often found himself as he either returned to or left Memphis.

Elvis was afraid of flying, especially in the early years, and he often rode the train when on tour or traveling to Hollywood. He almost always rode in a private car with an entourage of close friends, who were there to keep him company as much as offer any protection.

Colonel Parker sometimes came along and discussed business, but frequently it was just Elvis and the guys.

Many of Elvis's comings and goings were reported in the Memphis papers, usually after the fact. On occasion, staff photographers were given advance notice. Undoubtedly the Colonel knew the publicity value of Elvis and his girlfriend Anita Wood saying their lingering good-byes.

Likewise, the Colonel knew that Elvis's return from Germany in 1960 following his army service provided a rare opportunity for promotion. In fact, the Colonel felt it was an event that needed to be broadcast to the world because Elvis had been away from his audience for two years. No one yet knew what impact that would have on his career. Would his fans accept him again? Would they still rush out and buy his records?

The Colonel made sure that Elvis's return provided the excitement necessary to reignite his career. It was an event reported worldwide, but never in as much detail as in Memphis. The papers provided daily accounts of Elvis's whereabouts as the countdown continued. When the hour of his return approached, Elvis's fans and friends gathered at Union Station. On that snowy March 7th in 1960, more than 250 people waited for Elvis's arrival on the train that was due in at 7:40 A.M. More than fifty newsmen and photographers were present.

When the train rolled into the city, it stopped briefly at the Buntyn Station across from the Memphis Country Club on Southern Avenue. Elvis stepped onto the platform at the rear of the railroad car and waved to a group of a dozen or so people who had parked there in hopes of seeing him. Then the train rolled on toward downtown Memphis.

The scene at Union Station was electric. Elvis, wearing dress blues, stepped off the train, his hand held high in a friendly wave. He spotted his friend George Klein and others that he knew. Gary Pepper, a cerebral palsy victim and president of the Elvis Presley Tankers fan club (named in honor of Elvis's service with the Second Armored Division), sat in his wheelchair, holding a sign that said "Welcome Home Elvis." A sea of Elvis's fans pressed against an iron barrier, shouting "Elvis! Elvis!" Elvis made his way toward them to shake hands. He visited briefly with his friends, then he got into a police car and sped toward Graceland.

DOWNTOWN. FROM UNION AVENUE, DRIVE SOUTH ON SECOND STREET TO CALHOUN AVENUE. UNION STATION WAS DEMOLISHED TO MAKE WAY FOR THE POST OFFICE BULK MAIL FACILITY. THE STATION, LIKE THE POST OFFICE BUILDING TODAY, COVERED THE ENTIRE BLOCK ON CALHOUN AVENUE BETWEEN SECOND AND THIRD STREETS.

ANOTHER TRAIN STATION, CENTRAL STATION, IS LOCATED ON SOUTH MAIN STREET AT CALHOUN AVENUE, A FEW BLOCKS WEST OF THE SITE OF UNION STATION. ELVIS TRAVELED FROM CENTRAL STATION WHENEVER HIS DESTINATION WAS NORTH OR SOUTH OF MEMPHIS. TRAINS RUNNING TO DESTINATIONS EAST AND WEST STOPPED AT UNION STATION. TODAY, AMTRAK TRAINS DEPART OR ARRIVE AT THE REAR OF CENTRAL STATION, THOUGH THEIR SCHEDULE IS VERY LIMITED. THE STATION, IN DIRE NEED OF RENOVATION, IS NOT OPEN, EXCEPT FOR A SMALL AMTRAK TICKETING AREA.

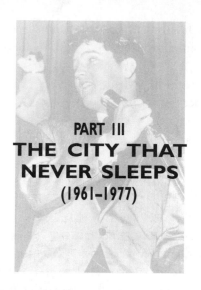

RECORDING STUDIOS

American Sound Studio
829 Thomas Street

At the end of the 1960s, Elvis's movie career was at an ebb, so he decided to perform on stage again. But first, Elvis decided to record some new material to support his concerts. The movie soundtracks had not been challenging, and he was especially hungry for songs that had feeling. Elvis was attracted to American Sound Studio, a Memphis recording studio. Part of the reason Elvis chose to record at American Sound was because some members of his Memphis Mafia were already involved in songwriting and music promotion there. The primary reason was the quality of music coming out of the studio—American Sound was churning out the hits.

The young studio was founded by Chips Moman, who had earned a reputation as a session musician and songwriter. With the financial backing of friends, he opened American Sound Studio in a decaying building. Studio musicians and songwriters liked to joke about the rats in the building. Still, they were drawn to Moman's talent and promise.

American Sound first found success with hit songs by local teen-age bands such as the Gentrys and the Box Tops. As word of the studio spread, singers from all over the world, including Neil Diamond, B.J. Thomas, Joe Simon, Dusty Springfield, Roy Hamilton, and the Sweet Inspirations, recorded hit songs there. From 1967 to 1971, approximately 120 hits songs were produced at the American Sound Studio. That success brought even more singers and musicians to Memphis. Chips Moman's little studio became a part of the Memphis sound legend.

This was the sound that Elvis tapped into in January 1969, making his first recordings in Memphis since leaving Sun Records at the end of 1955. During the sessions at American Sound, Elvis recorded some of his greatest material. Songs like "Kentucky Rain," "In The Ghetto," and "Suspicious Minds" put Elvis Presley back on the top of the music charts. Then and now, music critics have called the American Sound sessions the spark that launched his music career a second time.

For all the acclaim those sessions produced, Elvis did not return to American Sound Studio. Elvis preferred a producer like Felton Jarvis, who did not tell Elvis what to do in the studio. Chips Moman did not stay in Memphis long either. In 1972, angry that he did not receive the recognition in Memphis he felt he deserved, he left, moving first to Atlanta and then to Nashville. Today, nearly all the studio musicians and songwriters who worked for Chips enjoy successful careers in Nashville.

The studio itself sat unused for many years, a symbol of the declining fortunes of the Memphis music business. For a time, a local promoter operated tours of the building for Elvis fans, but he could not sustain that enterprise. The building was demolished in 1987 to make way for an auto parts store.

DOWNTOWN. FROM UNION AVENUE, TURN NORTH ON THIRD STREET AND CON-TINUE UNTIL YOU REACH ITS DEAD END AT CHELSEA AVENUE, ABOUT A MILE FROM THE PEABODY HOTEL. TURN RIGHT AND DRIVE ABOUT THREE BLOCKS TO THOMAS STREET. ON YOUR LEFT, AT THE NORTHWEST CORNER OF THOMAS STREET AND CHELSEA AV-ENUE, IS THE SITE OF THE STUDIO. TODAY A DAY CARE CENTER OPERATES ON THIS SITE.

Stax Records
928 East McLemore Avenue

Elvis Presley recorded music released for consumer sales at five locations in Memphis: Sun Records, American Sound Studio, a concert album at Mid-South Coliseum, at Graceland at the end of his life, and Stax Records. Each of the three Memphis studios where Elvis recorded had a distinctive sound. Sun Records blazed the trail for rockabilly. American Sound Studio mastered mainstream top forty. Stax Records was the birthplace of the city's own brand of soul music.

In 1960, Jim Stewart and Estelle Axton opened a small recording studio and retail record shop in what was once the Capital Theater. From the beginning, they recorded young black entertainers who had honed their skills in churches and nightclubs. The south Memphis studio was located in a neighborhood that was changing from white to black, and they often literally found talented performers at their door. Disc jockey and performer Rufus Thomas brought in his teenage daughter Carla, and her songs became the first national hits for the Stax label. David Porter, Booker T. Jones, and Isaac Hayes were among the many local performers who walked into the Stax recording studio and became stars. Five years later, a young Georgian singer named Otis Redding recorded his first hit song at Stax. That year, Atlantic Records brought in Wilson Pickett and Sam and Dave to record at Stax.

The recording studio became renowned for its unique style of soul music, a music that tapped into the Memphis sound. What made the success story more remarkable was that the studio founders, and many of the session musicians, were white. In a decade marked by racial tensions, Stax Records was a story of cooperation and harmony.

Unfortunately, those feelings would not last. The more success the company earned, the more difficulty Stax seemed to have managing its business. Old partnerships dissolved, and many of the Stax people moved away from Memphis. Stax filed for bankruptcy in 1975. Fifteen years later, the abandoned studio was torn down. Not enough

Stax Recording Studio
Courtesy of the Memphis and Shelby CountyRoom
Memphis/Shelby County Public Library and Information Center

people in Memphis cared to save it. A chapter in music history came
to an end.

Elvis recorded at Stax in two sessions held in June and December
of 1973. All but two of the songs on Elvis's *Raised on Rock* album
were recorded at Stax. The sessions were neither a highlight of his
recording career, nor in the history of the studio. Perhaps because of
personal matters that were troubling him, Elvis was not particularly
happy in the studio during those sessions.

SOUTH MEMPHIS. FROM GRACELAND, DRIVE NORTH ON ELVIS PRESLEY BOULEVARD
ABOUT THREE MILES TO MCLEMORE AVENUE. TURN LEFT AND DRIVE TO COLLEGE STREET.
THE STUDIO WAS LOCATED AT THE NORTHWEST CORNER OF MCLEMORE AVE-NUE AND
COLLEGE STREET. A TENNESSEE HISTORIC MARKER NOTING THE SIGNIFICANCE OF THE
STUDIO MARKS THE ABANDONED SITE.

Hi Records/Royal Sound Studio
1329 South Lauderdale Street

While Elvis Presley was not directly involved with the Hi Records story, it is worth telling here. There were three studios in Memphis that produced national hit songs during the '60s and '70s: Stax Records, American Sound Studio, and Royal Sound Studio (for Hi Records). All three studios contributed to creating the Memphis sound. Elvis knew a number of people who made Hi Records a success, and he often listened to the music that was recorded there.

The label was founded in 1956 by Pop Tunes co-owner Joe Cuoghi. Three years later, Bill Black recorded the song "Smokie–Part 2" at the studio with his band, the Bill Black Combo. The song went on to become Bill's first hit since leaving Elvis. Hi Records also released instrumental hits by Ace Cannon and Willie Mitchell. Mitchell became the key figure in the success of Hi Records. He had been a bandleader for some time, even playing at some of Elvis's private New Year's Eve parties at the Manhattan Club. His 1964 instrumental hit "20–75" established him as a star.

Mitchell became an influential leader within the record label following the death of Black in 1965. He renovated an old movie theater in south Memphis and named it the Royal Sound Studio. Mitchell, who is black, turned the label's attention towards the emerging soul music scene. He first recorded Ann Peebles, who had a hit with "I Can't Stand The Rain." His most important discovery was the artist Al Green, who recorded fifteen hits between 1971 and 1976. Like Elvis, Green shared a love for the standards, recording old favorites like "I'm So Lonesome I Could Cry" and "Funny How Time Slips Away." These were two of Elvis's favorite songs. Elvis first performed "I'm So Lonesome I Could Cry" at his "Aloha From Hawaii" television special in 1973, about the time that Green first released his version.

With Al Green, Hi Records soared to the top of the music business. Then the success ended abruptly. Green stopped singing commercial music in order to sing gospel and preach in his church. At the same time, popular tastes in music were moving away from soul towards disco.

Mitchell is still active in managing the Hi label and producing, though he has not had any hit songs for years. His Royal Sound Studio is the only survivor among the Memphis sound studios. Royal Sound is generally not open to the public. The best place to experience the history of the label is at Willie Mitchell's own nightclub, Willie Mitchell's Rhythm & Blues Club at 326 Beale Street. You can also still catch some of the entertainers from Hi's glory days playing around town on occasion. On most Sundays, you can hear Al Green preach at his church, the Full Gospel Tabernacle at 787 Hale Road. Reverend Green has returned to popular music, although he makes it a point to be in Memphis on Sundays.

SOUTH MEMPHIS. ROYAL SOUND STUDIO IS LOCATED ON SOUTH LAUDERDALE STREET BETWEEN TRIGG AVENUE AND SOUTH PARKWAY EAST. THE STUDIO IS CLOSED TO VISITORS AND THE AREA IS NOT INVITING TO TOURISTS. A BETTER PLACE TO SEE HIGHLIGHTS OF THE HI RECORDS STORY IS AT WILLIE MITCHELL'S NIGHTCLUB ON BEALE STREET BETWEEN THIRD AND FOURTH STREETS. THE CLUB IS ON THE NORTH SIDE OF THE STREET; MARKERS IDENTIFYING THE PALACE THEATER SITE ARE TO THE LEFT.

TO REACH AL GREEN'S CHURCH FROM ELVIS PRESLEY BOULEVARD, TURN WEST ON HALE ROAD AND DRIVE TO AUBURN ROAD. THE CHURCH IS ON THE LEFT SIDE OF HALE ROAD, JUST PAST AUBURN ROAD. VISITORS ARE WELCOME, HOWEVER, THE CONGREGATION ASKS THAT GUESTS ARE RESPECTFUL OF THEIR WORSHIP SERVICES.

*Elvis in concert at the Mid-South
Coliseum, June 10, 1975*
Courtesy of Carolyn White Scarberry

PERFORMANCES

Mid-South Coliseum
Mid-South Fairgrounds
Early Maxwell Boulevard

By 1974, thirteen years had passed since Elvis's last performance in Memphis, practically a lifetime in the career of an entertainer. Much had occurred since his last hometown concert in 1961. He had filmed twenty-five movies and released as many full-length albums, which had spawned countless singles and won two Grammy Awards. What's more, by that time his concert tour was a well-oiled, music-making machine; he had appeared in more than *seven hundred* concerts in Las Vegas and across the country by the time he stepped onto a Memphis stage again in 1974.

Why did Elvis bypass his hometown while selling out shows across the country? It certainly wasn't for lack of local interest. In 1972, one lady even sent a blank check to the coliseum box office in the hope that Elvis would someday perform in Memphis. She wanted to place the first order, she wrote in her letter. Remarkably, her order was eventually filled. When it was announced that Elvis would be

Elvis in concert at the Mid-South Coliseum, June 10, 1975
Courtesy of Carolyn White Scarberry

performing at the Mid-South Coliseum in March, ticket sales were so brisk that two more shows were quickly added to the three already planned.

The final show on March 21, 1974, was recorded and released as *Elvis Recorded Live On Stage In Memphis.* "I wanted to record a live session in my hometown of Memphis," Elvis explained on stage that night. "After all, this is where it all started out for me. I was a little worried for the first show last Saturday, but the audience knocked me out. They were great, and I appreciate it. It has always been said that a person cannot return to their hometown, but you have disproved that theory completely."

Elvis and Colonel Parker were so pleased by the audiences in Memphis that Elvis returned to the Mid-South Coliseum again fifteen months later. This show was recorded also, though not officially released as an album. Many of the songs were the same as those sung the previous year, although he did add Olivia Newton John's "Let Me Be There." That night he clowned with the audience, teasing the ladies and causing a near-riot by throwing scarves. "I got the worst bruise of my life trying to get a scarf," Carolyn Scarberry remembers. While bending to kiss a woman on the front row, Elvis split the seam of his jumpsuit. "Of all the places in the world to split my pants, it would be in my hometown," he said. "Is it bad?" he asked his band members. Assured that it wasn't, he continued the show.

By 1976, Elvis had taken his show to every major city in America, appearing in many of these cities several times. He appeared again in Memphis on July 6, wearing his Phoenix jumpsuit. As before, the show was sold out, and the audience reveled in his every move. "It never ceases to amaze me," he said, barely audible above the screams of adulation. Though the crowd obviously enjoyed the performance, a reviewer for the *Commercial Appeal* was not as kind, calling Elvis's rendition of "Fairytale" almost mechanical with the barest of feeling. Was Elvis tiring of the constant touring? Was his health suffering? For some reason, Elvis felt motivated to comment on stage. "The last time I was here I was sick a couple of weeks. But I'm over all that and I'm working and I'm happy." Despite the reference to his previous performance, the comment seemed to be addressed towards problems he was having at the time.

That was Elvis's last Memphis show. He was scheduled to appear in town again on August 27, 1977. Elvis died on August 16. Thousands of the tickets were never submitted to the coliseum ticket office for refunds. Instead, they were kept as souvenirs.

The Mid-South Coliseum was built in 1965 and seats eleven thousand for concerts. At the time of its construction, Elvis fan Gary Pepper led a petition to name the new arena Elvis Presley Coliseum. Some political leaders favored the idea, but most did not and another name was chosen. Nearby is the Liberty Bowl football stadium, where Elvis attended some professional football games in 1975. He owned a percentage of the short-lived Memphis Southmen football team.

MIDTOWN. FROM UNION AVENUE, DRIVE SOUTH ON EAST PARKWAY AND CONTINUE TO SOUTHERN AVENUE. TURN EAST ON SOUTHERN AVENUE; THE COLISEUM ENTRANCE IS THE NEXT LEFT.

AWARDS

Claridge Hotel
109 North Main Street

Despite his outwardly cool demeanor, Elvis was nervous as he prepared to go downtown on February 25, 1961. Governor Ellington had proclaimed the day "Elvis Presley Day" throughout Tennessee. That afternoon, he was scheduled to appear at Ellis Auditorium in his first live show since 1957. But first, he would attend an awards luncheon at the Claridge Hotel. At Graceland, he fretted about his appearance, changing his clothes at the last minute. An unmarked police car finally drove him through Graceland's gates five minutes after his scheduled arrival at the hotel.

Arriving fifteen minutes late, the car whisked into the alley, outwitting the crowd of five hundred waiting in the lobby to see Elvis. A guard opened the side door, and Elvis was escorted to a service elevator that carried him to the second-floor kitchen. He walked through the pantry and stepped out into the banquet room amid a rousing welcome.

The luncheon was a charity event, with guests paying a hundred dollars each for the privilege of dining with Elvis. That was the reason Elvis decided to participate in the luncheon, since he usually avoided ceremonies of any kind. The luncheon served as the preliminary fund-raiser to the two charity concerts Elvis would give that afternoon, with proceeds from all benefiting two dozen local charities.

While the purpose of the luncheon was to raise funds for a worthy cause, it gave others the opportunity to publicly recognize Elvis's accomplishments. RCA was first to honor Elvis with a plaque for his sales of seventy-five-million records. His latest record, "Surrender," had sold one million copies in just ten days. *Billboard* magazine presented Elvis with an award for his record "Now or Never," which they proclaimed the best single in 1960. The last of the music awards was a plaque sent from Dick Clark naming Elvis the top male vocalist on *American Bandstand*.

At the ceremony's end, the media was invited to ask questions. One reporter asked, "Do you always feel like you are coming home to Memphis?"

"Yes sir," Elvis replied. "I like to work in California, but when a picture is over I get out of there."

Then someone asked, "What will you be doing ten years from now?"

"I'll tell you, Mr. Johnson," Elvis said, obviously recognizing the reporter, "I would not say. Everything is changing. People change. Times change. I'm trying to make it acting. It takes a long time. It takes a lot of work and experience. I don't know how long the music will last."

Another reporter asked about the upcoming show. Elvis replied, "I have not been on such a stage in three years. I've almost forgotten the words of one of my songs. I'm a little nervous." But then, to put things in perspective, Elvis mentioned his appearance on the *Frank Sinatra Show* immediately following his release from the army. "I wasn't just nervous, I was petrified," he said.

DOWNTOWN. FROM UNION AVENUE, TURN NORTH ON THIRD STREET. CONTINUE TO ADAMS AVENUE AND TURN LEFT. DRIVE TWO BLOCKS TO THE INTERSECTION WITH

Holiday Inn-Rivermont
200 West Georgia Avenue

During his twenty-three-year career, Elvis won countless awards in nearly every category of music. He was given trophies, plaques, keys to cities, and virtually every honor imaginable, but none ever meant more to him than being named one of the "Ten Outstanding Young Men of America" by the United States Junior Chamber of Commerce, more commonly known as the Jaycees.

Elvis rarely accepted awards personally. However, for this occasion, he participated in all of the events associated with the award ceremony, beginning with the prayer breakfast held at the Holiday Inn-Rivermont. Here, he met the other recipients, including President Nixon's press secretary, a Harvard Medical School biologist, a National Cancer Institute scientist, a professor at West Point who had earned the medal of honor in Vietnam, and others with extraordinary accomplishments. Despite his success, Elvis was truly awed by these men and noticeably nervous. Furthermore, the humbled Elvis was determined that his fame would not overshadow their accomplishments in any way. This was one time in Elvis's life when he dearly wanted to be treated like everyone else, without the fanfare of media, fans, and photographers that usually accompanied his public appearances.

Of course, Elvis could not be anything but a celebrity, despite his best intentions. Arriving late by private jet the night before, he stayed in a suite at the Rivermont rather than drive the short distance from Graceland. Social breakfasts were not something that Elvis normally participated in; he was usually fast asleep at this time of day. Not surprisingly, he was late the next morning. With security carefully planned, his host, Harold Sterling, anxiously stood in the hallway

Holiday Inn-Rivermont
Courtesy of the Memphis and Shelby County Room
Memphis/Shelby County Public Library and Information Center

waiting for him. But Elvis had not overslept. He was agonizing over his appearance because he had lost a cufflink.

Harold was surprised when he saw Elvis. "It was overwhelming," Harold remembered. "I was just not ready for someone that theatrical. He had all these diamonds on, and his hair was long. Charlie Hodge was drinking and laughing. Red and his wife were there. Priscilla had long jet black hair. He was a taskmaster. People jumped. He had ideas on what he wanted and the impression he wanted to give. But he was a benevolent tyrant. He was so good, but he was demanding, too."

His entrance into the dining room was electric, filling the most staid businessmen and society wives with teenage enthusiasm; they all stopped their conversations to watch him enter the room. Just as he and Priscilla sat down, photographers rushed to their table. Graciously, Elvis allowed a couple of quick pictures. Then he asked the newsmen to leave.

A private question-and-answer session followed. The media were banned from the forum to allow honorees to speak openly about their views. On this occasion, Elvis spoke of religion and its importance to his life. In attendance was future President George Bush, who was then serving as ambassador to the United Nations and appearing at the luncheon as the featured speaker.

In the afternoon, Elvis hosted a cocktail party at Graceland for the other honorees and distinguished members of the Jaycees. He then treated them to dinner at the Four Flames Restaurant. Dinner was followed by the award ceremony at Ellis Auditorium. At the ceremony's end, Elvis returned to his suite at the Rivermont and invited his hosts from the Jaycees to join him. "He was more relaxed than I'd ever seen him," remembered Frank Taylor, the Memphis organizer of the Jaycees convention. "It was almost like the weekend was away from reality. He had never been exposed to the professional part of life. It was a new world for him. For once he shared the spotlight with others."

Being included in a group of men that were contributing great things to society moved Elvis. Although his own accomplishments were substantial, and his many gifts to charity were the primary reason for his nomination, he felt that his own success paled in comparison to those of the other honorees. And of all his many achievements, including those he later attained, none were as treasured by him as the Jaycees' presentation. He carried his trophy with him whenever he left Memphis, and the scrapbook given to him by Frank Taylor was proudly displayed on his desk.

The Holiday Inn-Rivermont was converted to condominiums several years ago. The green-neon-lit building towers over the Mississippi on Riverside Drive, a focal point to those crossing the bridge from Arkansas. A walkway built along the river bluff at the rear of the building provides one of the most scenic views in all of Memphis. This is a site where generations of Memphians have stopped to enjoy the river view, and most likely Elvis did the same. You can too, simply by stopping at Tom Lee Park and following the trail up the small hill.

♦

DOWNTOWN. FROM UNION AVENUE, TURN SOUTH ON RIVERSIDE DRIVE. THE MISSISSIPPI RIVER IS TO YOUR RIGHT. DRIVE ONE MILE TO THE INTERSECTION OF RIVERSIDE DRIVE AND GEORGIA AVENUE. THE BUILDING IS ON THE RIGHT SIDE OF THIS INTERSECTION. JUST BEYOND THE BUILDING IS THE EXIT FOR THE MEMPHIS-ARKANSAS BRIDGE.

Elvis and Priscilla at the Jaycees event honoring the
"Ten Outstanding Young Men of America"

RESTAURANTS

Four Flames Restaurant
1085 Poplar Avenue

Aside from his clothes, Elvis's tastes were very simple. He could have eaten every meal in five-star restaurants, enjoying the most expensive and exotic meals. But what he really enjoyed was sitting in an ordinary, working-class diner, eating the common foods that he grew up with. There was, however, one occasion when Elvis set aside his preferences to impress his guests.

In January 1971, Elvis was named one of the "Ten Outstanding Young Men of America" by the Jaycees. The night of the award ceremony, Elvis treated his fellow honorees to a dinner party. Elvis wanted the event to be flawless and chose the Four Flames Restaurant as the site for dinner.

The evening began with a cocktail reception at Graceland. Then, thirty automobiles and limousines led by a motorcycle escort carried the large party (the nominees and their wives, along with various Jaycees officials) to the Four Flames Restaurant. Bouquets of fresh flowers and candelabras adorned the center of the tables. A violinist played soft and elegant music as the guests were led to their seats, marked by place cards bearing Elvis's signature at the bottom. Steak knives positioned amid the formal setting were the only indication of Elvis's true tastes. Dinner was served by white-gloved waiters.

Although Elvis had been nervous at the cocktail party, he seemed at ease by the time dinner was underway. He enjoyed his guests so much that, at one point, he stood up and invited them all to come to Las Vegas to see his show. Of course, Elvis didn't have to work so hard to impress his guests; they were delighted to be in his company.

DOWNTOWN. THE RESTAURANT IS ON THE SOUTH SIDE OF POPLAR AVENUE AT THE INTERSECTION WITH WALDRAN STREET. THE NEW VETERANS HOSPITAL COMPLEX IS NEARBY. THE SITE IS NOW THE CHILD ADVOCACY CENTER, HOWEVER, VISITORS CAN STILL VIEW THE FOUR TOWERING COLUMNS, WHICH ONCE HELD FOUR FLAMES.

Chenault's Restaurant
1400 Elvis Presley Boulevard

It's hard to say what Elvis liked most about Chenault's. It may have been that it was convenient to Graceland, since it was just a few miles north. The food appealed to him (although there were many items on the menu, Elvis often ordered burgers), and the staff treated him and his friends well. These reasons were factors, but what probably made the restaurant a hangout was the fact it had a private dining room; Elvis and his buddies could be themselves here without fear of interruption.

The decor was more fitting to a lakeside lodge than an urban restaurant, contributing to the comfortable atmosphere. The interior featured tan brick and natural plywood paneling trimmed with redwood. A brick planter created an island in the dining room.

A get-together at Chenault's was usually an impromptu affair. Elvis had a car phone, and if he mentioned that he might like to stop at the restaurant, someone in his party would call ahead. Once one of these calls was received, the Chenault's staff would fly into preparations, not the least of which was to position someone at the back door to watch for Elvis's car. When Elvis arrived, the staff member at the back door would quickly let Elvis and his party in and escort them to the banquet room. Then, for as long as Elvis wanted, he could relax at the restaurant in privacy.

Elvis's friend Will McDaniel was running late one night, arriving at Chenault's only to find that Elvis and his gang were already sequestered in the banquet room. There was a hard and fast rule about hanging around with Elvis: if Elvis and his entourage were dining out, the door was closed just once. There was no mercy for latecomers; Elvis was not to be interrupted. McDaniel knew better than to beat on the door, so instead he decided to get Elvis's attention. He began looking over the songs on the jukebox. As soon as he spotted the song by Anita Wood, he knew that he had to play it. Sure enough, Elvis sent someone to look out the door and see who was playing Anita's song, and McDaniel was let inside.

SOUTH MEMPHIS. FROM GRACELAND, DRIVE NORTH ON ELVIS PRESLEY BOULEVARD ABOUT THREE MILES. THE SITE WAS LOCATED ON THE BOULEVARD BETWEEN KERR AVENUE AND SOUTH PARKWAY EAST. EUREKA'S DINING AND CATERING NOW OCCUPIES THIS SITE.

Leonard's Barbeque
1140 South Bellevue Boulevard

Though Elvis loved Southern food, there was one significant exception. According to George Klein, Elvis was not fond of barbeque. He didn't despise it, and would eat it on rare occasions, but considering most Southern males crave barbeque the way a baby needs milk, Elvis's tastes were unique in this regard.

Nonetheless, Elvis would find himself at Leonard's Barbeque occasionally. Priscilla claims that Elvis's cousin Patsy Presley introduced her to Leonard's, taking her there at least once a week while Elvis was in California. Perhaps Priscilla was the one who initiated Elvis's visits to the restaurant.

Typically, someone in Elvis's entourage would call the restaurant just before closing time and ask if they could stay open for them. They were always accommodated, and Elvis and his friends would have the entire restaurant to themselves.

It was a typical restaurant of its day. Chrome-and-vinyl stools were positioned at one end of the formica lunch counter. The dining room, rimmed with booths, seated two hundred. The restaurant also featured a private banquet room. Perhaps the most unique part of the decor was the thirty-five silver dollars randomly glued to the floor. When the restaurant was built in 1956, Leonard's owner, Leonard Heuberger, put the coins on the floor to represent each year he had been in the food service business. Newcomers to the restaurant always tried to pick up a coin.

During Elvis's visits to Leonard's, he and his friends would gather around a big table. Rather than the usual dinner plates, Elvis's group was served family style. Big bowls of barbeque, coleslaw, beans, potato salad, and buns would be set in the middle of the table to be passed among the party.

Leonard's has closed this restaurant and moved east to 5465 Fox Plaza Drive. The current restaurant is decorated in a Memphis '40s-and-'50s theme, with the silver dollars in place. The original site was demolished to make way for a Walgreen's store.

SOUTH MEMPHIS. TO REACH THE ORIGINAL SITE, DRIVE NORTH FROM GRACELAND ON ELVIS PRESLEY BOULEVARD ABOUT FOUR MILES TO THE INTERSECTION WITH MCLEMORE AVENUE. THE RESTAURANT WAS LOCATED ON THE RIGHT SIDE OF THIS INTERSECTION, WHERE THE WALGREEN'S IS NOW LOCATED.

THE NEW LEONARD'S BARBECUE IS IN EAST MEMPHIS. TO REACH THE NEW LOCATION, EXIT SOUTH ONTO MT. MORIAH ROAD FROM I-240. DRIVE ABOUT TWO MILES TO THE INTERSECTION OF MT. MORIAH AND MENDENHALL ROADS. PASS THROUGH THE INTERSECTION AND TAKE THE NEXT RIGHT ONTO FOX PLAZA DRIVE. LEONARD'S WILL BE TO YOUR RIGHT.

Colletta's Italian Restaurant
1063 South Parkway

With his own personal cooks at Graceland, Elvis rarely ate out.

On occasion, Elvis's friends would go by themselves. For this reason, Elvis kept a charge account at Coletta's Italian Restaurant. Elvis's tastes were purely American, and very Southern at that. That's not to say he didn't like spaghetti. He tended to like Italian foods that had been Americanized, but he didn't necessarily want them enough to suggest going out to eat them.

That's why Elvis's friend George Klein was surprised late one Sunday night when Elvis said, "Where are y'all going for dinner?"

George said, "Colletta's."

"Me and Priscilla will go with you. Do they have a little private dining room?" Elvis asked. George replied that they did, and he called ahead to reserve the room.

When Elvis's group arrived, they were quickly seated. Elvis looked at the menu for several minutes before he finally saw something that appealed to him, but when the waitress came to take the order, she informed Elvis they were sold out of that item. Elvis looked at the menu again and made another choice. "I'm sorry," the waitress had to tell him. "We don't have any left."

Eventually Elvis did find something to eat, and by all accounts enjoyed his meal. It was, however, one of the few instances when Elvis was treated exactly like everyone else at a restaurant. After all, it was late on a Sunday evening at the end of a very busy weekend. How could the people at Colletta's have known that Elvis would be dining there that night?

SOUTH MEMPHIS. COLLETTA'S CONTINUES TO SERVE ITALIAN FOOD. FROM GRACELAND, DRIVE NORTH ON ELVIS PRESLEY BOULEVARD TO SOUTH PARKWAY EAST. TURN LEFT ONTO SOUTH PARKWAY EAST AND DRIVE A FEW BLOCKS. THE RESTAURANT IS TO YOUR LEFT.

Western Steakhouse and Lounge
1298 Madison Avenue

There were at least two things that attracted Elvis to the Western Steakhouse and Lounge. First and foremost was the succulent steaks.

The second reason was that Elvis had known the restaurant's owner, Lil Thompson, since he was a child.

Lil once owned a restaurant called the 81 Club, named for its address at 81 North Second Street. "Elvis would come in and say, 'Mama Lil, if I play the guitar for you would you give me a quarter?'" Lil recalled. And she would always reply, "No, but I'll cook you a cheeseburger."

She proudly remembered an evening years later at the Western Steakhouse. Near closing time, Elvis's friend George Klein called to ask if Elvis could eat at the restaurant. "Give us an hour to get there," George said. About an hour later, Elvis's group of about twenty friends and girlfriends arrived. Lil waited tables and her husband Tommy cooked. The party stayed for a couple of hours, enjoying the food and each other's company.

When Elvis finally got up to leave, he asked Tommy how much he owed them. "Son, you don't owe us anything," Tommy replied.

Shortly after the party left, Elvis called. "Look in the back of the telephone directory," he said cryptically. Lil found five hundred dollars hidden there.

"I really loved Elvis," Lil said recently. "I've buried a son and a husband, but the saddest thing of my life was losing Elvis. When that hearse drove out of the gates of Graceland, it like to killed me, it was so sad."

Western Steakhouse still serves steaks. You can sit in Elvis's booth in the back of the music room and listen to country music on Friday and Saturday nights.

MIDTOWN. FROM UNION AVENUE, TURN NORTH ON MANASSAS STREET. DRIVE TWO BLOCKS TO MADISON AVENUE AND TURN RIGHT, THEN CONTINUE DRIVING EAST FOR ABOUT ONE MILE. THE RESTAURANT IS ON THE LEFT SIDE OF MADISON AVENUE BETWEEN NORTH BELLEVUE BOULEVARD AND CLEVELAND STREET.

Gridiron Restaurant
4101 Elvis Presley Boulevard

To say that Elvis was particular about his food is an understatement.

Elvis loved cheeseburgers. Not ordinary wimpy burgers with one measly slice of cheese, but a plump, juicy patty cooked to a crisp and topped with three slices of melted cheese. Preferably, the bun should be grilled in butter, while onion, tomato, and lettuce completed the sandwich.

The Gridiron cooked cheeseburgers the way Elvis liked them. What's more, it was open twenty-four hours a day, which suited Elvis's night-time rambles. According to waitress Ann Lyon, who began working at the Gridiron in 1960, Elvis sometimes took great pains not to be recognized, especially in later years, despite the lateness of the hour when he usually dined.

"He'd have on an old cap and baggy overalls so he could come in disguised," Lyons recalled. "He'd do anything to keep people from recognizing him. Elvis never knew all the girls here. I knew him when he first started out. I got him to autograph pictures for my children then."

This particular branch of the Gridiron restaurant chain has been in operation since 1954.

WHITEHAVEN. FROM GRACELAND, DRIVE SOUTH ON ELVIS PRESLEY BOULEVARD TO THE SOUTH PLAZA SHOPPING CENTER AT RAINES ROAD. LOOK TO YOUR RIGHT. THE GRIDIRON IS STILL OPEN TWENTY-FOUR HOURS A DAY, AND ITS CHEESEBURGERS ARE STILL COOKED THE WAY ELVIS LIKED THEM.

Hickory Log Restaurant
3795 Elvis Presley Boulevard

Beef and Liberty Restaurant
3765 Elvis Presley Boulevard

Since both of these restaurants were located in the shopping center across the street from Graceland, they were associated with Elvis more for their location than his patronage. Elvis rarely ate at either restaurant, though he did dine at the Hickory Log on one memorable occasion at 4:00 A.M. However, many people involved with Elvis did eat at both establishments, and for fans who wanted to catch a glimpse of their idol, the comings and goings of Elvis's entourage were important clues to his own plans.

Bonnie and Hobart Burnett, owners of the Hickory Log, made an effort to cater to Elvis's fans and friends. They were open twenty-four hours a day, convenient for people keeping Elvis's late hours, and the jukebox was filled with Elvis's songs. The restaurant became a place where many of the fans who watched the gates of Graceland met and became friends with some of Elvis's relatives and employees. This bond between fans and Elvis's entourage became even closer when Elvis died. The Burnetts continued their relationship with the Presleys when they bought Vernon's house in 1978, when Vernon decided to move to Graceland.

By 1983, both restaurants had closed. The new management of Elvis Presley Enterprises purchased every building in the shopping area. They wanted to use the property to manage the selling of tours and Elvis merchandise after Graceland was opened for tours. This area became the Graceland Plaza; it now contains the ticket office, gift shops, restaurants, and attractions like the Sincerely Elvis Museum. The site of the Hickory Log Restaurant became the Elvis Presley Automobile Museum.

WHITEHAVEN. THE GRACELAND PLAZA IS LOCATED ACROSS THE STREET FROM GRACELAND ON ELVIS PRESLEY BOULEVARD.

The Beef and Liberty Restaurant across the street from Graceland shortly after Elvis's death.

McDonald's
4237 Elvis Presley Boulevard

One of the greatest fallacies written about Elvis is that he lived his later years as a recluse. Certainly, his grueling concert schedule contradicts this statement; he was away from home for weeks on end. His life at home in Memphis seems to dispute this notion as well. Between tours, he frequently sought entertainment and services outside of Graceland.

Perhaps writers have stated that Elvis was reclusive because he sought periods of solitude. Like many people in the public eye, he occasionally retreated to a very private world. When he emerged revitalized, he would sometimes appear in the most unexpected of places.

During one such period of seclusion, Elvis's girlfriend Linda Thompson was concerned that the couple was spending too much time at Graceland. Thinking that Elvis would benefit from a trip outside, she said, "Why don't we go out for a hamburger?"

Elvis looked at her and said, "You know we can't do that. I'll be mobbed."

"Of course we can. No one will bother you," Linda insisted, knowing that there wouldn't be many people out in the middle of the night.

After much coaxing, Elvis finally agreed. They got into the car and drove down the street to McDonald's. Only a few cars were in the parking lot, none as fine as the one Elvis and Linda drove. They walked through the door and straight to the counter, where they placed their orders. Within minutes, they were carrying their trays to a small table. It seemed the handful of diners in the restaurant scarcely noticed them.

Elvis and Linda were almost finished with their meal when a man approached their table. "Who do you think you are?" the stranger said angrily. "I'm tired of you people dressing up like Elvis Presley. There's only one king."

Elvis was stunned. Moreover, he suddenly felt defensive, his fears of being recognized completely forgotten. "My name is Elvis," he said.

"No, you're not Elvis Presley," the man said, studying the "impostor's" casual clothes. "Elvis wouldn't eat at McDonald's."

"I am Elvis," Elvis insisted, but the man continued to look at him with a scowl of disbelief. Finally, in desperation, Elvis turned to his companion. "Linda, will you please tell this man who I am?" he said.

Remembering their earlier conversation, Linda wasn't about to ruin a quiet night. "Will you cut the crap, George?" she said to Elvis without hesitation.

Whether Elvis ate here again is as much a mystery as his identity remained to this gentleman. However, on at least this one occasion, Elvis strolled beneath the golden arches and ordered an ordinary meal just like everyone else.

WHITEHAVEN. FROM GRACELAND, DRIVE SOUTH ON ELVIS PRESLEY BOULEVARD TO MARLIN ROAD, ONE STREET PAST RAINES ROAD. THE RESTAURANT, STILL OPEN, IS JUST BEYOND MARLIN ROAD ON THE RIGHT SIDE OF THE BOULEVARD.

PARTIES

Manhattan Club
1459 Elvis Presley Boulevard

For Elvis, the '60s were, for the most part, the Hollywood years. During this decade, he filmed twenty-nine of his thirty-three movies. During this period, Elvis was living his childhood dream—he was a movie star with a life every bit as glamorous as the celebrities in California. At no time was this celebrity more evident than on New Year's Eve, when Elvis would throw lavish parties.

The Manhattan Club hosted several of these parties, beginning in 1962 when Priscilla first came to live at Graceland. Elvis loved occasions when he could dress up, especially when he had a beautiful girl at his side. He also enjoyed mingling with his guests. It was refreshing to listen to the entertainment, as opposed to *being* the scheduled entertainment, and the musicians who worked at Elvis's parties were always some of the finest. Willie Mitchell and his band worked more than one of these parties.

These were events in which Elvis could have a good time, and he did. And though Elvis always enjoyed himself at these lavish affairs, in truth, he wasn't much of a partier. For one, Elvis didn't really care for dancing. He was accomplished, but his trips to the dance floor were rare. It probably didn't help that everyone else usually stopped dancing whenever he and Priscilla took the floor. Secondly, Elvis wasn't much of a drinker. He might have one or two very weak cocktails over the course of a party, but for most of the night, he and Priscilla would sip soft drinks.

What Elvis did enjoy was being the host. He wanted everyone to have a good time. His parties were another measure of his generosity, not only in the sense that he paid for the events, but also in the number of people he invited. The parties were not limited to close friends or people who worked for Elvis. Often, invitations were sent to slight acquaintances with only remote connections to Elvis.

By the latter half of the '60s, Elvis's parties were getting out of hand. Smoochy Smith remembered one such party that Elvis didn't even attend. "There were so many people that found out that Elvis was gonna be there," Smith recalled. "There was such a big crowd that the place was crammed pack, and they had just as many people on the outside trying to get in or waiting to get a glimpse of him. When I got there, I couldn't even get in myself. I was just standing out there waiting for the crowd to get out of the way. Elvis come drivin' up, and he just waved and he said, 'Man, man. Y'all have a good time.' And he drove off. The truth is, he could not get in for those people at his own party."

SOUTH MEMPHIS. FROM GRACELAND, DRIVE NORTH ON ELVIS PRESLEY BOULEVARD ABOUT THREE MILES. THE NIGHTCLUB WAS LOCATED BETWEEN KERR AVENUE AND SOUTH PARKWAY EAST ON THE LEFT SIDE OF THE ROAD. BOURBON LIQUOR STORE NOW OCCUPIES THIS SITE.

Thunderbird Lounge
750 Adams Avenue

Ernie Barrasso, who once sold Elvis a Thunderbird at Hull-Dobbs Ford, became a nightclub owner in the mid-60s. His club, called the

Thunderbird Lounge, was located in the lobby floor of the Shelbourne Towers apartments. Half of the place, the Blue Room, was arranged with tables and barstools. The other half, the Red Room, had a dance floor. Ernie would book local bands for entertainment, including notable acts like Isaac Hayes and Sam and Dave.

Elvis chose the Thunderbird Lounge for his New Year's Eve parties of 1967 and 1968. He paid three thousand dollars to rent the club, brought his own security, and hired his own entertainment. Only those people who received an invitation could attend. Elvis's parties were a good deal for Ernie because they were the talk of the town. Many people crowded around the nightclub, even if they did not have an invitation. Though there was a lot of excitement before the parties began, Ernie remembers both events as being short. Elvis arrived late and left early. Once Elvis left, everyone else followed.

DOWNTOWN. FROM UNION AVENUE, TURN NORTH ON MANASSAS STREET AND CONTINUE TO ADAMS AVENUE. THE APARTMENT TOWER IS ON THE NORTHWEST CORNER OF THE INTERSECTION OF ADAMS AVENUE AND MANASSAS STREET. THE NIGHTCLUB NO LONGER EXISTS.

THIS IS A NEIGHBORHOOD THAT HAS REMAINED VIRTUALLY UNCHANGED FROM MEMPHIS'S EARLIER DAYS. CONTINUING ONE BLOCK WEST ON ADAMS AVENUE BRINGS YOU TO VICTORIAN VILLAGE, A COLLECTION OF MAGNIFICENT NINETEENTH-CENTURY HOMES.

T.J.'s Lounge
94 North Avalon Street

In 1969, T.J.'s Lounge was the hottest nightclub in Memphis. Elvis always held his New Year's Eve parties at popular clubs, but that reason alone was not why Elvis decided to move his party there that year. The truth was he had connections to T.J.'s. His friends and former employees Richard Davis and Alan Fortas were now working at the club, and they encouraged Elvis to move his party there. An important element of their argument was the quality of the house band.

At that time, Memphis was really rocking. American Sound Studio was cranking out the hits, and like pilgrims finding their way to mecca, songwriters and musicians flocked to the city to get a piece of this success. Many of these musicians worked at clubs while trying to get their own studio gigs. Earlier that year, Elvis had tapped into this sound to create one of his most popular records, *From Elvis in Memphis*. With the album's popularity, Elvis was riding a new wave of success.

This was the mood that extended all the way to New Year's Eve. In order to celebrate the year's accomplishments, the guest list included many of the people who had worked on the record with Elvis. Some of them even got up on stage to entertain. Mark James, who wrote Elvis's 1969 hit "Suspicious Minds," sang a couple of songs. But the highlight of the show was a performance by Ronnie Milsap, then an unknown studio musician who led T.J.'s house band. Milsap was familiar to Elvis because he had played piano and sung background vocals on Elvis's song "In The Ghetto."

Elvis seemed to truly enjoy the evening, and by all accounts, this was one of his better parties. Elvis was relaxed and having a good time, and the mood was as light as it had ever been.

MIDTOWN. FROM POPLAR AVENUE, TURN NORTH ON AVALON STREET. THE NIGHTCLUB SITE IS TO YOUR LEFT, WITHIN THE CENTER CITY SHOPPING CENTER. IT IS NO LONGER IN BUSINESS.

MOVIE THEATERS

Memphian Theater
51 South Cooper Street

Imagine getting up in the morning and deciding you want to spend the day watching movies. Now imagine that you can choose whatever movies you want to see, even those that aren't playing in your city yet, and you can watch them on the big screen in a theater open only to you and your friends. For Elvis, this was an ordinary occurrence. He often rented out the Memphian Theater for exactly such private movie parties, with the only difference being that he slept during the days and rented the theater after it closed at night.

Like many of Elvis's outings, the private movie parties turned into huge events, eventually reaching crowds of a hundred or more. As soon as Elvis decided his plans for the night, calls would go out to friends and acquaintances. By the time Elvis arrived, there was already a large crowd gathered at the theater.

Although guests were invited, the movies were clearly for Elvis's enjoyment. There was a certain protocol, the first rule being that Elvis had his own seat in the center of the fifth row. He always entered by a side door, and his guests waited until he sat down before claiming their seats. His personal entourage, known as the Memphis

Mafia, sat beside and behind him as if to shield him. No one was allowed to sit in front of him, and no one was to disturb him. Elvis alone chose the movie, and if he tired before it was over, he would wave his flashlight at the projectionist to signal that he wanted the film stopped and another begun. Likewise, one of his friends would jump up and get him a coke or popcorn if Elvis so much as snapped a finger.

For employees of the Malco theaters, the chain that owned the Memphian, working during Elvis's movie parties was optional. But when the call went out to all of the theaters in the chain for volunteers, there was never a shortage. Employees of the theater chain were allowed to watch the movie if they followed certain rules. The theater was divided into three sections, with a main group of seats in the center and two narrower arrangements of seats on either side, separated by aisles. Employees were allowed to bring one guest, and they were seated behind Elvis in the side sections. Anna Hamilton, who now owns Anna's Steakhouse, worked at the Crosstown Theater. She remembers the thrill of attending the movie parties. She always sat at an angle where she could watch Elvis watch the movie, only occasionally looking up at the screen.

Before Elvis got up to leave, all of the employees would file into the lobby and stand at the sides of the door. Elvis would then enter and greet everyone before he left. Anna fondly recalled these moments. "He was phenomenal," she remembered. "When he walked into the room, it lit up."

MIDTOWN. THE MEMPHIAN THEATER IS NOW CALLED PLAYHOUSE ON THE SQUARE AND IS USED FOR SMALL THEATER PRODUCTIONS. FROM UNION AVENUE, TURN NORTH ON COOPER STREET; THE THEATER IS ON YOUR IMMEDIATE LEFT.

Crosstown Theater
400 North Cleveland Street

During Linda Thompson's four-year relationship with Elvis, she watched many a movie with him, beginning with their first meeting at the Memphian Theater not long after his divorce from Priscilla. Years later, Linda said she couldn't even remember which movie they watched that first night together. She did, however, remember a particularly insightful anecdote about watching a movie with Elvis at the Crosstown Theater.

She told the anecdote in an interview with the *Commercial Appeal* newspaper shortly after Elvis's death. During the interview, Linda spoke eloquently about Elvis's character, his caring nature, and his spirituality. "Once Elvis Presley touched your life, you were never the same," she said, making her most famous statement about their relationship. She ended the interview with the story about their trip to the Crosstown Theater. Elvis and Linda had gone to the theater to watch the movie *Patton*, and she remembered the movie made quite a lasting impression on Elvis. "I shall always remember a line that Elvis used to quote from *Patton*," she said. "In it, General George S. Patton says, 'All glory is fleeting.' Elvis knew that."

MIDTOWN. FROM POPLAR AVENUE, TURN NORTH ON CLEVELAND STREET AND DRIVE TO OVERTON PARK AVENUE. THE THEATER BUILDING IS JUST BEYOND THE INTERSECTION TO THE RIGHT. THE THEATER IS NOW USED AS A WORSHIP HALL BY A SEVENTH-DAY ADVENTIST CONGREGATION.

PRISCILLA'S SCHOOL

Immaculate Conception High School
1725 Central Avenue

On display at Immaculate Conception High School are pictures of former students. However, the school's most famous student, Priscilla Beaulieu, who later became Mrs. Elvis Presley, is conspicuously absent. Priscilla attended the school while living with Elvis at Graceland. The couple met in Germany when Priscilla was just fourteen, and their relationship continued after he returned to America. Eventually, Elvis persuaded her father to allow Priscilla to move to Memphis. Part of the agreement was that Priscilla would live with Vernon and his wife Dee. Priscilla did live with Vernon for a very short while, but then moved into Graceland. Another part of the agreement was that Priscilla would continue her education at a school of Elvis's choosing. Vernon and Priscilla's father enrolled her in Immaculate Conception High School in 1963.

By Priscilla's own account, she was not an attentive student.

Furthermore, she was afraid of making friends with any of the other students because she thought they would use her to try to get close to Elvis. Besides, her experiences were so different from those of the other girls. She was living with the most famous rock star of our century, partying all night, then donning her school uniform in the morning. "I was leading a double life—a schoolgirl by day, a femme fatale by night," she said.

Although Priscilla didn't participate in school any more than was required, she did attend her high school graduation ceremony. Afraid that Elvis would disrupt the event, she asked him to wait outside for her while she received her diploma. When she stepped outside, she saw Elvis standing in front of the church. His black limousine was parked at the curb and several of his friends were nearby. A group of nuns surrounded him, asking for his autograph.

MIDTOWN. FROM UNION AVENUE, TURN SOUTH ONTO BELVEDERE BOULEVARD AND DRIVE TO CENTRAL AVENUE. THE SCHOOL IS AT THE INTERSECTION OF CENTRAL AVENUE AND BELVEDERE BOULEVARD.

Elvis horseback riding at Graceland
Courtesy of Linda Everett

RANCHING

Circle G Ranch
Intersection of MS 301 and Goodman Road
Walls, Mississippi

In 1967, Elvis found a new interest in his life—ranching. It began when Priscilla wanted a horse to ride at Graceland. Elvis complied, and in typical Elvis fashion, bought horses for himself and a number of his friends. Before he knew it, there was not enough room within Graceland's fourteen acres for all of the horses and their stable.

Elvis found the solution to this problem on a Sunday drive in Walls, Mississippi, a rural area only ten miles from Memphis. During the drive, Elvis saw a fifty-foot-tall white cross in a pasture. Under the cross was a pond, and several cattle grazed nearby. Elvis immediately drove onto the ranch. He found the owner, Jack Adams, and began to negotiate for the property. Adams asked for $437,000, a sum that made the frugal Vernon gasp. But Elvis wanted the ranch and agreed to the price.

Elvis named his new property the Circle G Ranch—the "G" for Graceland. Immediately after the sale, Elvis dived into outfitting his ranch. Because he wanted several of his friends to share the ranching experience, Elvis bought numerous mobile homes, pickup trucks, and assorted equipment for farming and riding.

By all accounts, the early months that Elvis and his entourage spent here were idyllic. Priscilla especially enjoyed horseback riding on the property. She and Elvis spent part of their honeymoon in the ranch cottage after their marriage on May 1, 1967. The little house was so close to the road that it offered little privacy from the fans who gathered there. Elvis had a ten-foot wooden fence constructed around the cottage, but even that wasn't enough. Elvis and Priscilla then took up residence in a three-bedroom mobile home on the property. The mobile home delighted the new bride because it was too small to accommodate Elvis's entourage, and for Elvis, trailer living was an exciting new adventure. He actually preferred it to the brick cottage.

For all of the ranch's simple pleasures, it soon became a burden. Privacy was much less assured than at Graceland because the property was not protected by brick walls. Eventually, the Memphis Mafia began complaining that their wives and children would rather be at home than at the ranch.

Only two years after its purchase, Elvis sold the ranch to a group of investors who turned the land into a hunting club. When the investors defaulted on their payments, Elvis resumed ownership until another buyer could be found. In 1973, the property was sold to the Boyle Investment Company, which turned it into a working ranch again.

Today, the ranch remains private and is off limits to visitors. For a brief time in the late '80s and early '90s, fans could visit the ranch because the owner allowed a businessman to open a restaurant and banquet hall there. That business failed, but recently a gift shop has opened in the cottage where Elvis and Priscilla enjoyed their honeymoon. From this vantage point, you can see the white cross and the white bridge that Elvis built across the pond. The decaying pink buildings that are visible from the shop were built by the hunting club, not Elvis. Less visible is the barbecue pit with the engraved initials, "EP," a gift from his friends.

WALLS, MISSISSIPPI. FROM WHITEHAVEN, TAKE I-55 SOUTH TO EXIT 289, THE GOODMAN ROAD/HORN LAKE EXIT. TAKE THE WEST EXIT AND DRIVE THROUGH THE TOWN OF HORN LAKE TO THE INTERSECTION OF MS 301 AND GOODMAN ROAD. THE HONEYMOON COTTAGE IS TO YOUR LEFT, ON THE SOUTHEAST CORNER OF THE INTERSECTION. THE COTTAGE GIFT SHOP IS THE ONLY PUBLIC ACCESS TO ANY PART OF THE RANCH AT THE TIME OF THIS WRITING. THE RANCH PROPERTY FRONTS BOTH ROADS ON YOUR LEFT.

FOOTBALL

Graceland School
3866 Pattie Ann Drive

In 1965, Elvis was asked by a Nashville reporter whether he had a hobby. Elvis replied, "I play touch football on weekends—whether I'm in L.A. or in Memphis. I play with a team of us fellows each place. You might say that's something I've always wanted to be—a football player."

Elvis loved football—the rougher the better. Sometimes, he and his friends played at Graceland, but often they played at Graceland School. The teams would reach as many as fifteen guys on each side. In the early years, games were loosely organized without referees, rigid boundaries, or rules for fouls. Nearly everything was fair game, at least until Elvis broke his little finger during one rowdy Sunday afternoon game.

"I got my man, too," Elvis told a reporter at the hospital, "and he was just a step or two away from a touchdown. I dived for him see, and after tagging him my hand landed in some mud and buried up in it. At first I didn't notice it—it didn't hurt me at all—until one of the fellows told me the little finger was bent all the way over the other fingers. No, it won't affect my strumming a guitar."

While Elvis took the injury in stride, his teammates became a little more cautious. "After the time we played and he broke the finger, no one from then on ever laid a finger on him," Buddy Wilson remembered. But that didn't dampen Elvis's passion for the sport, if in fact, he ever noticed any preferential treatment at all.

WHITEHAVEN. THE SCHOOL IS IN THE SAME NEIGHBORHOOD WHERE MANY OF ELVIS'S FAMILY AND FRIENDS LIVED. FROM GRACELAND, DRIVE SOUTH ON ELVIS PRESLEY BOULE-VARD TO THE NEXT LEFT, DOLAN DRIVE. TAKE DOLAN DRIVE TO HERMITAGE ROAD AND TURN LEFT (THE SECOND LEFT ON DOLAN). DRIVE ONE BLOCK TO LEHR DRIVE. TURN RIGHT ONTO LEHR DRIVE AND CONTINUE FIVE BLOCKS TO PATTIE ANN DRIVE. TURN RIGHT ONTO PATTIE ANN DRIVE; THE SCHOOL WILL BE TO YOUR LEFT.

Whitehaven High School
4851 Elvis Presley Boulevard

Elvis never did anything halfway. Whatever captured his interest had his full attention, a fact that was often reflected in his checkbook expenditures. This was certainly the case with football. As Elvis's enthusiasm for the sport grew, so did his desire to play on a real team. Eventually, the E.P. Enterprises team, duly outfitted in matching jerseys, was formed. Elvis rented the football stadium at Whitehaven High School for the games. To complete the atmosphere of a real game, he hired Memphis Park Commission football referees.

The teams were made up of an assortment of Elvis's friends and associates. Charles and John Bramlett, friends from Alabama Street, often played against Elvis's team. Like most of the players, they had high school and college football experience. John even played in the National Football League for several years. Charles Bramlett remembers that Ricky Nelson played on Elvis's team when visiting Memphis. Ricky was also a regular in Elvis's games in California.

WHITEHAVEN. FROM GRACELAND, DRIVE SOUTH ON ELVIS PRESLEY BOULEVARD FOR TWO MILES UNTIL REACHING SHELBY DRIVE. WHITEHAVEN HIGH SCHOOL AND ITS FOOT-BALL STADIUM IS TO THE RIGHT, JUST SOUTH OF SHELBY DRIVE.

BOATING

McKeller Lake
At the Mississippi River

According to Elvis's cousin Gene Smith, Elvis didn't know how to swim. As much as Elvis loved the water, this comes as a surprise. He seemed absolutely fearless on boats, especially when he donned his yachting cap and powered his boat on McKeller Lake.

McKeller Lake is actually an old channel bed of the Mississippi River located southwest of downtown Memphis. The Corps of Engineers dredged and shaped the channel bed to create the new Port of Memphis. The new lake was named in honor of Senator McKeller, who supported the harbor project. The surrounding dock facilities and industrial sites make this an unusual place for water recreation.

Elvis was no stranger to this small recreational area. Bob Neal and his family liked to boat here, and Elvis often joined them. In 1960, after Elvis's return from the army and the filming of *GI Blues*, he was ready for a little rest and relaxation. In the middle of a steamy July in Memphis, Elvis bought his first boat, a sixteen-foot speedboat, for two thousand dollars.

With typical enthusiasm, he launched the boat on McKeller Lake, with four friends and a writer from the *Memphis Press-Scimitar* accompanying him. The boat roared to life as Elvis manned the wheel. As the craft reached its top speed, nearly forty miles per hour, the nose rose high above the water. With the throttle on full, Elvis sped around the lake, banking sharply and passing other boats amid cries of "Hey! That's Elvis!" Finally, he directed the boat towards the marina and casually said to the reporter, "This is the first time I ever drove a boat." It was a statement that seemed all the more ominous as Elvis's boat raced at full speed toward the rapidly approaching dock. Elvis cut the motor and threw the gearshift into reverse, but it was hopeless. The boat crashed into the dock. "Well, that's one way of stopping it," Elvis said as he got out to survey the damage. Aside from a smashed mooring ring, his boat was intact.

Just a couple of days later, it was reported that Elvis had his boat inspected by McKeller Lake's safety director as part of National Boat Safety Week. It seemed an innocent public service announcement meant to encourage others to practice safe boating. However, anyone who read the earlier reports would have to wonder whether the safety director had witnessed Elvis's first outing.

SOUTH MEMPHIS. TO REACH THE PLEASURE BOAT LAUNCH FOR MCKELLER LAKE, TAKE I-55 NORTH FROM GRACELAND FOR ABOUT FIVE MILES TO THE SOUTH PARKWAY WEST EXIT. DRIVE WEST TO THE RIVERSIDE PARK ENTRANCE AND TURN LEFT. FROM THE PARK ENTRANCE, FOLLOW THE SIGNS TO THE LAUNCH RAMP. RIVERSIDE PARK IS ONE OF THE PLACES WHERE ELVIS COURTED DIXIE LOCKE IN THE SUMMERS OF 1953 AND 1954.

AUTOMOBILES

Hull-Dobbs Ford
115 South Third Street

In October of 1961, Elvis was watching football with friends one Sunday when he noticed an advertisement for the Ford Thunderbird. The ad depicted the fantasy life one could enjoy with the Thunderbird Landau, a special edition of the car. Elvis was curious. "We have one on the showroom floor," said his friend Ernie Barrasso, a salesman for Hull-Dobbs Ford. Only two hundred of these special cars were made by the company, but because Hull-Dobbs was one of the top Ford dealers, it had one on display.

The next day, Elvis arrived at Hull-Dobbs. He asked Ernie about the price of the car. Ernie answered $6,100. Elvis replied, "Great. When can you get it ready for me? I want it now."

Elvis told Ernie he would pay for the car with a countercheck. At that time, auto dealers offered counterchecks to buyers, who would fill in a bank account number and the amount of the transaction. The dealer would then cash the check at the appropriate bank. Ernie asked, "Which bank do you want me to fill in?"

Elvis and Ernie Barrasso with Elvis's new Ford Thunderbird
Courtesy of Ernie Barrasso

"Any bank," Elvis replied. "I have money in all of them."

"Well, how about the First Bank of Hong Kong?"

"Sure," Elvis deadpanned.

When all the details of the sale were completed, Elvis took possession of the car. By that time, a crowd had gathered outside the dealership. A newspaper reporter who had been tipped off about the sale asked, "Just one picture, Elvis?" Elvis agreed and was photographed seated in his new car, with Ernie, the proud salesman, standing beside it. The photo was published by wire services around the world, prompting Mr. Edsel Ford, Jr., to congratulate the Hull-Dobbs dealership on their publicity coup.

A short time later, Elvis had a problem with the car. A wheel cover was damaged, and Elvis wanted it replaced. No one within Ford Motor Company could find a replacement because the parts manufacturer had gone out of business. Elvis finally called Mr. Ford, who

NEW CAR INVOICE AND BILL OF SALE

Hull-Dobbs Company

Stock # 178
GR # 7566
SP# F53686

THIRD AT GAYOSO   TELEPHONE JACKSON 6-8871

MEMPHIS 3, TENN.   10-17-61

SALESMAN   **Barrasso**

KEY NO.

SOLD TO

ENGINE NUMBER   **2Y85Z-107109**

FULL NAME
Elvis Presley

SERIAL NUMBER

STREET OR R.F.D.
3736 Hiway 51 South(Graceland)Ford S/Road

MAKE   BODY

CITY OR TOWN
Memphis 16, Tennessee

MODEL   YEAR
T Bird   1962

DATE OF PURCHASE   WEIGHT   No. CYLS.
10-17-61   Plus 3600   8

FORMER TITLE No.

DELIVERED PRICE   6100.00

EXTRAS
**Radio
M.A. Heater
C/O/Matic
P.Steering
P.Brakes
P.Seats
W/S/ Washers
W Tires
H.D. Battery
Sport Road. Package
Movable Steering Col.
O/S Mirror**

NEW USED

LIEN HOLDER
None

AMOUNT   **New**

ADDRESS

KIND
DATE

ADDITIONAL LIEN

NAME STATE LAST REGISTERED

INSURANCE COVERAGE INCLUDES
☐ FIRE AND THEFT   ☐ PUBLIC LIABILITY AMT.
☐ COLLISION—AMT. DEDCT.   ☐ PROPERTY DAMAGE AMT.

THE UNDERSIGNED DEALER HAS THIS DAY SOLD UNDER CONDITIONAL SALES CONTRACT TO THE ABOVE NAMED PURCHASER, THE HEREINABOVE DESCRIBED MOTOR VEHICLE, WARRANTS AND COVENANTS THAT THE UNDERSIGNED DEALER IS THE LAWFUL OWNER THEREOF WITH A GOOD RIGHT TO SELL SAME, THAT THERE IS NO LIEN OR ENCUMBRANCE THEREON EXCEPT CONDITIONAL SALES CONTRACT OR CHATTEL MORTGAGE, SIGNED BY ABOVE PURCHASER AND TO BE ASSIGNED TO ABOVE LIENHOLDER, AND UNDERSIGNED WILL WARRANT AND DEFEND TITLE AGAINST ALL PERSONS EXCEPT ABOVE LIENHOLDERS.

HULL-DOBBS COMPANY

BY
OWNER(S)-PRES.-VICE PRES.-SECTY. TREAS.

SWORN TO AND SUBSCRIBED AND ACKNOWLEDGED BEFORE ME THIS **17th** DAY OF **Oct.**   19 **61**

NOTARY PUBLIC IN AND FOR COUNTY OF **Shelby**   STATE OF **Tenn**

MY COMMISSION EXPIRES

**STATE OF TENNESSEE
COUNTY OF**

ON THIS____DAY OF____   19____ PERSONALLY APPEARED
BEFORE ME, THE UNDERSIGNED AUTHORITY____
AND/OR____WITH WHOM I AM PERSONALLY ACQUAINTED,
WHO, UPON OATH SAY THEY ARE____OF THE____
A CORPORATION, AND THAT THEY ARE THE OFFICIALS NAMED, BEING AUTHORIZED SO TO DO, EXECUTED THE FOREGOING INSTRUMENT FOR THE PURPOSES THEREIN CONTAINED, BY SIGNING THE NAME OF SUCH CORPORATION AS ITS____AND AFFIXING THE CORPORATE SEAL.

Title   1.00
FACTORY INSTALLED
DEALER INSTALLED
FED. EXC. TAX—ON EXTRAS   183.00
TOTAL SALES TAX
TOTAL CASH PRICE   6284.00
INSURANCE CHARGE

TIME PRICE DIFFERENTIAL
RECORDING FEE
TOTAL TIME PRICE   6284.00
SETTLEMENT:
DEPOSIT
CASH ON DELIVERY   6284.00
USED CAR STOCK No.

TYPE
MOTOR No.
SER. No.
BAL. DUE
PAYMENTS

TOTAL   6284.00

RECEIVED FEES FOR TITLE AND FOR RECORDING LIEN____   **W. H. Ewing**
COUNTY COURT CLERK

Invoice for Elvis's Thunderbird
Courtesy of Ernie Barrasso

gladly returned his money; the purchase price was of less value to the company than the photograph of Elvis in the car.

DOWNTOWN. FROM UNION AVENUE, TURN SOUTH ON SECOND STREET. BECAUSE OF THE ONE-WAY STREETS, YOU WILL HAVE TO CIRCLE THE BLOCK, TURNING LEFT ON GAYOSO AVENUE AND LEFT AGAIN ON THIRD STREET. THE FORMER LOCATION, AT THE

Southern Motors/Madison Cadillac
341 Union Avenue

Elvis was celebrated for the cars and other luxury items he bought then gave away. Particularly during the early '70s, it was not unusual to read in the daily papers that Elvis had bought six or eight cars the previous night. Most of these cars were given to family and friends, but sometimes they were awarded to complete strangers.

Of all the luxury cars, Elvis loved Cadillacs more than any other. One of his first Cadillacs, purchased at Southern Motors, was a gift for his mother that he had painted pink. Throughout his life, Elvis disposed of many cars, but not that pink Cadillac. It remains on display today at Graceland's Automobile Museum.

No one knows exactly how many Cadillacs Elvis bought over the years. Robert Short, a salesman and sales manager in Memphis, estimated that Elvis bought thirty cars from him. Southern Motors, which was renamed Madison Cadillac after Bert Madison bought the dealership in 1966, kept Elvis's patronage over the years by catering to his odd habits. If necessary, the salesmen would keep the showroom open after hours so Elvis could shop undisturbed.

One night in July 1975, Elvis made an exception to his usual shopping habits and stopped by before closing hours. While Elvis was shopping, another customer, Mrs. Minnie Pearson, stopped to admire his limousine. Elvis approached Mrs. Pearson and told her the car was not for sale, but that she could have another. He accompanied her to the showroom lot and told her to pick out any car. She chose a white-and-gold Cadillac El Dorado worth $11,500. He insisted on paying everything, telling salesman Howard Massey, "I want her to do nothing but drive the car." When Elvis discovered that her

birthday was near, he also gave her a check to buy some new clothes.
This story has been told so many times it is now part of the Elvis
Presley legend. Many of his friends speculate that Elvis bought her
the car because the expression on her face as she looked at the car
reminded him of his life years ago. When he had little money, Elvis
often looked longingly through the showroom windows at the new
cars. Ironically, Mrs. Pearson was not destitute, but instead worked
as a bank clerk and was the owner of a year-old Cadillac at the time.

Madison Cadillac was one of many auto dealers on this part of
Union Avenue, though it had the most distinctive showroom—an
eight-foot-tall stuffed polar bear stood on display facing the street.
In 1986, Bert Madison sold the dealership and the new owners moved
it to 2177 Covington Pike. Since then, the dealership has been sold
a number of times. It is now called Cadillac of Memphis. Sadly, there
is nothing at the dealership to remind one of the days when Elvis
was its most famous customer.

DOWNTOWN. THE ORIGINAL LOCATION OF SOUTHERN MOTORS/MADISON CADILLAC
WAS AT THE INTERSECTION OF UNION AVENUE AND DANNY THOMAS BOULEVARD. PYRA-
MID TIRE AND AUTO SERVICE CENTER NOW OCCUPIES THE BUILDING THAT ONCE
HOUSED THE CADILLAC DEALERSHIP.

Schilling Lincoln-Mercury
987 Union Avenue

Foxgate Lincoln-Mercury
2660 South Mt. Moriah Road

Elvis liked Lincoln Continentals almost as much as he liked
Cadillacs. On several occasions, Elvis bought Lincoln Continentals
from Schilling Lincoln-Mercury, including perhaps the last two cars
he ever purchased.

On one shopping spree, Elvis drove away with one Lincoln Continental, then called the salesman to order three more. Elvis made another car salesman's dreams come true on September 22 and 23, 1974. Raymond Struber, the salesman at Schilling who waited on Elvis that weekend, had only been in the business two years and had certainly never seen a shopper as compulsive as Elvis. During that fall weekend, Elvis made five trips to the dealership and bought the entire stock of Lincoln Continental Mark IVs, at a total cost of more than sixty thousand dollars. Elvis gave away each of those cars as a gift.

Elvis always shopped for cars at night, after the dealership had closed. The reason for these unusual shopping habits was made evident one day in the early '70s. On this day, Elvis visited a branch office of Schilling, Foxgate Lincoln-Mercury, during regular hours, while many customers were still present. Unfortunately, a crowd surrounded him, and Elvis had to leave.

Charles Russell, a salesman who sold many cars to Elvis, was so accustomed to the hoopla surrounding Elvis's visits that he did not pay attention to a phone call in the summer of 1977. The caller said that Elvis wanted to buy cars that night, but because Charles had received prank calls like this before, he did not take the request seriously. However, a second phone call convinced him the request was real.

Charles drove to the showroom where he met some of Elvis's entourage. Together, they picked out two Lincoln Continental Mark IVs and drove them to Graceland. Elvis came downstairs to approve the purchases. Many other people were there anticipating some sort of event. Elvis signed a check for over twenty-two thousand for the two cars, then gave one to Kathy Westmoreland, one of his backup singers, and the other to Larry Geller, his hairdresser.

That night, Charles remarked to Elvis, "No one has ever given me a car."

To which Elvis replied, "Me neither." Elvis then invited Charles to stay for the ensuing party, but it was now 2:00 A.M., and Charles wanted to go home. Kathy drove him back to the showroom in her new car. That evening was probably the last time Elvis ever bought a car.

Schilling Lincoln-Mercury on Union Avenue was the last car

dealership remaining on what used to be known as "automobile row." A copy of one of Elvis's checks was on display at the dealership.

DOWNTOWN. SCHILLING LINCOLN-MERCURY IS LOCATED AT THE INTERSECTION OF UNION AVENUE AND EAST STREET. ACROSS THE STREET IS BAPTIST MEMORIAL HOSPITAL.

EAST MEMPHIS. FOXGATE LINCOLN-MERCURY IS NOW ALSO CALLED SCHILLING LINCOLN-MERCURY. IT IS LOCATED AT 2660 SOUTH MT. MORIAH ROAD. FROM I-240, EXIT SOUTH ONTO MT. MORIAH ROAD.

Robertson Motors
2950 Airways Boulevard

Although Elvis preferred American-made luxury cars, he learned to appreciate the craftsmanship of German automobiles during his army service in Germany. On two or three occasions, Elvis bought cars at Robertson Motors, the first Mercedes-Benz dealership in Memphis. Just before Christmas in 1970, Elvis bought nine Mercedes there. He gave most of these cars away. One was a gift for Bill Morris.

The Presley and Morris families had known each other in Mississippi. Morris had convinced Elvis to accept a nomination from the Jaycees as one of the Ten Outstanding Young Men of America, an award Elvis received a few weeks later on January 16, 1971. Perhaps as a gesture of his appreciation, or simply as an act of good will, Elvis wanted to give Bill Morris a car. One night, Bill and some other guests were at Graceland. Elvis sent word that he wanted Bill to come outside. The first thing that Bill noticed was the beam from Elvis's flashlight aimed into a large tree. Bill looked up and saw one of Elvis's peacocks perched on a limb. Then Elvis swung the flashlight around until it shone on a silver Mercedes. "How do you like it?," Elvis asked. When Bill replied that he thought it was a beautiful car, Elvis said, "Good, I'm glad. It's yours."

As Elvis often handed out impressive gifts with little fanfare, he did not expect the recipients to suffer any consequences. However, Elvis's gift to Bill Morris created quite a stir in Memphis because

Morris had just completed his term as sheriff of Shelby County and was contemplating his future in politics. He would later serve as mayor of Shelby County.

WHITEHAVEN. FROM GRACELAND, DRIVE NORTH ON ELVIS PRESLEY BOULEVARD TO BROOKS ROAD. TURN RIGHT ONTO BROOKS ROAD AND DRIVE TO AIRWAYS BOULEVARD. TURN LEFT ONTO AIRWAYS BOULEVARD AND LOOK TO YOUR RIGHT. THE DEALERSHIP WAS SOLD IN 1981 AND WAS RENAMED AUTORAMA. AT THE TIME OF THIS WRITING, THE PROPERTY IS FOR SALE AND THERE ARE PLANS TO MOVE THE DEALERSHIP TO ANOTHER LOCATION.

Sid Carroll Pontiac
1011 Union Avenue

A typical day with Elvis often left those around him reeling with excitement. No one ever knew what Elvis was going to do next, and some days it seemed that even he didn't have a plan. Few complained about his spontaneity, especially when he was in a generous mood.

One day in 1974, Elvis was feeling particularly charitable. He had decided to buy his cook, Mary Jenkins, a house and arranged for the realtor, Portia Fisher, to come to Graceland. The last thing Portia Fisher expected was to end the day at a car dealership.

Feeling a bit nervous at meeting Elvis, Portia asked her mother to come along with her for support. After some quick introductions, everyone piled into Elvis's Cadillac station wagon. Elvis's cousin Billy Smith and his wife Jo came along for the ride, as did George Klein's wife Barbara. With Mary and the two ladies from the real estate company, the car was nearly full.

Elvis headed down Elvis Presley Boulevard and pulled into a camper dealership at the intersection of Brooks Road. He was thinking of buying a camper for his uncle Vester, he said. After he talked to the salesman for a few minutes, they drove off again. The roads were busy with rush hour traffic, and Elvis sped along quickly. Portia's mother held on tightly and said, "You may can sing, but you can't drive." Elvis laughed and said she reminded him of his own mother.

They then drove to Devant Street and looked at a piece of property. Mary liked the house and the deal was closed. Instead of traveling back to Graceland, Elvis headed the car north until he reached Sid Carroll Pontiac. He told Portia's mother to pick out anything she liked. For Portia, he personally picked out a 1975 LeMans. Then he bought Mary a 1975 Bonneville.

Just a few hours later, Elvis was at the airport, flying out of Memphis and leaving a wake of excitement behind him.

DOWNTOWN. SID CARROLL PONTIAC IS NO LONGER IN BUSINESS. THE FORMER LO-CATION WAS AT THE INTERSECTION OF UNION AVENUE AND PAULINE STREET. THE DEALERSHIP WAS LOCATED BETWEEN THE PRESENT-DAY BURGER KING AND EXXON STATION.

Elvis riding his motorcycle on South Parkway
Courtesy of Linda Everett

MOTORCYCLES

Super Cycle
624 South Bellevue Boulevard

Elvis was a typical joyrider. He liked power and speed, and one day when he lost both in his three-wheeler, he rushed into the Super Cycle motorcycle dealership and repair shop to find out what the problem was.

Ron Elliott spotted the problem immediately. Elvis and his companion, Ginger Alden, were riding on a bike that was ideally designed for one person. The motorcycle originally was built with one seat, and a second seat had been added. The small motor just couldn't handle the added weight. Ron showed him a two-seat Volkswagen three-wheeler that was equipped with a powerful automobile engine. Elvis said that he would think about it.

A day or two later, Elvis walked into the shop and asked Ron to take him for a ride. Ron took him for a spin on his own bike, the same model as the one he had shown Elvis. Elvis liked it and bought one for himself. A couple of days later, he bought the other model Ron had on the showroom floor.

Ron wanted to personalize Elvis's bike and suggested putting a crown or his name on the front. Elvis wasn't particularly interested, but Ron went ahead and painted "TCB" on the front, putting a lot of effort into the design. The next time Ron saw the bike, he was disappointed that Elvis had put a radio antenna right in the middle of the artwork. "I guess he didn't need to show off," Ron remarked.

"He was a customer for two years," Ron said. "He was a perfect gentleman. He called me and my brother Mr. Elliott. He was never presumptuous at all. He was always so appreciative of everything we did."

During those two years, Super Cycle took care of all of Elvis's bikes. Elvis always asked that they send him a bill for their service, but because Elvis was always so grateful for the work they did, Ron never charged him for upkeep.

Billy Smith, Elvis's cousin and assistant, called Super Cycle shortly before Christmas one year. Elvis wanted to give his daughter, Lisa Marie, a golf cart. Could they customize it for her? he asked. For several days, Ron and his brother worked hard on the cart, sanding and painting the cart Lisa's favorite color, baby blue. As a finishing touch, they added a painted rose. They delivered the cart on Christmas Eve.

Ironically, Elvis bought his first bike from Super Cycle exactly two years before his death. His check for that purchase was dated August 16, 1975. Elvis was last in the shop two weeks before his death.

Since then, Super Cycle has restored several of Elvis's vehicles for display at Graceland, including the two three-wheelers, Elvis's '66 Harley Chopper, his snowmobiles (which were mounted with wheels since there is so little snow in Memphis), and his pink jeep. They also built a replica of Elvis's '57 Harley, which is on display at the Heartbreak Hotel Restaurant at Graceland.

MIDTOWN. FROM GRACELAND, DRIVE NORTH ON ELVIS PRESLEY BOULEVARD ABOUT FOUR MILES. AS YOU DRIVE NORTH, THE BOULEVARD'S NAME CHANGES TO BELLEVUE BOULEVARD. THE SHOP IS TO THE RIGHT SIDE OF BELLEVUE BOULEVARD, JUST NORTH OF THE LAMAR AVENUE INTERSECTION. SUPER CYCLE WELCOMES ELVIS FANS.

AIRPLANES

Memphis Aero
Memphis International Airport

In his younger days, Elvis avoided flying, even though his travel schedule was demanding. However, when Elvis resumed his concert touring in 1970, he was forced to overcome his fear of flying. There was no way to avoid flight because tour dates were arranged with little travel time between shows.

At first, Elvis chartered jets for his tours. Scenes from the 1972 concert film *Elvis On Tour* included footage of his charter aircraft. But Elvis never felt comfortable with air travel until he purchased his own plane and hired his own pilots. On April 18, 1975, he bought a Convair 880 jet formerly owned by Delta Airlines. He then spent eight hundred thousand dollars to redesign the interior. Space was made for a galley, a conference room, a guest bedroom, and two rest rooms. All the rooms were decorated in suede, leather, and inlaid gold. Elvis named the plane the "Lisa Marie." A crew of four, led by Captain Elwood David, were on call to fly whenever Elvis wanted.

In September of 1975, Elvis bought a Lockheed Jetstar for nine hundred thousand dollars to use on business flights. He had it decorated like the "Lisa Marie." Another crew, led by Captain Milo High, was hired to fly the Jetstar.

All of Elvis's planes, chartered or his own, were stored and maintained at Memphis Aero, a flight terminal and hanger space available for charter and corporate flights. Elvis rarely used passenger terminals because he believed that security within a crowded terminal was impossible. Memphis Aero was based on Memphis International Airport property north of Winchester Road, well away from the passenger terminal. This allowed Elvis and his passengers a chance to arrive or depart in privacy. At every airport Elvis flew into, he would have a car waiting to pick him up as he left the airplane. Often more than one car was made available to confuse the onlookers who always followed him.

WHITEHAVEN. FROM GRACELAND, DRIVE NORTH ON ELVIS PRESLEY BOULEVARD TO WINCHESTER ROAD. TURN RIGHT AND DRIVE ONE MILE. THE ENTRANCE TO THE SITE OF MEMPHIS AERO IS TO YOUR LEFT; ON THE OPPOSITE SIDE IS THE ENTRANCE TO THE AIRPORT TERMINAL. THE MEMPHIS AERO PROPERTY WAS ORIGINALLY THE PASSENGER TERMINAL FOR THE MUNICIPAL AIRPORT, UNTIL THE NEW TERMINAL, SOUTH OF WINCHESTER ROAD, WAS OPENED IN 1963. TODAY, THE MEMPHIS AERO PROPERTY IS KNOWN AS AMR-COMBS MEMPHIS INCORPORATED. A NUMBER OF OTHER AIRCRAFT CHARTER, EQUIPMENT, AND SALES COMPANIES DO BUSINESS NEARBY.

STORES

Goldsmith's Department Store
123 South Main Street

In the days when downtown Memphis bustled with shoppers, Goldsmith's was one of the city's most popular department stores. It wasn't the sort of place where one ran in and grabbed a hurried purchase. Rather, the store was designed to accommodate the shopper who preferred to savor the experience. Tastefully arranged merchandise was arranged throughout the five floors of departments. On the fifth floor were the dining rooms, including an elegant thousand-seat restaurant that occasionally held fashion shows with local celebrity models such as Anita Wood. A men's dining room, decorated in masculine colors and hunting motifs, was separate.

Shoppers flocked to the store year round, but at no time was Goldsmith's more busy than at Christmas. Then, the store was transformed into a fantasyland, complete with mechanical figures and Santa himself.

The season was not lost on Elvis and Priscilla, who had their own lists of Christmas presents to buy. When Elvis and Priscilla wanted to shop, the store opened after hours to allow them plenty of time to choose their purchases undisturbed.

DOWNTOWN. GOLDSMITH'S STOOD AT THE NORTHWEST CORNER OF MAIN STREET
AND GAYOSO AVENUE. THIS LOCATION IS NOW CLOSED.

GOLDSMITH'S NOW HAS SEVERAL OTHER LOCATIONS AROUND MEMPHIS, INCLUD-
ING THE SOUTHLAND MALL AT ELVIS PRESLEY BOULEVARD AND SHELBY DRIVE, SOUTH
OF GRACELAND, AND THE OAK COURT MALL AT 4545 POPLAR AVENUE. RUMOR HAS IT
THAT LISA MARIE AND MICHAEL JACKSON SHOPPED AT THE OAK COURT MALL LOCA-
TION WHILE IN TOWN FOR THE ELVIS TRIBUTE CONCERT IN OCTOBER 1994.

Lowell Hays Jewelers
4872 Poplar Avenue

The phone call was every merchant's dream. "Come down to the Memphian Theater tonight. Elvis wants to look at some jewelry," the caller said to Lowell Hays, a Memphis jeweler. Although Lowell was acquainted with several of the men who worked for Elvis, he had never met the singer. However, he knew this could be an important moment, so he carefully selected some of his finest pieces and took them to the theater.

Elvis liked the jeweler and bought several items that night. It was an auspicious beginning to a relationship that would last four years, until Elvis's death. For Lowell, it was the most unusual association of his career, and his most profitable. Their relationship developed into a unique blend of friendship and business—one in which Elvis was very caring and generous, though at the same time could be exasperatingly demanding.

Lowell made himself available whenever Elvis was in the mood to shop for jewelry, even if this meant rising from a sound sleep in the early morning hours to rush to wherever Elvis was at the time—at Graceland or on tour. Lowell would travel with as much as a quarter-million-dollars worth of jewelry in an effort to be prepared for Elvis's latest whim.

Many of the items Elvis purchased were carefully selected gifts, with Elvis often matching a stone to a person's birthday. For himself, Elvis favored rings, preferring bold designs. Some of the pieces Elvis bought from Lowell were custom-made. Elvis designed the ring he wore on his last tour—a heavy, square face with four large black sapphires in each corner and diamonds between the stones.

Lowell estimates that Elvis bought between five hundred and seven hundred thousand dollars worth of jewelry from him. He always paid by check and usually on account. When Lowell came to Graceland, Elvis frequently asked if he had been paid yet. The few times when Lowell answered no, Elvis asked for his checkbook and made the check out himself.

In exchange for being such a good customer, Elvis expected a certain level of service. In 1977, when Elvis proposed to his girlfriend, Ginger Alden, he called Lowell at 1:00 A.M. Elvis told Lowell he wanted a ring with a large diamond. Lowell replied that what he wanted was impossible because all of the diamonds were secured in a vault. Elvis would not be dissuaded. "Look, I do all my business with you, and when I need something special, I need it special. I want this diamond and I want it tonight and I want you to get it for me."

Lowell delivered the eleven-and-a-half carat ring seven hours later. Its price tag was fifty thousand dollars. Although this would have been ample compensation, Elvis showed his appreciation by giving Lowell a navy blue Lincoln Continental Mark V.

EAST MEMPHIS. LOWELL HAYS CONTINUES TO SELL JEWELRY AT HIS STORE. FROM I-240, TAKE THE POPLAR AVENUE WESTBOUND EXIT. DRIVE WEST ON POPLAR AVENUE TO THE INTERSECTION WITH ERIN ROAD; THE STORE IS TO YOUR RIGHT.

Sears Roebuck and Company
495 North Watkins Street and Southland Mall

If a single retailer could be called typically American, it would be Sears Roebuck, and the Presleys, like millions of ordinary Americans, were regular customers of the store, utilizing both their catalog services and their retail locations.

When Priscilla redecorated Graceland after marrying Elvis, she purchased the blue drapes for the living and dining rooms from Sears. According to Priscilla, Elvis personally shopped in the basement of Sears when he was outfitting the Circle G Ranch. He was in the mood to buy tools, Priscilla remembered, and where better to buy power tools than Sears? Priscilla didn't specify which Sears location Elvis visited on that occasion, but it was most likely the Sears Crosstown store at North Watkins Street. This was the closest store to Graceland. The Poplar Avenue branch was a bit further away, and the Southland Mall store didn't have a basement.

Vernon Presley was also a frequent customer at Sears, probably patronizing the Southland Mall store most often. When Vernon died in 1979, an accounting for his will revealed that he owed Sears Roebuck and Company sixteen hundred dollars.

MIDTOWN. SEARS CROSSTOWN LOCATION IS NO LONGER IN OPERATION. TO REACH THE SITE OF THE STORE FROM POPLAR AVENUE, TURN NORTH ONTO CLEVELAND STREET, WHICH MERGES INTO NORTH WATKINS STREET. THE MULTI-STORY BUILDING THAT ONCE HOUSED THE SEARS IS VISIBLE TO YOUR LEFT AFTER THE MERGE.

WHITEHAVEN. SOUTHLAND MALL IS LOCATED AT ELVIS PRESLEY BOULEVARD AND SHELBY DRIVE. FROM GRACELAND, DRIVE SOUTH ON ELVIS PRESLEY BOULEVARD FOR ABOUT TWO MILES UNTIL REACHING SHELBY DRIVE. THE SOUTHLAND MALL ENTRANCE IS TO YOUR LEFT, JUST PAST SHELBY DRIVE.

POLICE DEPARTMENT

Memphis Police Station
128 Adams Avenue

Elvis often joked that if things didn't work out in the entertainment business, he could always go back to driving a truck. What he really would have liked to have been was a police officer. His passion for law enforcement was deep-seated, born out of a respect for authority and kindled by his own experiences with police officers. Very early in Elvis's career, he began relying on police protection in crowds. On numerous occasions, he was driven to or from events in police vehicles. Police escorts for his limousine became almost a way of life. In times of crisis, as in the death of his mother, the police shielded him from the prying public and press. Elvis knew that he could rely on the police no matter where he traveled, but in Memphis, he considered many of these fine gentlemen as friends.

It was not uncommon for Elvis to stop in at the police station in the wee morning hours; on occasion, he even rode on patrol. He admired the selflessness with which the policemen performed their duties and their kindness to the public. Perhaps Elvis admired these traits because he was such a caring person himself. One Christmas, while he could have been home at Graceland, he visited the police station. While he joked that it was the only place open, the truth was that he had been thinking about the officers who were working the holiday for the good of the community.

Jerry Schilling, who worked for Elvis, recalled Elvis's fondness for police officers. "In Las Vegas, you could have some of the biggest personalities in the United States there where Elvis could talk to them, and you'd find him over in the corner talking to two policemen," Jerry said.

At heart, Elvis wanted to be a policeman. In a way, he got his wish. Elvis's friend Bill Morris gave him an honorary title during his term as sheriff. For a time, being an "honorary" policeman satisfied Elvis. Then he began thinking what it would be like to carry a real badge, to hold identification that named him a member of the police force, and even to be licensed to carry a weapon, just as the men on the beat. In 1970, Sheriff Roy Nixon commissioned Elvis as a special deputy, presenting him with a badge and identification card in a serious ceremony at the sheriff's office. Elvis was required to post five thousand dollars bond and to qualify at the shooting range, which wasn't a problem. "He was an expert shot," Sheriff Nixon recalled.

Jerry Schilling's brother, Billy, who also served as a sheriff, remembered that Elvis wasn't given everything he asked for in regards to his law-enforcement aspirations. "He was just like a kid about law enforcement," Billy Schilling said. "He always wanted blue lights for his cars." Though Elvis's request were occasionally denied, he was always respectful to the police. "During the time that I was sheriff and on the county court, he said several times that if there was ever anything law enforcement needed that he could do, he was available," Billy remembered.

DOWNTOWN. FROM UNION AVENUE, TURN NORTH ONTO THIRD STREET AND DRIVE FIVE BLOCKS TO ADAMS AVENUE. TURN LEFT ONTO ADAMS AND DRIVE TO THE NEXT STREET, SECOND STREET. THE POLICE STATION IS AT THE NORTHWEST CORNER OF ADAMS AVENUE AND SECOND STREET. ACROSS SECOND STREET IS THE SHELBY COUNTY COURTHOUSE.

THE BEST PLACE TO SEE SOME OF ELVIS'S LAW ENFORCEMENT MEMORABILIA IS AT THE POLICE SUBSTATION AT 169 BEALE STREET, LOCATED BETWEEN SECOND AND THIRD STREETS ON THE SOUTH SIDE OF BEALE. A WORKING POLICE STATION, IT ALSO SERVES AS AN INFORMAL MUSEUM ON MEMPHIS LAW ENFORCEMENT HISTORY.

KARATE

Kang Rhee Institute for Self-Defense
1911 Poplar Avenue

While in the army, Elvis took some karate classes. Elvis enjoyed martial arts and became an enthusiastic student of the sport for the rest of his life. Elvis learned quickly, earning a black belt in 1960. At the time, Elvis was one of the few Americans who had attained a black belt. He would demonstrate his skills by breaking boards with karate kicks or displaying hand chops to anyone who was interested. Soon, many people in his entourage were taking lessons and sparring with him.

Elvis began to incorporate his karate skills into the fight scenes in his movies. *International Fighter* magazine credits Elvis with contributing to the popularity of martial arts in action movies. And the popularity of martial arts in the movies led to a tremendous interest among the general public during the 1970s. During his later concert tours, Elvis included various karate movements into his stage performance.

Elvis often talked about the benefits he derived from martial arts training. Karate's emphasis on self-discipline and meditation appealed to his interests in religion and philosophy. In 1974, Elvis even worked on a documentary film about the martial arts, but it was never completed.

Kang Rhee is a Korean master of tae kwon do, the most widely known type of karate. He began his school, or dojo, in Memphis in 1964. Elvis trained with Kang Rhee for a longer period of time than he trained with any other master of karate. They became good friends. Kang Rhee admired Elvis's enthusiasm for martial arts, calling him "The Tiger." He promoted Elvis to an eighth-degree black belt, though other instructors thought the promotion was not justified by Elvis's ability. Elvis in kind lavished Kang Rhee with many gifts. Later, Kang Rhee admitted the title was really honorary.

MIDTOWN. THE KANG RHEE INSTITUTE FOR SELF-DEFENSE WAS LOCATED ON POPLAR AVENUE, JUST WEST OF THE INTERSECTION WITH TUCKER STREET. THE MEMPHIS COLLEGE OF ART NOW USES THE BUILDING. OVERTON PARK IS ACROSS THE STREET.

TODAY, KANG RHEE OPERATES HIS DOJO AT 706 GERMANTOWN PARKWAY #70—A SUBURBAN LOCATION. HE IS VERY INVOLVED WITH ELVIS FANS. VISITORS TO HIS DOJO CAN BUY A NUMBER OF PHOTOS AND OTHER MEMENTOS OF KANG RHEE'S RELATIONSHIP WITH ELVIS. FROM I-240, TAKE THE WALNUT GROVE ROAD EASTBOUND EXIT. DRIVE EAST ON WALNUT GROVE ROAD TO THE GERMANTOWN PARKWAY INTERSECTION. EXIT NORTH ONTO GERMANTOWN PARKWAY AND CONTINUE TO THE INTERSECTION WITH TRINITY ROAD. KANG RHEE'S CURRENT DOJO IS IN THE SHOPPING CENTER ON THE RIGHT SIDE OF THIS INTERSECTION.

Tennessee Karate Institute
1372 Overton Park

Elvis trained at the Tennessee Karate Institute because of his friendship with Red West, the institute's owner. Elvis and Red had known each other at Humes High School, and Red was one of the first people to work security for Elvis during those frantic early tours. Red continued to serve as Elvis's chief of security until 1976.

Elvis with Red and Pat West at their wedding
Courtesy of the Mississippi Valley Collection

Like Elvis, Red was also a karate enthusiast. After Elvis left the army in 1960, he and Red staged karate fight scenes for Elvis's movies. In 1974, Red and a business partner opened the Tennessee Karate Institute. Advertisements for the institute featured Elvis and Red, both black belts, facing each other in a fighting stance. This is one of the few occasions Elvis endorsed a business or product through advertising.

Red's partner was kick-boxing champion Bill Wallace. Kick boxing is a full-contact sport pitting opponents who both kick and punch each other in a boxing ring. Wallace, called "Superfoot" for his speed at kicking, won the world title from 1974 to 1980. Red believed Wallace's association with the school would draw customers, a plan that worked well. Soon a number of kick boxers and stunt men from Hollywood were training at the school.

When Elvis was in good shape and in the mood, he loved to practice karate for a crowd. Twice he allowed the media to cover his workouts, once for the Memphis papers, and the last time for a *People* magazine story on his fortieth birthday in 1975.

Although Bill Wallace and Elvis were not close friends, Elvis did help him overcome a serious injury. The fighter had suffered a bruise to his kicking leg that did not respond to medical treatment. If the wound did not heal, Wallace could not compete in fights. Elvis invited him to Graceland to meet an acupuncturist Elvis had flown in from Los Angeles. Fifteen minutes after the acupuncture needles were inserted into his leg, Wallace's pain had disappeared.

Eventually, Red sold his part in the institute to Patrick Wrenn, who still teaches martial arts in Memphis. Wrenn helped create the Elvis Presley Memorial Karate Tournament, which was held for a number of years. The Tennessee Karate Institute closed in 1977 when Wrenn suffered a serious injury and Bill Wallace could no longer devote the time to manage it.

MIDTOWN. FROM POPLAR AVENUE, TURN NORTH ONTO CLEVELAND STREET AND CONTINUE TO THE INTERSECTION WITH OVERTON PARK AVENUE. THE TENNESSEE KARATE INSTITUTE WAS ON THE UPSTAIRS FLOOR OF THE BUILDING AT THE NORTHEAST CORNER OF THIS INTERSECTION.

RACQUETBALL

Presley Center Courts
Mendenhall Road at Mt. Moriah Road

During the '70s, Elvis became interested in the new sport fitness trend of racquetball. He played the sport at the Memphis Athletic Club and the Jewish Community Center, but it was difficult for him to play with privacy at these facilities. Finally, Elvis had his own court, complete with piano and hot tub, installed at Graceland.

Dr. George Nichopoulos, Elvis's doctor, and Joe Esposito, Elvis's road manager, as well as another investor sought to capitalize on Elvis's name and his enthusiasm for the sport by opening a chain of racquetball courts to be called Presley Center Courts. Elvis approved the idea at first. Paperwork was drawn up, plans were detailed, and business cards and letterheads were printed in anticipation of the expected investment. Ground was even broken at the site of the first location in April 1976. Then Elvis backed away from the idea, apparently uncomfortable with the financial commitment expected of him. The other investors sued Elvis in 1977 but dropped the suit before it went to trial.

Eventually, the court was opened under the name of baseball star Don Kessinger, who also invested in other fitness centers in Memphis. Kessinger managed the racquetball court and fitness centers until 1982.

EAST MEMPHIS. FROM I-240, TAKE THE MT. MORIAH ROAD SOUTHBOUND EXIT. DRIVE SOUTH TO THE INTERSECTION OF MT. MORIAH AND MENDENHALL ROADS (A FORK IN THE ROAD), AND FOLLOW THE RIGHT FORK. THE BUILDING THAT HOUSED THE COURTS IS NOW THE RANGEMASTER SHOOTING RANGE; IT IS LOCATED PAST AND BEHIND PERFORMANCE TOYOTA USED CARS.

HIDEAWAY

Howard Johnson's Motor Lodge
3280 Elvis Presley Boulevard

When Elvis wanted to escape Graceland and the many demands people made on him, he would occasionally travel a quarter mile up Elvis Presley Boulevard to the Howard Johnson's Motor Lodge, where he kept two rooms year-round. Though Elvis could have had his choice of luxury accommodations, the rather ordinary quarters suited him as well as any penthouse suite. More importantly, he knew the motor lodge would provide him with complete privacy.

He first met the hotel's manager, Mrs. Norrine Mitchell, during the 1950s when he would visit one of her coworkers at the Hicks Composition Company. A few years later when Elvis moved to Audubon Drive, he and his parents occasionally saw Mrs. Mitchell when she visited one of the Presley's neighbors. More than a decade later, another mutual acquaintance, Jerry Schilling, led Elvis to Mrs. Mitchell's Howard Johnson's. Jerry knew Mrs. Mitchell through her daughters. He often stayed at the hotel, and one day he brought Elvis with him.

Elvis remembered Mrs. Mitchell immediately. That day, he told her he wanted to book a couple of rooms year-round for out-of-town guests. An account was established, and Room 127 and Room 111 were set aside for the Presleys. The arrangement proved convenient. Elvis's friends and business associates could stay close to Graceland, and Elvis could let himself into the rooms whenever he wanted to be alone. He did not have to check in at the desk, so his presence often went unnoticed by the staff and other hotel guests.

Only Mrs. Mitchell knew about Elvis's arrangement at the hotel, and she guarded her secret faithfully until his death. The hotel continued to serve the Presley family when it was used as the lodging for family and friends staying in Memphis for Elvis's funeral.

WHITEHAVEN. FROM GRACELAND, DRIVE NORTH ON ELVIS PRESLEY BOULEVARD FOR LESS THAN A MILE TO THE INTERSECTION WITH GATEWAY DRIVE. THE MOTEL ENTRANCE IS TO YOUR RIGHT, JUST PAST GATEWAY DRIVE. IT IS NOW A GUEST HOUSE INN. ELVIS FAN EVENTS ARE USUALLY HELD AT THE MOTEL EVERY AUGUST DURING TRIBUTE WEEK.

FAMILY AND FRIENDS

Vernon Presley's Homes
3650 Hermitage Road and 1266 Dolan Drive

Vernon Presley married Dee Stanley two years after Gladys died. For Elvis, the marriage was troublesome. He wanted his father to be happy, but he had no desire for Dee to assume the role of his mother. Vernon, Dee, and her three sons lived at Graceland for a while, but it eventually became evident they could not coexist in the same house with Elvis, so the couple and Dee's sons moved out. Despite the tensions created by the situation, Vernon and Elvis remained close, with Vernon continuing to watch over his son's personal finances.

In 1961, Vernon bought a home at 3650 Hermitage Road. The two-level, three-bedroom home was close to Graceland and large enough to accommodate Dee's three children. It was decorated in very modern colors, with bright green and red walls and Oriental accents.

Vernon soon tired of the house on Hermitage Road. In 1964, he found a home on Dolan Drive that was perfect for everyone's needs, since the home adjoined the Graceland property. A gate was installed through the fence so that Vernon could walk from his home to his office in the backyard of Graceland. The gate was also convenient for Elvis's occasional visits to the home. A separate fence and gate in front of Vernon's house afforded him some privacy.

The house was enlarged until it was considerably larger than the neighboring ranch-style homes. Certainly it was the most unique home in the subdivision—it had an eight-foot square whirlpool bath in the main bedroom, probably one of the first in the city.

Eventually, all of Dee Presley's sons went to work for Elvis and continued to do so until his death. Dee and Vernon's marriage ended in 1976. Vernon sold the house in 1978 when he moved into an apartment on the Graceland property. The home's buyers were the owners of the Hickory Log Restaurant. Ever since, the home has been owned by Elvis fans. Today, it is unoccupied for much of the year, except in August. Then, fan club or group events surrounding Tribute Week are held there.

1266 DOLAN DRIVE: WHITEHAVEN. FROM GRACELAND, DRIVE SOUTH ON ELVIS PRESLEY BOULEVARD TO DOLAN DRIVE. TURN LEFT ONTO DOLAN DRIVE AND LOOK FOR THE TAN, BRICK HOUSE—THE ONLY ONE WITH A WALL IN FRONT.

3650 HERMITAGE ROAD: WHITEHAVEN. FROM THE HOUSE AT 1266 DOLAN DRIVE, CONTINUE TO THE NEXT STREET, CHARLES DRIVE, AND TURN LEFT. DRIVE TO HERMITAGE ROAD. TURN LEFT ONTO HERMITAGE ROAD AND CONTINUE UNTIL CROSSING OVER OLD HICKORY ROAD. THE HOUSE IS TO THE RIGHT ON THIS BLOCK. PLEASE RESPECT THE PRIVACY OF BOTH OWNERS.

Linda Thompson's Home
1254 Old Hickory Road

Of all of the women in Elvis's life, Linda Thompson, with her fun-loving personality, seems to have been the best influence on him. At least, that is the consensus among many who were close to Elvis. After Priscilla asked Elvis for a divorce, Linda quickly filled a void in his life during a time of depression and loneliness. The two would go on to live together for over four years. Elvis was so enamored with her and her family that he even bought separate homes for her parents and her brother. In 1974, he bought this home for Linda, even though she had redecorated Graceland and continued to live with him there. The cost for the house was fifty-two thousand dollars.

The house is a large, ranch-style home set on a wooded lot some distance from the street. In the back was a swimming pool that was the scene of many parties. The interior of the home reflected Elvis and Linda's tastes for bold, extravagant colors. The front room is decorated in bright green shag carpet and matching wallpaper. Shag carpeting was even installed in the kitchen. Linda's bedroom was a little more subdued, with white-and-gold colors and a brass bed.

Linda left Elvis in December 1976 and has since moved on with her life. She is now the wife of record producer David Foster and the mother of two sons by her former husband, Bruce Jenner. Linda shares songwriting credit with her husband on the score of the recent blockbuster movie *The Bodyguard*. Today, she rarely speaks about Elvis and has turned down numerous offers to write exposé books on their relationship.

In 1981, Linda sold the house on Old Hickory Road to Elvis collector Jimmy Velvet. The home is currently owned by another Elvis fan named Marie Nersesian, who retained the original carpet and wallpaper.

WHITEHAVEN. FROM GRACELAND, DRIVE SOUTH ON ELVIS PRESLEY BOULEVARD AND TAKE THE NEXT RIGHT ONTO OLD HICKORY ROAD. THE HOUSE IS ON THE LEFT, ABOVE A CIRCULAR DRIVEWAY. PLEASE RESPECT THE PRIVACY OF THE OWNER.

Sam Thompson's Home
1317 Favell Road

When Linda Thompson began dating Elvis in 1972, her younger brother, Sam, was a Shelby County deputy jailer. Sam lived with his wife, Louise, in an apartment that was quite a distance from Graceland, so the couple did not visit Linda and Elvis often. At the time, Sam was recuperating from a serious leg injury and was on disability leave.

Elvis knew their situation and wanted to help. Without realizing Elvis's intention, Sam and Louise accompanied Elvis in his Stutz Blackhawk on a leisurely drive to the Circle G Ranch. It was a hot August afternoon, and Elvis could not resist stopping at a nearby watermelon stand. There, he bought the stand's entire watermelon inventory after failing to convince the young black entrepreneur to reduce his price. On the way back to Graceland, Elvis made the pretense of stopping for an errand in front of a house for sale on Favell Road.

Elvis knocked on the front door. The shocked homeowner offered to let Elvis and his friends tour her house. After Elvis understood that Sam and Louise liked the home, he merely said, "Great. It is yours."

An unbelieving Sam could only mutter, "You can't do this."

Elvis replied, "Yes I can. I am rich." A quick phone call brought the real estate agent to the house. Another phone call brought Elvis's checkbook, and the transaction was completed within minutes.

Not long after this incident, Sam left the sheriff's department to work for Elvis as a bodyguard. Sam and Louise lived in their home on Favell Road until 1978. After Elvis died, Sam returned to the department and then entered law school. Today, he is a general sessions judge.

WHITEHAVEN. FROM GRACELAND, DRIVE SOUTH ON ELVIS PRESLEY BOULEVARD TO DOLAN DRIVE. TURN LEFT ONTO DOLAN DRIVE AND THEN TURN RIGHT AT THE FIRST STREET, FAVELL ROAD. THE HOUSE IS ON YOUR LEFT. PLEASE RESPECT THE PRIVACY OF THE OWNER.

Elvis's Other Properties
1576 Lehr Street
4152 Royalcrest Place

Elvis owned just four pieces of property at the time of his death, a surprisingly low number for someone who could have owned most of Shelby County. These holdings included Graceland and eleven acres of undeveloped land across the street and immediately north of Graceland. The other two properties were homes for the parents of two of his girlfriends. In both instances, Elvis apparently purchased the homes with the intention of generously giving them away, yet neglected to have the deeds transferred.

Linda Thompson's parents, Samford and Margie Thompson, lived in one of these homes at 1576 Lehr Street. Elvis purchased the small ranch house in 1974 for thirty-four thousand dollars. For whatever reasons, the Thompsons were under the impression the house belonged to them and were shocked to learn after Elvis's death that it was still in his name. As such, it became part of Elvis's estate, and the Thompsons moved out soon after his death. Elvis's uncle Vester Presley eventually moved into this house and lived there until his death in 1997.

Ginger Alden's parents faced a similar situation. The deed to their home at 4512 Royalcrest Place remained in Elvis's name. They claimed Elvis intended to pay off the forty-thousand-dollar mortgage and give the house to them. Vernon Presley, the executor of Elvis's estate, claimed the estate was not obligated to pay the debt. Eventually the two parties reached an agreement, and the Alden family kept the house for many years.

In both cases, it is possible Elvis did not fully protect his intentions. He did not concern himself with business arrangements of any kind, whether relating to his career or his household. He operated on impulse, often without attending to the details. Perhaps he simply assumed someone would dot the i's for him, or maybe he didn't think it was necessary. For whatever reason, these two residential properties were part of Elvis's unresolved business.

1576 LEHR STREET: WHITEHAVEN. FROM GRACELAND, DRIVE SOUTH ON ELVIS PRESLEY BOULEVARD TO DOLAN DRIVE AND TURN LEFT. CONTINUE DRIVING ON DOLAN DRIVE UNTIL REACHING HERMITAGE ROAD. TURN LEFT ONTO HERMITAGE ROAD AND DRIVE TO THE INTERSECTION WITH LEHR STREET. TURN LEFT ONTO LEHR STREET; THE HOUSE IS ABOUT THREE BLOCKS DOWN ON THE LEFT SIDE OF THE STREET. PLEASE RESPECT THE PRIVACY OF THE OWNER.

4152 ROYALCREST PLACE: SOUTHEAST MEMPHIS. FROM GRACELAND, DRIVE NORTH ON ELVIS PRESLEY BOULEVARD TO WINCHESTER ROAD. TURN RIGHT ON WINCHESTER ROAD AND DRIVE SIX-AND-A-HALF MILES TO RIDGEWAY ROAD. TURN RIGHT ONTO RIDGEWAY ROAD, THEN TAKE THE THIRD LEFT ONTO SCARLETCREST LANE. TAKE THE NEXT RIGHT ONTO ROYALCREST PLACE; THE HOUSE IS ON THE LEFT SIDE OF THE STREET.

BANKING

National Bank of Commerce
One Commerce Square
45 South Second Street

Like most young people starting out in life, Elvis opened a checking account to pay his expenses. Elvis chose the National Bank of Commerce for his banking needs. Whether he was depositing his meager thirty-five-dollar-a-week salary from his truck-driving job or the tiny receipts from those first club appearances, he probably did not receive much attention at the bank aside from the teller's pleasant greeting. In those early days, no one at the bank could have imagined he would become the National Bank of Commerce's most famous, if not wealthiest, client.

His bank transactions were private, of course, but at the time of his death, his finances became public record. It was revealed his checking account at National Bank of Commerce held a little more than a million dollars. He also had a few minor savings accounts, amounting to about thirty-five-thousand dollars, at various banks around town. His smallest, at First Tennessee Bank, held just thirty-nine dollars.

Elvis was one of the few individuals in life blessed with the knowledge that there would always be enough money to satisfy his needs. Sometimes that meant going on tour again, or cutting another album, but he was always confident the money would be there. He didn't concern himself with money management or investments. His father, Vernon, was his financial advisor, despite his limited schooling and banking experience. To them, it made sense to leave a million dollars sitting in a low-interest-bearing checking account. They knew exactly where it was, and they knew that the bank could be trusted.

After Vernon's death, the National Bank of Commerce served as the executor of his will. Ultimately, it took over as executor of Elvis's will as well.

DOWNTOWN. FROM UNION AVENUE, TURN NORTH ON SECOND STREET AND DRIVE ONE BLOCK. THE BANK OCCUPIES THE BLOCK OF SECOND STREET BETWEEN MADISON AND MONROE AVENUES.

THE LOSS
OF A LEGEND

Baptist Memorial Hospital
899 Union Avenue

For Elvis fans, Baptist Memorial Hospital will always be associated with his final hour—it was here that Elvis was pronounced dead at 3:30 P.M. on August 16, 1977. The event practically shook the towering hospital; reporters from radio and television stations swarmed upon the medical center, and police were called in to secure the area. A few hours later, when Elvis's body was removed for transport to Memphis Funeral Home, a side street was blocked off.

Baptist was equipped to deal with the publicity and disruption surrounding Elvis's death because they had protected his privacy for years. He had been hospitalized there on several occasions, often for what the press reported as fatigue, but what in truth were a variety of problems ranging from colon ailments to hypertension. Whenever Elvis was admitted to the hospital, he always occupied the same suite of rooms. From the street, fans could tell immediately when Elvis was there because of the unusual glare coming from the window in his room—at his request, the window was covered with tin foil to darken it. Vernon stayed in this same room in 1975 while he recuperated from a heart attack, but his presence was less obvious. Vernon died at the hospital in 1979.

It was a challenge for the staff to protect Elvis's privacy. Hospital employees hovered around his room hoping to catch a glimpse of their idol, while reporters scoured the halls looking for an inside scoop. Occasionally, Elvis would meet with the reporters. When he spent a night at the hospital in 1960 after breaking a finger in a football game (unheard of today), he granted interviews and posed for pictures.

While the mood during that particular stay was light, it was absolutely jubilant when Priscilla delivered Lisa Marie on February 1, 1968. The proud father paced the waiting room in anticipation of the delivery. Vernon, his wife Dee, and several members of the Memphis Mafia waited with him. It might have seemed a perfectly ordinary birth, except for the guards stationed outside the waiting and maternity rooms. As was customary then, Priscilla stayed in the hospital for four days, with Elvis frequently at her side.

Perhaps the birth of his child is the best image of Baptist Memorial Hospital to associate with Elvis. Just as it is appropriate to remember how Elvis lived, instead of the details of his death, perhaps we should also remember Baptist Hospital as the place where he experienced one of his greatest joys, the birth of his only child.

DOWNTOWN. BAPTIST MEMORIAL HOSPITAL, ONE OF THE LARGEST HOSPITALS IN THE COUNTRY, IS LOCATED AT THE INTERSECTION OF UNION AVENUE AND EAST STREET. IT IS NEXT TO THE UNIVERSITY OF TENNESSEE MEDICAL SCHOOL.

Memphis Funeral Home
1177 Union Avenue

Memphis Funeral Home's stately building on Union Avenue was the site of many funerals, but none were as newsworthy as those of

Gladys Presley's grave at Forest Hill Cemetery

the Presley family. In 1958, Gladys's body was released from nearby Methodist Hospital to National Funeral Home, Memphis Funeral Home's predecessor. After the body was prepared for viewing, it was moved to Graceland for the night. In the morning, it was returned to the funeral home, where nearly three thousand people filed past the casket.

The funeral service for Gladys, held in the chapel, was limited to three hundred guests. Elvis and his father sat in an alcove where their privacy was protected. Reverend James Hamill of the Assembly of God Church gave the eulogy. The Blackwood Brothers sang "Rock of Ages" and "Precious Memories." At the end of the ceremony, sixty-five policemen escorted the procession to Forest Hill Cemetery.

The next day, as Elvis wrestled with his own grief, he returned to the funeral home to support a friend. Red West, a friend from high school, was preparing to bury his father. Red remembered, "Elvis told me, 'My mama was here yesterday just where your daddy is, Red.' He couldn't say too much more. He was so badly broken up. We just sort of held on to each other, and I thought, This is one helluva guy to go through what he did the day before and then face it all over again to pay his respects to my daddy."

Like so many Memphians, Elvis visited the Memphis Funeral Home many times throughout the years for the funerals of friends, loved ones, and acquaintances. He came to know many staff members, who always shielded him from the public.

The challenge to protect Elvis's privacy was never greater than when he died. At 8:15 P.M. on August 16, 1977, Elvis's body was released to the funeral home. The hearse he was transported in was escorted by two police cars and four police motorcycles. Vernon asked that Elvis be buried in a coffin like the one used for Gladys. This particular coffin was not in stock in a size large enough for Elvis, so the funeral home had one flown in from Oklahoma City. During the night, Elvis's friend and former bodyguard Sam Thompson guarded the body. In the morning, Charlie Hodge, a longtime employee of Elvis's, styled his hair. Elvis was dressed in a white suit chosen by Vernon. At 10:30 A.M. on August 17, Elvis's remains were transported to Graceland for public viewing and a private service the following day. Elvis was interred in a mausoleum in Forest Hill Cemetery. Later, the body was removed and buried at Graceland.

The mausoleum at Forest Hill Cemetery

R. Max Snow, who managed Memphis Funeral Home for more than thirty years, recalled that in many ways, Elvis's funeral was like any other. Except, in the days and years following this particular funeral, fans would visit Memphis Funeral Home just to see the white hearse that carried Elvis's body on his last journey down Elvis Presley Boulevard. Snow remembered that on several occasions, the hood ornament from the hearse disappeared. "We replaced the hood ornament about a half-dozen times," he said. "We finally just gave up and left it without one."

MIDTOWN. MEMPHIS FUNERAL HOME HAS CLOSED THIS LOCATION AT 1177 UNION AVENUE AND PUT THE BUILDING UP FOR SALE. THE BUILDING IS LOCATED ON UNION AVENUE BETWEEN THE I-240 INTERCHANGE AND BELLEVUE BOULEVARD. METHODIST HOSPITAL CENTRAL IS NEARBY.

THE LEGACY
CONTINUES

Elvis Presley Trauma Center
877 Jefferson Avenue

The Elvis Presley Trauma Center is the only public institution named after Elvis Presley. The trauma center is devoted to critical, emergency care and operates as a special part of the Regional Medical Center. The trauma center opened in 1983, replacing the outdated John Gaston City Hospital. Shelby County mayor Bill Morris played a key role in the construction of the hospital, and in naming it for his good friend. Over the years, the center has developed a reputation as one of the best hospitals in the country.

It is a cause that Elvis fans have embraced, donating over $150,000 to the hospital in the last six years. The hospital places recognition plaques on an interior wall in honor of those donors who contribute one thousand dollars or more. Elvis fans will recognize many of the clubs and individuals who have been honored. Visitors are encouraged to see this wall, with restrictions: because this is a busy trauma hospital, visitors should check in at the security post and let security officers guide you to the display of plaques.

DOWNTOWN. FROM UNION AVENUE, TURN NORTH ONTO MANASSAS STREET. CONTINUE TO JEFFERSON AVENUE AND TURN RIGHT, THEN DRIVE ONE BLOCK. YOU ARE WITHIN THE REGIONAL MEDICAL CENTER; THE ELVIS PRESLEY TRAUMA CENTER IS TO YOUR RIGHT.

Le Bonheur Children's Hospital
50 North Dunlap Street

Back when the Le Bonheur Children's Hospital was just a dream of the members of the Le Bonheur Club, Elvis was an early supporter of their efforts. Each year he would give between $50,000 and $100,000 to charity. The money was divided among several local organizations, and the Le Bonheur Club was always remembered.

After the hospital became a reality, Elvis, on occasion, would visit or telephone sick children at the hospital. Each year, he donated thousands of stuffed animals. The hospital honored Elvis's contributions by naming its ward for teenagers after him.

Today, Elvis fans continue his legacy by contributing to the hospital. A wall in the front reception room is decorated with plaques honoring the hospital's donors.

DOWNTOWN. FROM POPLAR AVENUE, TURN NORTH ON DUNLAP STREET AND CONTINUE TO ADAMS AVENUE. THE HOSPITAL FRONTS BOTH DUNLAP STREET AND ADAMS AVENUE. NEARBY IS THE ELVIS PRESLEY TRAUMA CENTER.

St. Jude Children's Research Hospital
332 North Lauderdale Street

The St. Jude Children's Research Hospital held a special place in Elvis's heart, and he supported its cause through the years. His affinity for the hospital was not due only to the soft spot he held for children, though that was certainly an important factor. He was especially pleased that St. Jude was built in Memphis when, as a national institution, it could have been built anywhere in the country. It was an added bonus to him that the facility was built in his old neighborhood, just a stone's throw from his family's apartments in Lauderdale Courts and on Alabama Street.

When the hospital's founder, Danny Thomas, was in the early stages of raising funds to build the research center, Elvis attended a benefit show at Russwood Park. He couldn't perform because of his film contracts, but he excited the crowd by walking on stage and wiggling his hips.

In 1964, Elvis supported St. Jude in a most unusual way. Elvis had purchased Franklin D. Roosevelt's presidential yacht *Potomac* at auction for fifty-five thousand dollars, and he donated the yacht to the hospital. He presented Danny Thomas with the bill of sale in a ceremony in Long Beach, California. St. Jude sold the yacht for sixty thousand dollars, turning Elvis's gift into sizable donation. Today the yacht is berthed in Oakland, California.

Elvis did not cross paths with Danny Thomas again until they became neighbors in Beverly Hills. Danny Thomas always appreciated Elvis's support of the hospital. In turn, Elvis considered the comedian a great humanitarian.

Today, in the pavilion at St. Jude, just steps from the crypt where Danny Thomas is buried, there is a museum highlighting Danny Thomas's career. Amid all the photographs of entertainers and Hollywood celebrities, the photo of Elvis and Danny Thomas aboard the *Potomac* stands apart from the rest.

DOWNTOWN. FROM UNION AVENUE, TURN NORTH ONTO THIRD STREET AND CONTINUE TO JACKSON AVENUE, WHICH IS JUST PAST THE I-40 INTERCHANGE. TURN RIGHT ONTO JACKSON AVENUE, WHICH CHANGES ITS NAME TO LAUDERDALE STREET, AND LOOK TO YOUR LEFT. ST. JUDE CHILDREN'S RESEARCH HOSPITAL IS TO THE RIGHT OF ST. JOSEPH HOSPITAL AND TO THE LEFT OF LAUDERDALE COURTS.

APPENDIX

Getting Around Town

Memphis is unlike any other city you will ever visit. It is the musical melting pot of the South, a place where rock-and-roll, blues, and gospel share street corners, barrooms, and recording studios. It is a place that sometimes bursts with creativity. And for all of that, it is a place of such hardship that music becomes the soul's release. Nowhere is this more evident than in the places Elvis knew as a teenager. These areas were impoverished even then, and time has not been kind to them. Nor has the decline of the inner city happened overnight. In 1969, when Elvis recorded "In The Ghetto" at American Sound Studio, he was literally in one of the poorest slums in Memphis.

As in most American cities, much of the growth in Memphis over the past few decades has taken place outside of the city limits. The suburbs are flourishing, just as they were when Elvis bought his dream home in the suburb Whitehaven. But demographics are constantly changing in this city. Even Elvis's beloved Whitehaven, once the shining jewel of Memphis's suburban communities, has declined.

With few exceptions, most of the places listed in this book are within seven miles of Graceland. Getting around town can be a bit tricky though, unless you have an automobile or hire a taxi, because public transportation is minimal. We do not advise walking; if you do choose to walk, please be cautious, particularly at night.

Expect the best and worst of service because we have both in ample supply. Unless following specific recommendations, we recommend you rely on the name-brand hotels and restaurants, especially in the Graceland area. For those willing to travel a small distance from Graceland, the best values can often be found in neighboring Southaven and other parts of the city. If planning to visit Memphis during January or August, when so many of Elvis's fans will be in town, be certain to make your reservations well in advance.

For all of the big-city problems in Memphis, it is still very similar to a small town—a place where beauty can be found, where people are more often kind to each other than not, and where Southern hospitality is always in evidence. Best of all, it is a place unlike any other, for there is only one Memphis, Tennessee.

Graceland

Those who think the tour of Graceland consists of a quick walk around the mansion are badly mistaken. Since there is so much to see, including several museums, visiting Graceland is an experience worth several hours.

Tickets to attractions are sold either individually or in packages. The Graceland Mansion Tour ($10.00 for adults; $9.00 for seniors over age sixty-two; $5.00 for children ages seven to twelve; free for children six and under) includes the basic tour of Elvis's home. The Platinum Tour ($18.50 for adults; $16.65 for seniors over age sixty-two; $11.00 for children ages seven to twelve; free for children six and under) grants admission to all of the Graceland attractions: the mansion, the Elvis Presley Automobile Museum, the Sincerely Elvis Museum, the film *Walk a Mile in My Shoes*, and the *Lisa Marie* Jet and *Hound Dog II* JetStar Planes Tour.

The mansion is, of course, the star attraction, visited by nearly seven hundred thousand people a year. It is the second-most-visited house in America, surpassed only by the White House. Priscilla Presley is fond of saying that Elvis was Graceland's original tour guide because he enjoyed showing people his home. Today, the same rooms that Elvis would have shown his guests are the ones open to the public. The bedrooms and bathrooms are all closed. What is open are: the living room (with its view of the music room), the dining room, the TV room (so named for its three televisions along one wall), the billiard room, the kitchen, and the jungle room.

While these rooms accommodate thousands of visitors a day, there is still a sense of privacy here; in fact, one almost feels they are intruding on that solitude. Despite the museum-like quality the mansion has developed, these rooms practically breathe Elvis, in ways that go far beyond his wild decorating schemes or extravagant tastes.

It is the subtleties that speak loudest about him, the touches that say this was a home: the photograph of his parents in the living room, probably placed there by his mother; the Sam Cooke record "Shake" on the turntable in the TV room, the last record that Elvis ever played; and the tear in the pool table, the result of a rambunctious game. These nuances continue even as one steps out of the house towards the business office and past Lisa Marie's swing set, the one marred by a stray bullet from Elvis's target-shooting days.

Just as the mansion reflects Elvis's everyday life, the trophy room is testimony to his phenomenal career. The eighty-foot-long Hall of Gold is named for the walls lined with Elvis's gold records—and even this room isn't enough to display all of them. His Grammy awards are on display here, as well as virtually every other music award imaginable. The awards reflect Elvis's crossover appeal in all types of music—rhythm-and-blues, country, rock-and-roll, and gospel—along with his international appeal. Japan, Norway, Denmark, and Germany are just a few of the nations that presented him with gold records and awards on display here. As visitors turn the corner into the Big Room, stage costumes, movie scripts, and jumpsuits remind them of the diversity of Elvis's career. "Kid Galahad's" robe, the "'68 Comeback" leather suit, and the "Aloha from Hawaii" jumpsuit are just a few of the items on display in the Big Room.

The tour continues to the raquetball building where Elvis's awards continue to line the walls. More than a 110 gold, platinum, and multiplatinum records are displayed on this part of the tour, all presented to Elvis's estate by RCA in 1992. It is here that visitors can view the place where Elvis sang his last songs. Early in the morning of August 16, 1977, he sat at the piano in the racquetball building and sang "Blue Eyes Crying in the Rain" and "Unchained Melody."

The tour ends at the Meditation Garden, where Elvis, his mother, his father, and his grandmother are buried. A small marker reminds visitors of his brother, Jessie Garon, who is buried in Tupelo. Vernon decided on the placement of the graves, which is why Elvis is not buried next to his mother. However, Vernon did not design the Meditation Garden; this was Elvis's creation, and it was one of his favorite places.

Today, Elvis fans can enjoy the peace of the Meditation Garden during special walkups. Every day, year round, the gates of Graceland open an hour before tours begin to allow visitors to view Elvis's grave. Evening walkups are held during fan events in January and August. These are the only times that one can walk up the hill and experience the Graceland property as Elvis knew it, with the sound of the traffic dying to a soft murmur.

For those returning to the visitor center on the shuttle bus, there is more to see. In the Elvis Presley Automobile Museum, one can view the pink Cadillac Elvis gave to his mother, his purple '56 Cadillac Eldorado, his '73 Stutz Blackhawk, his '71 Mercedes, his '57 Harley Davidson, and the pink jeep used in the movie *Blue Hawaii*, to name a few.

Elvis's planes, the *Lisa Marie* and the *Hound Dog II* are parked nearby, and the *Lisa Marie* is available for boarding.

The Sincerely Elvis Museum exhibits many of Elvis's personal possessions. Here, one can look at a collection of his records, his books, signed boxing gloves given to him by Muhammad Ali, furnishings from his bedroom, and many other momentos from his life.

If all of this touring has worked up an appetite, there are two restaurants and an ice cream parlor open at the visitor center. A post office is open for mailing postcards and buying stamps. Numerous shops offer merchandise. And if you are just plain weary at this point, there are plenty of places to rest, all with a view of Graceland.

Hours:

From Memorial Day through Labor Day, Graceland is open seven days a week, 8:00 A.M. to 6:00 P.M. Winter hours are 9:00 A.M. to 5:00 P.M., with the mansion closed on Tuesdays from November through February. Graceland is closed New Year's Day, Thanksgiving Day, and Christmas Day.

For further information, call 800-238-2000; in Memphis call 332-3322.

Beale Street

One could not possibly appreciate Memphis without a day or a night on Beale Street. Daytime reveals a wealth of information through the many historic markers along the street. One discovers that Beale Street was once a center of commerce, where immigrant Irish, Italian, and Jewish families opened shops alongside African-Americans. The most prominent remnant of this mercantile past is A. Schwab's Dry Goods (163 Beale Street). Opened in 1876, Schwab's doesn't look like it has changed since. It is part museum and part merchandise store, selling things you thought had disappeared long ago.

One can study the region's past at the Center For Southern Folklore (209 Beale Street). Inside the center are a number of exhibits and gift items. The center offers music, entertainment, and other live events on a variety of folklore themes. For information, call 901-525-3655.

Recently, Sun Studio has opened a second museum in the Old Daisy Theater (333 Beale Street). The museum exhibits concentrate on Memphis music before 1950. You can also record your own songs on studio equipment for a nominal fee. The Old Daisy Theater was the first movie theater for African-Americans in Memphis, and also served as a stage for vaudeville performances. For information, call 901-527-6008.

W. C. Handy, who has been called the "Father of the Blues," made Beale Street famous when he wrote the songs "Memphis Blues" and "Beale Street Blues" before World War I. In 1960, two years after Handy's death, the city erected a statue of him within a park named in his honor. Today, the park, located at Beale and Hernando Streets, looks more like a vacant lot, but it comes alive on weekends when bands play for free under Handy's gaze. Ten years ago, W. C. Handy's home was saved from demolition and brought to the corner of Beale and Fourth Streets. The small shotgun home is filled with artifacts and memorabilia relating to his life.

Also of interest is the Police Substation (159 Beale Street), a working police station that also houses museum exhibits. Visitors can see Elvis's application to become a sheriff's department special deputy and have their picture taken inside an old jail cell.

During Beale Street's heyday, nighttime was when the musicians gathered to perform and party. At one time, Memphis had a reputation for the rawest nightlife in the country, and Beale was where the action happened. Today, one can experience a slightly tamer version of Beale's nighttime revelry. The talented musicians who play on Beale Street are of equal quality to internationally famous rock stars, locals like to brag. In fact, many rock stars participate in or listen to Beale Street performances when they are in town.

The best-known club on Beale Street today is named for the most popular bluesman alive, B.B. King. Blues acts of national prominence play here, including the club's namesake. The well appointed, two-story club offers a private loft for special guests. B.B. King's Blues Club (143 Beale Street) also offers good food for lunch and dinner. Across the street, the Blues City Cafe (138 Beale Street) offers similar music and food in scruffier surroundings.

Nightclubs have come and gone since Beale Street underwent a revitalization in 1983. Two clubs have survived by offering a consistent party atmosphere. Rum Boogie Cafe (182 Beale Street) is festooned with guitars donated by rock legends. Above the stage is the famous Stax Studio marquee, salvaged from the ruins of the fallen studio. Alfred's On Beale (197 Beale Street) has an Elvis room in the back. The club hosts George Klein's (Elvis's friend and classmate) disc jockey show on Sunday nights. Klein's shows in August are reunions for Elvis's Memphis Mafia. Look for Elvis's musical note embedded on the sidewalk at the front entrance. Elvis's note is part of a series all along Beale Street honoring the city's music legends, much like Hollywood's Walk of Fame.

OTHER RECOMMENDED SITES

Downtown

There is a lot to see in downtown Memphis, but it is a long walk from the Pyramid Arena and the North Main neighborhood that Elvis knew to Beale Street on the south side. The Main Street Trolley is an easy and inexpensive way to cover downtown. All of the attractions listed below are serviced by the trolley, or are within two blocks of service.

Tennessee Welcome Center. The intersection of Jefferson Avenue and Riverside Drive. This brand-new visitor center for travelers on Interstate 40 is where the city of Memphis placed the famous Elvis statue that stood on Beale Street from 1980 to 1994. The statue was refurbished and placed here along with a new statue of B.B. King. Stop here to admire the views of the Mississippi River, Mud Island, and the Pyramid Arena. This is also a good spot to pick up some free brochures of local and area attractions.

Mud Island Park. 145 North Front Street. This popular attraction is not actually an island, but instead a peninsula of land jutting into the Mississippi River. Opened in 1982, the park offers the most intimate view of the river (without boarding a boat) in town. The park has a mix of attractions. The Mud Island Amphitheater seats five thousand for summer concerts. The River Museum has several exhibits on the Mississippi River. Also on exhibit is the *Memphis Belle* B-17 bomber made famous during World War II which was also the subject of a recent movie. You can enter the park by way of the monorail which begins at this Front Street address. Hours of operation vary by season; for information, call 901-521-1265.

National Civil Rights Museum. 450 Mulberry Street. On April 4, 1968, Dr. Martin Luther King, Jr., was assassinated on the balcony of the Lorraine Motel. The motel is now a museum honoring the civil rights movement of the 1950s and 1960s. For hours of operation and details of special exhibits on human rights issues or African-American cultural issues, call 901-521-9699.

Memphis Queen Line. 45 Riverside Drive. Ever wanted to ride on a Mississippi River paddle-wheel boat? Well, you can with the Memphis Queen Line. They offer a variety of tours and special boat trips. Most visitors take the two-hour afternoon cruise. The boats can be rented for your own party. In recent years, the Memphis Queen Line has offered a night-party cruise for Elvis fans during the month of August. For information, call 901-527-5694.

The Peabody Hotel. 149 Union Avenue. A writer once said the

Mississippi delta begins at the lobby of the Peabody Hotel, meaning that anyone who was anyone in the South would be found at the lobby bar. It is still true today. Whenever a major entertainment event happens in Memphis, you can bet that a number of celebrities will lodge at, or imbibe at, the Peabody. Everyday people gather to watch the grand procession of the Peabody ducks enter the lobby at precisely 11:00 A.M., then exit at 5:00 P.M. The ducks reside in their own penthouse suite. Also on the hotel's rooftop is the Peabody Skyway nightclub, where in the late 1940s, a young Sam Phillips helped engineer radio broadcasts of big-band music.

Second Street and Union Avenue. This area of downtown, just west of the Peabody Hotel, is one of the most interesting areas of the city. Of the many bars and restaurants to choose from, Automatic Slims (83 South Second Street) offers an exotic decor to match a menu unique to Memphis. Next door, Huey's showcases a number of contemporary blues artists, without imposing a cover charge. A few doors south is the Memphis Music Hall of Fame Museum (97 South Second Street). Memphis may not have been chosen as the home of the Rock and Roll Hall of Fame, but collector John Montague has created his own worthy version. His museum has seven thousand square feet of exhibits on Memphis music, covering the turn of the century to the present. In the same storefront are the museum's gift shop, stocked with great old records, and Rod and Hank's Guitars, where Eric Clapton shopped during his last Memphis visit.

Whitehaven

Graceland Crossing Shopping Center. 3727 Elvis Presley Boulevard. For some people, there are never too many places to buy Elvis souvenirs. Fortunately, there are many shops to choose from in Memphis, including this shopping center just north and across the boulevard from the Graceland mansion. Because these shops are not affiliated with Elvis Presley Enterprises, they offer merchandise that one cannot find at the Graceland Visitor Center shops. For example, many shrewd fans look to stores like the Wooden Indian, Memories of

Elvis, Loose Ends, and Souvenirs of Elvis for out-of-print books on Elvis. The Hot Rod Diner offers a convenient place to eat and meet friends. In the summer, entertainers (singing Elvis's songs, of course) perform in the diner's outdoor patio. In August during Elvis Week, entertainment is scheduled virtually around the clock. The shops also stay open to accommodate the fans during Elvis Week.

Marlowe's Restaurant and Ribs. 4381 Elvis Presley Boulevard. Another gathering place for Elvis fans is this restaurant and bar located one mile south of Graceland. Graceland employees often unwind at Marlowe's after a hard day's work. Many Elvis fans also enjoy this refreshing change from hotel restaurants and fast food joints. Marlowe's is open for lunch and dinner; the bar stays open late. During August, Marlowe's tries to schedule many parties for Elvis fans.

East Memphis

Pink Palace Museum. 3050 Central Avenue. Memphis has been the home of many an eccentric individual. One of those characters, Clarence Saunders, helped invent the supermarket with his Piggly Wiggly stores. The city opened its first museum in his home, the Pink Palace, after he lost it to bankruptcy. Today, some of the exhibits in the renovated old mansion illustrate what Memphis was like during Saunders's day. The exhibits include memorabilia on Elvis, on loan from the estate of Elvis Presley, covering his early life up to his return from the army. In August, the museum planetarium offers a laser-light show scored with Elvis's music. For information, call 901-320-6320.

Mall of Memphis. 4451 American Way. This is one of the most popular shopping malls in Memphis and is easily accessible from Graceland.

Anna's Steak House. 875 West Poplar Avenue, Collierville. In her new restaurant, Anna Hamilton (Class of '65) has created a Humes

High School class reunion, filling her walls with photographs and memorabilia of the school. Since Anna is an Elvis fan, many of the photographs are of Humes's most famous alumnus, and the restaurant will only play Elvis's music. Every fourth Friday, several former Humes students get together for an informal reunion and dinner. Come to dinner that night and you may meet someone who went to school with Elvis. Open seven days a week for dinner; Saturdays and Sundays 5 to 10 P.M., the rest of the week 5 to 9 P.M.

Pig-N-Whistle Barbecue Restaurant. 7144 Winchester Road. Elvis probably ate at the original version of this restaurant, then at 1579 Union Avenue, as did most everyone else in Memphis. Pig-N-Whistle was open on Union Avenue from 1929 to 1966. Today you can enjoy the experience of eating at the new Pig-N-Whistle, where the new owners have recreated the atmosphere of one of the most famous roadside diners in Memphis. Even the recipe for pork barbecue is exactly the same. Photographs on the wall show you what Memphis looked like during the Pig-N-Whistle's heyday. The restaurant is open for lunch and dinner seven days of the week.

Tunica County, Mississippi

Hollywood Casino, Robinsonville, Mississippi. The latest craze in the Memphis area is casino gaming in Tunica County, thirty miles south of downtown Memphis. Altogether, a billion-dollars worth of gaming attractions have been built in less than five years on land once used for cotton farming. Of the twelve casinos to chose from in Tunica, we picked the Hollywood to feature in this book. Inside, gaming patrons will notice the movie memorabilia throughout the large casino building. Prominently displayed at the casino entrance is a display of Elvis's guitars and one of his jumpsuits. Near the hotel entrance is the car Elvis drove in the movie *Spinout*. The Hollywood Casino offers a variety of dining experiences, lodging, and live entertainment.

BIBLIOGRAPHY

This book would not have been possible without the assistance of the Memphis/Shelby County Public Library and the University of Memphis Library. The public library maintains an invaluable collection of documents and reference work about Memphis in its Memphis Room, located in the library's main branch. The Mississippi Valley Collection at the University of Memphis Library contains the Jerry Hopkins archives of Elvis-related material used in his 1971 and 1977 biographies, as well as the *Memphis Press-Scimitar* newspaper files. At both libraries, we used the microfilm files of *Memphis Commercial Appeal* and *Memphis Press-Scimitar* back issues—it is impossible to research Elvis's life without referring to those two newspapers.

We relied on several magazines for our research, many of which were special editions devoted to Elvis. These magazines included: *Elvis Presley* by the editors of *TV Radio Mirror* magazine, published in 1956; *Elvis Presley: Hero Or Heel?* by Richard Gehman, published in 1957; *Memphis Downtowner* magazine; *Movie Teen's Elvis Yearbook* by the editors of *Yearbooks*, published in 1960; *The Official Elvis Presley Album* by the editors of Charlton Press, published in 1956; and *Tiger Magazine*.

Finally, the following books proved invaluable in our research into Elvis's life in Memphis.

Burk, Bill E. *Early Elvis: The Humes Years*. Memphis: Burk Enterprises, 1990.

Clayton, Rose M., and Dick Heard, eds. *Elvis Up Close*. Atlanta: Turner Publishing, Inc., 1994.

Cotton, Lee. *All Shook Up*. Ann Arbor: Pierian Press, 1985.

Fortas, Alan. *Elvis From Memphis To Hollywood*. Ann Arbor: Popular Culture, Inc., 1992.

Gregory, Neal and Janice. *When Elvis Died*. Washington, D.C.: Communications Press, 1980.

Gruber, Richard J., ed. *1948–1958: Memphis Memories*. Memphis: Memphis Brooks Museum of Art, 1986.

Guralnick, Peter. *Last Train To Memphis*. New York: Little, Brown and Company, 1994.

Hopkins, Jerry. *Elvis: A Biography*. New York: Warner Books, 1972.

Lacker, Marty and Patsy, and Leslie Smith. *Elvis: Portrait of a Friend*. Memphis: Wimmer Brothers Books, 1979.

Loper, Karen. *Elvis Clippings*. Self-published, n.d.

Presley, Priscilla, with Susan Harmony. *Elvis and Me*. New York: Berkeley Books, 1986.

Smith, Gene. *Elvis's Man Friday*. Nashville: Light of Day Publishing, 1994.

Staten, Vince. *The Real Elvis: Good Old Boy*. Dayton: Media Ventures, Inc., 1978.

Worth, Fred L., and Steve D. Tamerius. *Elvis: His Life From A To Z*. Chicago: Contemporary Books, 1990.

Yancey, Becky, with Cliff Linedecker. *My Life With Elvis*. New York: St. Martin's Press, 1977.

INDEX

A. Schwab's Dry Goods, 39, 228
Ace Appliance, 98, 99
Adams, Jack, 175
Adams, Nick, 16, 34, 89, 122
Adler, Justin, 57
Alabama Street, 3-8, 37, 179, 223
Alden, Ginger, 191, 192, 197, 213
Aloha From Hawaii, 226
American Bandstand, 152
American Sound Studio, 142, 143, 144, 224
Americana Club, 75
Anna's Steak House, 171, 232, 233
Arnold, Eddy, 94
Arthur Godfrey Show, The, 46
Atlanta, 143
Atlantic Records, 144
Axton, Estelle, 144

B.B. King's, 40, 229
Bailey, Loyd, 121
Baptist Memorial Hospital, 216, 217
Barrasso, Ernie, 166, 167, 182, 183, 184
Beale Street, 39-43, 54, 68, 69, 103, 104, 110, 111, 114, 115, 121, 131, 132, 133, 134, 147, 228, 229
Beef and Liberty Restaurant, 162, 163
Bel-Air Night Club, 73
Bellevue Boulevard, 51, 137, 138, 157-60, 191, 192, 219, 220
Bill Black Combo, 96, 99, 146
Black, Bill, 20, 44, 61, 71-78, 86, 94-99, 138, 146

Black, John, 20, 21, 96
Blackwood Brothers Gospel Quartet, 46-50, 69, 80-82, 218
Blackwood Brothers Record Shop, 46-49
Blackwood, Cecil, 48
Blackwood, Terry, 48
Bland, Bobby "Blue," 55
"Blue Eyes Crying In The Rain," 93, 226
Blue Light Studio, 102, 103
"Blue Moon Of Kentucky," 65
"Blue Suede Shoes," 87
Blues City Club, 229
Blues Shop, 43, 44
Bon-Air Club, xv, 71, 72
Box Tops, The, 143
Bradley, Anna Mae, 7, 8
Bramlett, Charlie, 36, 37, 38, 84
Bramlett, John, 37, 38, 179
Bramlett, Odell, 37, 38
Brenston, Jackie, 97
Brewer, Johnny, 101
Brewster, Reverend Harper, 52, 53
Brindley, T.C., 14
Britling's Cafeteria, 9, 10
Brown, Aubrey, 117
Brown, Ruth, 90
Bruce, John, 74
Burke's Florist, 138
Burlison, Paul, 23, 34, 43, 88, 89
Burnett, Bonnie and Hobart, 163
Burnette, Johnny and Dorsey, 23, 43, 88, 89, 96
Bush, George, 155

Cadillac, 185, 227
Calloway, Cab, 54

Cannon, Ace, 146
Cash, Johnny, 58, 61, 62
Centenary A.M.E. Church, 51, 52
Center For Southern Folklore, 111, 228
Central High School, 124
Central Station, 141
Chenault's Restaurant, 157, 158
Cherry, Ruben, 42, 43
Christine School, 12
Circle G Ranch, 175-77, 198, 211
Claridge Hotel, 151, 152, 153
Clark, Dick, 152
Clearpool, 74, 75, 129
Clement, Jack, 58, 73
Coffee, Guy, 80
"Cold Cold Icy Fingers," 13
Colletta's Italian Restaurant, 159-60
Columbia Mutual Tower, 24
Convair 880 (jet), 193
Country Music Hall of Fame, 112
Crosby, Bing, 54
Crosstown Theater, 171-72
Crown Electric Company, 33, 34, 35
Crump, E. H. "Boss," 55, 124-25
Crump Stadium, 106, 124-25
Culpepper's Chicken Shack, 54-55
Cuoghi, Joe, 44-45, 145

Dance Party, 100
Danny Thomas Boulevard, 1-5, 35
David, Captain Elwood, 193
Davis, Richard, 168
Dean, James, 28, 123
Diamond, Neil, 143
Dodgem Cars, 127, 128

Doug Poindexter's Starlight Wranglers, 71-72, 73, 94, 96

Eagle's Nest, xv, 74-75, 129
Earl's Hot Biscuits, 56
East Trigg Baptist Church, 52, 53
Eckstine, Billy, 94
Ed Sullivan Show, The, xv
Ellington, Governor Buford, 151
Elliot, Ron, 191, 192
Ellis Auditorium, 80-83
"Elvis '56," 84, 107, 108
Elvis Hour, 67
Elvis On Tour, 193
Elvis Presley Automobile Museum, 163, 227
Elvis Presley Memorial Karate Tournament, 204
Elvis Presley Memorial Tribute Week, 210, 224, 227
Elvis Presley Statue, 43, 230
Elvis Presley Tankers Fan Club, 140
Elvis Presley Trauma Center, 221, 222
Elvis Presley Youth Center, 82
Elvis Recorded Live On Stage In Memphis, 149
Elvis Presley, The King of Rock and Roll: The Complete 50s Masters, 44
Emmons, Dixie Locke, 51, 55, 129, 181
Esposito, Joe, 205

Fairgrounds Amusement Park, 126-27, 128

"Fairytale," 150
Fashion Curtain Company, 10, 11
Fernwood Records, 95
First Assembly of God Church, xiv, 49, 50, 51, 80
Fisher, Portia, 189
572 Poplar Avenue, 1-2
Fontana, D. J., 86
Forbess, Evan "Buzzy," 23, 24, 25, 38, 44
Ford Thunderbird Landau, 167, 182, 183, 184
Ford, Edsel, Jr., 182, 183, 184
Forest Hill Cemetery, 136, 137, 218, 219, 220
Fort Chaffee, 135
Fortas, Alan, 168
Foster, David, 211
Foster, Jean Lazenby, 4, 20, 21
Four Flames Restaurant, 155, 156, 157
462 Alabama Street, 7-8
1414 Getwell Road, 86-87
Foxgate Lincoln Mercury, 186-88
Frank Sinatra Show, 152
Frayser, 96
Friedman, Judge Sam, 117, 118
From Elvis In Memphis, 169
Fruchter family, 7, 8
Full Gospel Tabernacle, 147
"Funny How Time Slips Away," 146

Gale, Albert, 131
Geller, Larry, 187
Germany, 140, 173
GI Blues, 180
Gleaves, Cliff, 113

Godsey, James, 92
Goldsmith's Department Store, 195, 196
"Got A Lot Of Loving To Do," 121

Graceland: attractions at, xiii, 8, 224-27, 231-32; Elvis's grave, 219; Elvis's life at, 90-93, 111, 114, 131, 134, 137, 145, 151, 153, 155-60, 162-67, 175-76, 205, 185, 187, 188, 189, 192, 205; Gladys's grave, 137-38; Priscilla's life at, 173
Graceland Crossing Shopping Center, 231, 232
Graceland Elementary School, 178, 179
Graceland Plaza (visitors center), 163, 225, 226, 227
Graceland School, 178-79
Green, Al, 146, 147
Green Owl, 37, 38
Gridiron Restaurant, 161, 162
Groom, Arthur, 28, 29

Haertel, Joe, 6
Hall's Grocery, 26
Hamill, Reverend James E., 50, 51, 137, 218
Hamilton, Anna, 171, 232, 233
Hamilton, Roy, 143
Handy, W.C., 38, 39, 40, 228
Harley-Davidson Motorcycles, 122, 123, 191, 192
Harris, Mrs., 30, 34
Harry Levitch Jewelers, 109-10
Hayes, Isaac, 41, 144, 168

Hearn, Barbara, 120
"Heartbreak Hotel," 87
Heartbreak Hotel Restaurant, 192
Herenton, Dr. W. W., 56
Hi Records, 44, 146, 147
Hickory Log Restaurant, 162, 163, 210
High, Captain Milo, 194
High Noon Roundup, 47, 69
Hodge, Charlie, 154, 219
Holden, William, 54
Holiday Inn-Rivermont, 153-55
Hollywood, California, 139, 152, 178
Hollywood Casino, 233
Home for Incurables, 24
Home of the Blues Record Shop, 43-44
Hopper, Edd, 116
Hotel Chisca, 64-67
Hotel Men's Improvement Club, 40
Hound Dog II, 225
Howard Johnson's Motor Lodge, 207-8
Howling Wolf, 97
Hull-Dobbs Ford, 182-85
Humes High School, 6, 12-17, 109, 124, 202, 232, 233
Hy Gardner Calling, 107

"I Can Help," 96
"I Can't Stand the Rain," 146
"I'm So Lonesome I Could Cry," 146
Immaculate Conception High School, 173, 174
Imperials, The, 48
"In The Ghetto," 143, 169, 224

International Fighter, 201

Jackson, Mahalia, 53
Jailhouse Rock, 28, 29
Jamboree Attractions, 103
James, Mark, 169
Jarvis, Felton, 143
Jaycees, 153-56, 188
Jenkins, Mary, 189, 190
Jenner, Bruce, 211
Jimmy and Tommy Dorsey's *Stage Show*, 87, 103
Jim's Barber Shop, 131-32
Johnny Long Band, 74
Jones, Booker T., 144
Johnson, Robert, 65, 152
Jordanaires, 83

Kang Rhee Institute for Self-Defense, 201-2
Katz Drug Store, 76, 77
Keisker, Marion, 31, 43, 60, 61, 78, 128
Kennedy Veterans Hospital, 24, 134, 135
"Kentucky Rain," 143
Kessinger, Don, 206
Kid Galahad, 226
King, B.B., 39, 44, 45, 55, 68, 97
King Creole, 133
King, Dr. Martin Luther, 40, 53, 230
Klein, Barbara, 189
Klein, George, 13, 28, 110, 113, 122, 126, 140, 160-61, 189, 229
Krystal Restaurant, 113-14
K's Drive-In, 55, 56

Lacker, Marty, 14

Lamar Avenue, 74-78, 85, 86, 95, 104, 129, 130

Lamar-Airways Shopping Center, 76, 77, 109

Lansky Brothers' Men's Store, 14, 104, 110, 111

Lansky, Guy and Bernard, 110, 111

Las Vegas, 148, 200

Lauderdale Courts, xiii, 1, 3-6, 10, 11, 17, 19-21, 23, 35, 123, 223

"Lawdy Miss Clawdy," 87

Lazenby, Joan, 4

Le Bonheur Children's Hospital, 222

Leek, Ed, 44

Leonard's Barbeque, 158-59

Lepley, "Sleepy-Eyed" John, 74, 77

"Let Me Be There," 149

Lewis, Jerry Lee, 44, 58, 61, 62

Liberace, 74

Liberty Bowl Stadium, 125, 150

Libertyland, 126-28

Lincoln Continental, 186, 187, 197, 227

Lion's Club, 124-25

Lisa Marie, The, 193, 194, 227

Local Draft Board 86, 133-34

Lockheed Jetstar (plane), 194

Loew's State Theater, 27-29, 36, 57, 121

Love Me Tender, 16, 122, 130

Loving You, 120-21

Lowell Hays Jewlers, 196-97

Lyles, Bill, 48

Lyn-Lou Music Publishing, 96

Lyon, Ann, 162

M.B. Parker Company, 30, 31-32

Madison, Bert, 186

Madison Cadillac, 185-86

Malco/Orpheum Theater, xiii, 132, 133

Mall of Memphis, 232

Manhattan Club, 166-67

Market Mall in Lauderdale Courts, 20, 96

MARL Metal Company, 10, 29-30

Marlowe's Restaurant and Ribs, 232

Martin D-18 guitar, 112

Massey, Howard, 185, 186

McDaniel, Will "Bardahl," 130, 158

McDonald's, 113, 164-65

McKeller Lake, 180-81

McLemore Avenue, 49, 51, 144, 145, 159

Meditation Garden at Graceland, 138, 219, 226

Memphian Theater, 170-71, 172

Memphis Aero, 193, 194

Memphis Commercial Appeal, 84, 150, 234

Memphis Cotton Carnival, 82

Memphis Funeral Home, 137, 216-20

Memphis Harley-Davidson, 122-23

Memphis Housing Authority, 3, 4, 5, 19, 21

Memphis International Airport, 75, 193, 194

Memphis Light, Gas and Water Building, 43, 66, 115, 134

"Memphis Mafia," 142, 170, 176, 178, 179, 229

Memphis Police Museum, 200, 229

Memphis Police Station, 199, 200
Memphis Press-Scimitar, 91, 100, 103,
    131, 137, 181
Memphis Queen Line, 230
Memphis Recording Service, 7, 31,
    43, 58-63, 73, 78, 128
Messerschmidt motorcycle, 111
Methodist Hospital, 106, 125, 136,
    137, 220
Mid-South Coliseum, 148-49, 150
Mid-South Fair, 126, 128
Milsap, Ronnie, 169
Milton Berle Show, The, 87
Mississippi River, 155, 180, 181, 230
Mitchell, Norrine, 207, 208
Mitchell, Willie, 40, 146, 147, 229
Moman, "Chips," 142, 143
"Money Honey," 87
Moore, Scotty, 59, 61, 71-74, 77, 86,
    94, 95, 96, 98, 99, 100 Morris,
    Bill, 188, 189, 200, 221
"Move On Up A Little Higher," 53
Mud Island Park, 230
"My Happiness," 43

Nashville, 58, 71, 95, 143, 178
National Bank of Commerce, 214-15
National Boat Safety Week, 181
National Civil Rights Museum, 230
Neal, Bob, 69, 70, 78, 79, 102, 103,
    105, 180
Neal, Helen, 102, 103
Nelson, Ricky, 179
Nerserian, Marie, 211
New York, 111
Newborn, Calvin, 39, 40
Nichopoulos, Dr. George, 205

Nixon, Roy, 200
North Lauderdale Street, 5, 8, 21, 23,
    45, 223, 224,
North Main Street, 36-38, 43, 44, 80,
    83, 151, 153, 229
Novarese, John, 44

O.K. Houck & Company, 112
Oak Court Mall, 196
Odd Fellows Hall, 23-24
Old Camp Meeting In The Air, 53
Old Daisy Theater, 228
185 Winchester Avenue #328, 3, 4,
    5
Orbison, Roy, 58, 61
Overton Park Shell (Rauoll
    Wallenberg Shell), 78-80, 102

Palace Theater, 40, 41
Parker, Colonel Tom, 70, 84, 86, 90,
    98, 99, 103, 105, 106, 133, 140
Patton, 172
Peabody Hotel, 17, 18, 70, 103, 112,
    114, 118, 185, 230, 231
Peabody Place, 29, 110, 121
Peanut Shop, 57
Peebles, Ann, 146
Pepper, Gary, 140, 150
Perkins, Carl, 58, 61, 62
Person, Minnie, 185, 186
Phillips, Dewey, 37, 41, 45, 64-67,
    74, 77, 114, 115
Phillips, Jerry and Knox (Sam's
    sons), 97
Phillips, Sam, 44, 58-62, 65, 66, 97-
    98

Pieraccini, Doris and Joe, 75, 129, 130

Pig-N-Whistle Restaurant, 233

Pink Palace Museum, 232

Pittsburgh Courier, 69

Playhouse on the Square, 171

Plaza Cinema, 118-20

Pop Tunes, 5, 44-45, 146

Poplar Avenue, 1, 2, 5-8, 10, 33-35, 44-45, 108, 112, 119-20, 122-23, 156-57, 169, 195-98, 202

Poplar Plaza Shopping Center, 119, 120

Porter, David, 41, 144

Potomac, 223

Precision Tool, 32-33, 74

Presley Center Courts, 205, 206

Presley, Dee Stanley, 209, 210, 217

Presley, Elvis Aaron: army duty, 133-35, 139-41; autos owned by, 182-90; awards, 151-56; churches attended, 49-53; death of, 137, 138, 216-20; employment of, 27-35; homes of, 1-8, 85-93, 175-77; hospitals 136, 137, 216, 217, 221-23; hotels visited, 17, 18, 151-55, 207, 208; motorcycles, 122, 123, 191, 192; movie theaters, xiii, 27-29, 36, 37, 119-21, 170-72; music, 37-45, 46-53, 64, 65, 68, 69; nightclubs visited, 37-41, 166-69; performance locations, 19-24, 71-84, 148-50; police and legal, 116-18, 199, 200; radio stations, 64-70; record stores, 42-45; recording studios, 60-64, 92, 93, 145, 148-50; recreation, 19-25, 126-30, 175-78,

180, 181; restaurants, 26, 54-59, 113-15, 156-65; retail stores visited, 42-45, 109-12, 122, 123, 182-92, 195-99; sports, 24, 25, 124, 125, 178, 179, 201-6

Presley, Gladys: death of, 48, 51, 136-38, 217-19, 226; life of, 1-8, 10, 11, 13, 32, 36, 37, 85, 88-91, 96, 109, 121, 123, 209

Presley, Jesse Garon, 226

Presley, Lisa Marie, 92, 128, 217

Presley, Minnie Mae, 2, 4, 7, 226

Presley, Priscilla Beaulieu, 91-92, 104, 110, 154-58, 160, 166, 173-76, 195, 198, 210, 216

Presley, Vernon: homes of, 163, 209, 210; life of, 1-10 12, 32, 38, 50, 85, 88-91, 131, 137, 138, 173, 176, 198, 213, 215, 217, 219, 226

Presley, Vester, 32, 213

Prisonaires, The, 97

Public Works Administration, 5

Raised On Rock, 145

Raquetball (at Graceland), 205, 226

RCA-Victor, 45, 46, 61, 86, 87, 90, 98, 112, 152, 226

Recreation Hall (Lauderdale Courts), 21, 23

Red Hot and Blue, 64-66

Redding, Otis, 144

Regional Medical Center, 221, 222

Richardson, Jane, 3, 4

Riverside Park, 180, 181

Robertson Motors, 188, 189

Royal Sound Studio, 146, 147

Russell, Charles, 186, 187

Russwood Park, 83, 84

St. Joseph's Hospital, 6, 10, 11, 223
St. Jude Children's Research Hospital, 7, 10, 11, 223
Sam and Dave, 168
Schilling, Billy Ray, 200
Schilling, Jerry, 200, 207, 209
Schilling Lincoln Mercury, 188, 189
Scotland Inn, 37
Scrivener, Mildred, 13-16
Sears Roebuck and Company, 197-98
Second Armored Division, 140
Second Street, 18, 30, 40, 104, 112, 117, 141, 184, 200, 231
Shelby County Courthouse, 116-18, 200
Short, Robert, 185
Sid Carroll Pontiac, 189-90
Simon, Joe, 143
Sincerely Elvis Museum, 226
"'68 Comeback Special," 226
698 Saffarans Avenue, 6
Smith, Billy and Jo, 189, 192
Smith, Gene, 26, 32, 52, 55, 121, 180
Smith, "Smoochy," 166
Smith, William Edward, 26
"Smokie-Part 2," 96, 99, 146
Snow, Hank, 82, 95
Snow, R. Max, 220
Songfellows, The, 47, 48
South Main Street, vi, xi, 27, 29, 57, 64, 67, 109-10, 120-21, 131-33, 141, 195-96
Southern Motors, 185, 196

Southland Mall, 196, 198
Speer, William and Vancil, 3, 105, 106
Spinout, 233
Springfield, Dusty, 143
Stafford, Jo, 95
Stars, Inc., 103
State Café, 114-15
Stax Records, 144-45
Sterling, Harold, 153, 154
Steve Allen Show, The, 82, 107
Stewart, Jim, 144
Strand Theater, 120-21
Struber, Raymond, 187
Sumner, J.D., 48, 82
Sun Records, 7, 44, 58-63, 65, 73, 78, 94-98, 103, 144
Sun Studio, 59, 63, 228
Super Cycle, 191-92
"Suspicious Minds," 143, 169
Sutton, Margaret, 103
Suzore #2 Theater, 36-37, 65
Swan, Billy, 99
Sweet Inspirations, 143

T.J.'s Lounge, 168-69
Taylor, Frank, 155
Taylor, Tommy, 122, 123
Taylor's Café, 58-59
Ten Outstanding Young Men of America (award), 80, 153-57, 188
Tennessee Employment Security Office, 30, 31, 34
Tennessee Karate Institute, 202-4
Tennessee Welcome Center, 230

1034 Audubon Drive, 87-90
"That's All Right," 37, 61, 65, 71, 81
"That's Where Your Heartaches Begin," 43
Third Street, 5, 11, 20, 116, 118, 131, 132, 141, 143, 182, 184, 200, 223
Thomas, B.J., 143
Thomas, Carla, 41, 144
Thomas, Danny, 223
Thomas, Rufus, 41, 68, 69, 144
Thompson, Alex, 121
Thompson, Lil and Tommy, 160, 161
Thompson, Linda, 92, 164, 165, 171, 172, 210-13
Thompson, Sam and Louise, 211-13
Thompson, Samford and Margie, 213
398 Cypress Avenue, 6
Thunderbird Lounge, 167, 168
Time magazine, 45
Tipler, Gladys and James, 30, 33-35
Tom Lee Park, 155
Toof family, 90
"Tragedy," 95
Triangle (Lauderdale Courts), 20, 21
Tunica County, Mississippi, 233
Tupelo, Mississippi, 1, 9, 12, 49, 82, 120, 226
Turner, Ike, 97

"Unchained Melody," 93, 226
Union Mission, 2
Union Station, 139-41
United Paint Company, 9, 10
University of Tennessee Medical School, 217
University Park Cleaners, 99-100

Velvet, Jimmy, 211

Victorian Village, 168

Walker, Opal, 76, 77
Wallace, Bill, 203, 204
Wallis, Hal, 121
Walls, Mississippi, 175-77
Wayne, Thomas, 95
WDIA, 53, 68, 69
Wertheimer, Alfred, 107
West, Mae, 55
West Memphis, Arkansas, 56
West, Red, 14, 109, 154, 202-4, 217, 218
Western Steakhouse and Lounge, 160-61
Westmoreland, Kathy, 187
WHBQ, 37, 64-67, 100, 114
White House, xiv
White Station, 107-8
Whitehaven, 90, 93, 161-65, 177-79, 198, 207-13
Whitehaven High School, 179
Whitman, Slim, 77
Williams, Mrs. Hank, 84
Williams, Professor Nat D., 39, 40, 68, 69
Wilson, Buddy, 179
Wilson, Regis, 17, 18
WMPS, 47, 69, 70, 102-3
WMPS Farm Report, 69
Wood, Anita, 100, 101, 105, 113, 114, 121, 140, 158, 195
Wood, Natalie, 89, 122, 123
WREC, 97
Wrenn, Patrick, 204

Zippin Pippin, 127, 128

Just as our book was going to publication, we learned that Lauderdale Courts is in danger of being demolished by the Memphis Housing Authority. Elvis's former apartment will be turned into a parking lot as part of MHA's de-densification program. We need your help to stop the bulldozers from destroying this important piece of Elvis's history.

Please write to the following addresses and tell them that you want them to save Lauderdale Courts.

Mr. Jerome Ryans, Executive Director
Memphis Housing Authority
P.O. Box 3664
Memphis, TN 38103

Ms. Wynona Batson
U.S. Department of Housing and Urban Development
251 Cumberland Bend
Nashville, TN 37228